VICTORY OVER THE WIND

Don Berliner

VICTORY OVER THE WIND

A History of the Absolute World Air Speed Record

VNR VAN NOSTRAND REINHOLD COMPANY
NEW YORK CINCINNATI TORONTO LONDON MELBOURNE

Printed in the United States of America
Designed by Paul Chevannes

Published by Van Nostrand Reinhold Company Inc.
135 West 50th Street
New York, New York 10020

Van Nostrand Reinhold
480 Latrobe Street
Melbourne, Victoria 3000, Australia

Van Nostrand Reinhold Company Limited
Molly Millars Lane
Wokingham, Berkshire RG11 2PY, England

16 15 14 13 12 11 10 9 8 7 6 5 4 3 2 1

Library of Congress Cataloging in Publication Data

Berliner, Don.
  Victory over the wind.

    Includes index.
    1. Airplanes—Speed records. I. Title.
TL537.B47 1983   621.13'09   83-1275
ISBN 0-442-21301-8

Contents

When I can get up into the air on a monoplane like that, and drive it through the air at 100 miles an hour, I shall be able just to laugh at contrary gusts. It will be not only a conquest of the air, but a complete victory over the wind. Passing so swiftly through the atmosphere, my craft will be altogether unaffected by even the highest of winds. And imagine what this will mean! Picture the uses to which the aeroplane will then be put! — John B. Moisant, 1910

Acknowledgments

To the following individuals and organizations, the author owes a deep debt of gratitude, for without their assistance and encouragement, this work could never have been completed:

Dustin W. Carter; U.S. Air Force Office of Public Affairs, Magazine and Corp., Ltd.; Hawker Siddeley Aviation, Ltd.; Royal Air Force Staff, British Embassy, Washington; Musée de l'Air, Paris; Lockheed-California Co.; Rockwell International; Central Museum of Aviation and Cosmonautics, Moscow; Albert F. Simpson Historical Research Center, Maxwell Air Force Base, Montgomery, Ala.; The National Air and Space Museum (in particular, Phil Edwards and Bob Mikesh); National Aeronautic Association (Col. Milton Brown, Secretary, Contest and Records Board); Jay Miller, Aerofax; Truman ("Pappy") Weaver; McDonnell Douglas Corp.; Grumman Corp.; Lt.Col. Eldon Joersz; Air Historical Branch, Ministry of Defense, London; Maurice P. Marsh; H. R. Robinson; Office of Naval History; Sr. Luigi Colani; Betty Skelton Frankman; Jacqueline Cochran; Kawasaki Heavy Industries, Ltd.; Gen. Leigh Wade; Don Lefferts, Vintage Auto Restorations, Inc.; Fritz Wendel; Hans Dieterle; Messerschmitt-Bolkow-Blohm; Don Black; Al Chute; Jim Larsen.

In addition, the following publications were used for research purposes, mainly with the assistance of the staff of the Historical Research Center of the National Air and Space Museum:

Journal of the Royal Aeronautical Society, Flug Revue + Flug Welt, Flight International, The Aeroplane, Aeroplane Monthly, Journal of the American Aviation Historical Society, Air Britain Digest, Sport Aviation, Interavia, Air Service Newsletter, Air Classics, l'Aerophile, Aeronautical Digest, Aero and Hydro, Aerial Age, L'Aeronaute, American Machinist, Aircraft, Aero, Scientific American, The Aero, Model Aviation, the FAI Bulletin, and *Fly.*

Two books were of special help: *The Speed Seekers,* by Tom Foxworth, a thorough history of the early 1920s, and *The Invention of the Aeroplane,* by the late Charles H. Gibbs-Smith, which covers the beginnings of powered flight in a useful, complete manner.

Introduction

Fliers have lived and fliers have died for just a few more miles per hour. Some were test pilots intent on justifying, in a few quick dashes near the ground, their employers' confidence in some new idea or design. Others were military pilots assigned to a well-organized technical effort aimed almost as often at propaganda as at progress. Still others were adventurers or experimenters for whom a successful run at a record brought fame and fortune.

Since the earliest days of flying, the airplane has been seen as a special device for achieving speed. Not forced to drag four rubber tires across the pavement like a car nor push a hull through thick, choppy water, it is free to go as fast as power and shape and nerve permit.

Speed is of immediate and significant value in flying an airplane, in sharp contrast to other forms of transportation. Whereas doubling the speed of a car or a boat yields little in terms of increased utility, any increase in the speed of an airplane quickly translates into the saving of time and money. The airplane depends on speed for efficient performance. Thus the search for even greater speed in the air is far more than just a sport. The most recent, dramatic example of this statement is the Anglo-French Concorde supersonic transport. When the plane raised the cruising speed of commercial airliners from 600 mph to 1,300 mph (965 km/h to 2,100 km/h), it halved the time for most long journeys.

The first truly official Absolute World Air Speed Record was set Alberto Santos-Dumont in a rickety biplane at 26 mph (41 km/h). At that time, in 1906 by the land speed record was 128 mph (206 km/h), set 10 months earlier with a Stanley Steamer. It wasn't until the postwar impact of progress in aeronautical science during World War I that an airplane flew faster than an automobile had been driven. In 1920, when Sadi Lecointe piloted a French Nieuport-Delage Racer at 171 mph (275 km/h), the land speed record was still less than 150 mph (240 km/h).

From then on, there was no question which type of vehicle was faster. Rather, the questions became: Whose airplane is the fastest? Is it powered by a radial or an in-line engine? Is it a biplane or monoplane? And later, is it pulled through the air by its propellor or pushed by a jet engine?

There are genuine speed records, and there are *claims* of speeds greater than the mark recognized. Unless a record is established under standard international rules, there is no sure way to determine whether the record is accurate, whether it is an exaggeration, or whether it is pure fabrication. Even if the record is accurate, it may have been set under special conditions, making comparison with other records, at best, difficult and possibly misleading. Almost since the formation of the International Aeronautics Federation (FAI) in Paris in the autumn of 1905, a standardized set of rules has existed for setting most air-speed records. The distance that must be flown is not negotiable, nor is the accuracy of the distance measured. The maximum altitude of the flight is prescribed, along with restrictions on diving the airplane to increase its speed artificially. Moreover, the FAI demands great precision in timing and recording the performance, as well as considerable experience and skill on the part of officials who supervise it.

It is for these reasons that serious consideration will be given only to records set under FAI rules, hence, true Absolute World Air Speed records. Such claims as 507 mph (816 km/h) by a U.S. Army Air Force XP-47J Thunderbolt, experimental fight plane during World War II (the official record was then 469 mph, or 755 km/h) must be disregarded because the mark was achieved at high altitude, where the thinner air contributed to the speed attained. Also not recognized by the FAI as true Absolute World Air Speed records are the numerous flights made at speeds in excess of 4,000 mph (6,400 km/h) by the X-15 rocket-powered research plane. Because the plane has never taken off under its own power, but was launched by a mother plane already flying at considerable speed, its speed was not entirely of its own making.

What *will* be considered are the scores of occasions when airplanes took off, flew the required number of passes over a properly calibrated course, were timed with great accuracy, and achieved speeds in excess (by a specified margin) of previously recognized speeds over a similar course anywhere in the world. In addition, many unsuccessful attempts, and even some unsuccessful airplanes, will be reviewed, for they sometimes contributed almost as much to the advancement of speed in the air as did the airplanes and flights that worked. Often, the attempts that failed reveal more about the people and problems involved in setting records than do operations that went like clockwork.

During most of the 75 years of Absolute World Air Speed Record attempts, the classic event was the 3-kilometer (1.86-mile) straightaway run. It was the shortest of all the tests open to airplanes and could be completed at the highest speed. In the early 1950s, when the record was well above the speed of sound (roughly 750 mph, or 1,200 km/h at sea level), the FAI recognized that flying at such speeds within 100 meters (328 feet) of the ground was too dangerous. The 3-kilometer record, though not abandoned, was replaced by the 15/25-kilometer (9.3/15.5-mile) record, which could be flown at any altitude at which radar-tracking devices functioned.

Because of the intense human effort expended in the drive for greater speed, the airplane has grown from a crude piece of equipment that could barely get off the ground into a sophisticated and, perhaps sadly, impersonal means of efficient transportation. The most glamorous, and dynamic, period of speed-record setting is clearly behind us. Yet the race goes on. While it is hardly possible for an individual or even a group to challenge the Absolute World Air Speed Record (governments, too, are losing interest in such expensive and potentially secret-revealing projects), there are still opportunities for men and women with imagination and dedication. The FAI record book lists much more than absolute records. There are hundreds of straightaway and closed-course records that can be set by aircraft of many types, weight categories, and engine types. These are constantly contested and are being surpassed with increasing frequency, as the appeal of being "fastest of all," if only for a few days in a restricted category, regains much of its supposed old-fashioned appeal.

The desire and need to record the speed of an airplane arose even before there were airplanes, before there was a National Aeronautic Association to supervise an American speed run and rush the data to Paris to a yet unformed Federation Aeronautique Internationale.

As they waited for the snow and freezing rain to subside, Orville and Wilbur Wright kept busy building instruments to measure what they confidently believed would be the first flight of a man-carrying, heavier-than-air machine. An automatic stopwatch would record the elapsed time of the first flight, and the rotating cups of the anemometer would tell them the distance they had flown through the air. A tachometer would count the engine and propellor revolutions, while a simple tape measure would be used to determine the distance traveled over the ground.

When, on December 17, 1903, the skies cleared and a steady wind blew across Kill Devil Hills, near the Atlantic coast and Kittyhawk, North Carolina, men and machine were ready. Late that morning, Orville Wright climbed aboard the fragile craft, which resembled a box kite more than it did a flying machine. Handlers swung the two homemade propellors, and the handmade engine came to life.

The machine slowly accelerated along the 60-foot (18-meter) launching track, easing into the air after just 40 feet (12 meters) thanks to a headwind of about 25 mph (40 km/h). The airplane (for that it now was, having lifted off the ground) pitched erratically up and down as Wright struggled to keep it aloft long enough to get some feel for the controls. After 12 seconds, a sudden lunge brought the "Wright Flyer" back into contact with the sand. The first flight of a heavier-than-air machine was over.

Orville Wright had flown 120 feet (37 meters) in 12 seconds, against a wind estimated to have averaged 35 feet (10.7 meters) per second. His speed over the ground was no more than 7 mph (11 km/h), roughly the speed of a casual jogger. The calculated speed through the air, however, was slightly more than 30 mph (48.3 km/h), and that was what counted.

Three more flights were made that day in 1903 before the Flyer was badly damaged in a hard landing. The fastest flight was the second; Wilbur Wright averaged slightly over 10 mph (16 km/h). The longest flight was the third, when Wilbur flew at just under 10 mph for almost a full minute.

That none of those flights has ever been recognized as an official record means little; their significance can hardly be enhanced by an ornate piece of paper containing a few fancy signatures. The Wrights flew in a machine of their own design and manufacture. Whether they flew twice as fast or twice as far, the achievement remains the same: at that stage of powered flight, merely to fly was a supreme accomplishment. What enabled the Wright brothers to get in the air was their methodical, scientific approach to a set of problems others had sought to conquer more with inspiration than with calculation. Early in their study of flight, the Wrights discovered that much of the available data were wrong; they were forced to repeat experimental work in order to verify data and eliminate incorrect data. While others moved impetuously from dream to drawing board to workshop (and usually to the junkyard), Orville and Wilbur Wright took one cautious step at a time, measuring and recording as they went.

First came kites, then tethered gliders, man-carrying and free-flying gliders, and finally, an engine. By the time they were ready to attempt powered flight, Orville and Wilbur Wright had made more than a thousand glider flights, accumulating about five hours in the air. Throughout, they noted how long and how far, for only when they knew "why" could they discover the answer to the question, "How better?"

A spirit of competition was in the air as the Wrights returned to their bicycle shop in Dayton, Ohio to begin work on improving their machine. Not that any other aerial experimenter was close on their heels; it would be several years before anyone else, in the United States or Europe, approached the Wright brothers' flights made that first day, December 17, 1903. The Wrights had already shown that they were capable and eager. Beginning in May 1904, near Dayton, they experimented with the second Flyer, and immediately surpassed their earlier records for speed, distance, and duration. Before the year ended, they had made a flight of 2.75 miles (4.4 km) in just over five minutes, averaging approximately 32 mph (51 km/h). They did their own timing and measuring of distance; thus there was never any chance that the marks set would become official. In light of subsequent achievements, and a knowledge of the men involved, though, there is little reason to doubt their accuracy.

Forging ahead, the Wright brothers built a third Flyer in 1905, logging times, distances, and speeds unequaled for three years. By 1908, the Wrights had far surpassed the records set in 1905. Their best flight of 1905 was made on October 5, when Wilbur flew about 24 miles (38 kilometers) in 38 minutes, averaging 38 mph (61 km/h). At this time, they were still the only humans who had flown in a powered machine.

Only nine days after the flight of October 5, 1908, there occurred in Paris an event that would lead to clarification of a growing number of claims and an equal number of challenges: the formation of the FAI under the leadership of Prince Roland Bonaparte. The idea of such an organization originated in a meeting during the Olympic Congress in Brussels in June 1905. There, Count de la Vaulx, vice-president of the Aero Club of France, Fernand Jacobs, president of the Aero Club of Belgium, and Major Moedebeck, of the German Airship League, proposed that a "Universal Aeronautical Federation" be formed to "regulate the various Aviation meetings and advance the science and sport of Aeronautics." These gentlemen established the FAI before a single airplane had flown anywhere in Europe, at a time when few of their contemporaries took seriously reports of the Wright brothers' flight in that bastion of exaggeration, the United States. What reaction would they have had if someone had suggested that within the lifetime of their children, an airplane would fly more than 2,000 mph (3,200 km/h), its speed recorded with as yet unimagined accuracy by tiny electrical devices? Theirs was the first in a long series of far-sighted moves which have since become the story of the Absolute World Air Speed Record.

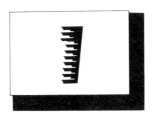

The Early Birds

In the first decade of the twentieth century, speed became an American sport. The automobile speed record belonged to Frank Marriott, who drove a Stanley Steamer almost 128 mph (206 km/h) at Daytona Beach, Florida. The record for motorcycles was even faster: 136 mph (219 km/h), held by Glenn Curtiss, driving a V8-powered two-wheeler.

In aviation, no one had come close to the achievements of the Wright brothers, though many, especially in France, were trying. By late 1905, the Wrights were flying their third Flyer at 37 to 38 mph (60 to 61 km/h) almost routinely. Their flight on October 5, 1905, near Dayton, covered more than 24 miles in just over 38 minutes, at an average speed of 38.2 mph (61.5 km/h). That, of course, wasn't an official record. The Aero Club of America, which became the documenter of records in the United States, was not founded until November 1905, and FAI wasn't founded until the next year (even then, it was at first so dominated by Europeans that it paid little attention to the Wright brothers).

In 1905, France was the center of aviation interest in Europe, even though no one there had made more than a brief airplane flight; nor had an airplane shown itself capable of sustained, controlled flight. At midsummer 1906, the closest anyone had come to flight was the Paris-based Romanian Trajan Vuia, who had struggled 79 feet (24 meters) through the air before crashing. Vuia's airplane was repaired and used for a few more short hops before being retired. Today, it is on display in the Musée de l'Air, southwest of Paris.

In America, the Wrights had withdrawn from public view to experiment and plan the commercial exploitation of the airplane. They made no flights in 1906 or 1907.

Until Alberto Santos-Dumont arrived on the scene, little progress was made in European flying. The charismatic Brazilian electrified the Continent with a series of flights in his powered lighter-than-air craft, including a flight around the Eiffel Tower. Having achieved both technical and social success with airships, Santos-Dumont next turned his attention to airplanes.

On September 13, 1906, he got his Type 14 tail-first biplane off the ground for the first time. It traveled only 26 feet (7.9 meters). Even though it was far short of the Wrights' first flight, Santos-Dumont's "flight" was later recognized by the FAI as the world's first aerial distance record. But he *had* flown, at least by FAI standards. In late October, Santos-Dumont bettered this distance, flying 200 feet (61 meters) at about 20 mph (32 km/h), to win the Archdeacon Prize of 3,000 francs. It was the first officially observed flight of more than 25 meters (about 82 feet) in Europe.

Finally, on November 12, he fired up the 50-horsepower Antoinette V8 engine in his modified Type 14-bis airplane for a try at the prize offered by the Aero Club of France for the first observed flight of more than 100 meters (328 feet). According to a report in the January 1907 *Journal of the Royal Aeronautical Society:*

> Regarding the actual achievements of M. Santos-Dumont with his machine, there has been a great discrepancy in the reports of the distances he has flown. Therefore, I have obtained . . . the exact measurements of his third and fourth ascents of November 12th, 1906, at Bagatelle. The first and second ascents took place in the morning, and were not chronometrically registered. The third and fourth ascents, which took place in the afternoon of the same day, were officially checked by the Sport Committee of the Aero Club.
>
> In the third attempt, the start was at 4:09 P.M. There were two flights. The first, of about 50 meters, [was] not chronometrically registered. The second, of 82 meters 60 [82.6 meters] in 7.5 seconds, which is at the rate of 11 meters 47, the second [11.47 meters/second], or 41 kilometers 292, the hour [41.292 km/h].
>
> In the fourth attempt, the start was at 4:45 P.M. There was a flight of 220 meters in 21 seconds 1/5, chronometrically recorded, that is, 10 meters 38 the second [10.38 meters/second], or 37 kilometers 358, the hour [37.358 km/h].
>
> The third experiment, therefore, . . . is the official record of speed, and the fourth the official record of distance and time in the air.

It was later determined that the time for the third flight, which was reported as "7.5 seconds," was apparently a misprint for 7.2 seconds, as the latter works out to exactly 41.292 km/h. Because the flight was formally supervised by the Aero Club of France, Santos-Dumont received credit for the first French air speed record. When the FAI began keeping records, it accepted this mark as its first official Absolute World Air Speed Record. At 25.66 mph (41.29 km/h), it was considerably slower than the Wrights had flown a year earlier. The Wright brothers had, however, timed themselves — a critical difference even in 1906, though no one today seriously questions the Wrights' achievement.

The Type 14-bis airplane was a canard (tail-first) biplane built mainly of pine and bamboo and covered with unbleached cotton cloth. Its wingspan was 36 feet 9 inches (11.2 meters), its length 31 feet 10 inches (9.7 meters), and its height about 11 feet (3.4 meters). The steel-and-aluminum, two-bladed pro-pellor, located the the extreme rear of the airplane, was driven by a water-cooled Antoinette V8 engine generating approximately 50 horsepower. At takeoff the plane weighed about 660 pounds (299 kilograms), including a small pilot and a few liters of gasoline.

There is no doubt that Orville and Wilbur Wright could have made a short, straight flight at least 50 percent faster than Santos-Dumont made; but they didn't. Regardless of what the Wrights might have done in the air (and most Europeans were highly skeptical of their claims), the flights in France were recorded, and the public responded with enormous enthusiasm — making Santos-Dumont's impact on aviation much greater in Europe than that of the Wright brothers.

Among the first positive results was the offering of a large cash prize to the first person to fly the English Channel. Of less tangible value was the prestige suddenly granted heretofore ridiculed aeronautical experimenters in Europe. Now that a European had shown that it was possible to fly a heavier-than-air machine, it was no longer the height of foolishness to try.

Santos-Dumont flew his Type 14-bis only one more time before setting it aside in favor of a newer design. In late 1907, he flew the first of a series of Demoiselles, an unusually small airplane recognized today as the world's first light plane. The prototype flew only three times, but its successors flew as long as 11 minutes, igniting worldwide interest in airplanes of minimum size even though planes of other's designs had by then achieved greater flights.

Santos-Dumont's last flight came in late 1909; then, suffering from the onset of a form of multiple sclerosis, he retired to his native Brazil. His ac-complishments with airships and airplanes have earned him a place as an effec-tive pioneer in the history of early flight. Today, an accurate reproduction of Santos-Dumont's Type 14-bis hangs in the display hall of the Technical Museum in Paris, and a real Demoiselle is housed in the Musée de l'Air.

When Santos-Dumont set the first Absolute World Air Speed Record, no re-quirements were specified other than the flight must be observed, measured, and certified by officials of the Aero Club of France. No minimum distance was set, nor did anyone care what the direction of the wind was or whether the pilot dived his airplane to increase its speed artificially. In those days, flying was difficult enough without a committee of bureaucrats telling a pilot how to fly. Whatever the pilot did was a glorious feat, to be rewarded with flowers, champagne, and medals.

Once the first official flights had been made in France, that country became the focus of aeronautical activity. The first to produce a significant airplane in Europe (in contrast to Santos-Dumont, whose designs were inspirational but did not lead directly to long-term technical progress) were the brothers Gabriel and Charles Voisin. Their fragile biplanes, flown by many of Europe's top pilots, figured in more pioneering flights than any other airplanes except those of the Wright brothers.

The first Voisin flew in March 1907; in September the second one was built for Henry Farman, an Englishman living in France. The Voisin-Farman, as it was called, was powered by a 50-horsepower Antoinette V8 of high reliability and resembled the Wright Flyers more than anything created by Santos-Dumont. The plane had two wings amidship, a horizontal tail out front, and a vertical tail in back, along with another horizontal member. The pilot came in for more attention than in most airplanes of the time; he was provided with a semienclosed compartment for his "comfort."

As a young man, Henry Farman was an art student in Paris, as well as an accomplished bicycle racer who, by 1892, had won major championships. With his brother, Maurice, Farman went into the automobile business around 1900, then turned to the manufacture and sale of airplanes.

Only four weeks after flying his Voisin for the first time, Farman set records for both speed and distance on a single flight at Issy-les-Moulineaux, near Paris. With several short warm-up flights, he became proficient enough to achieve a flight of 770 yards (704 meters), performed in 48.1 seconds on October 26, 1907. He thus increased Santos-Dumont's Absolute World Air Speed Record of 25.66 mph (41.29 km/h) to 32.74 mph (52.68 km/h). Farman, however, was still well below the speeds achieved by the Wright brothers two years earlier.

The Voisin-Farman was the first in a long line of successful airplanes from the Farman factory. It had a wingspan of 32.8 feet (10 meters), a wing area of 430 square feet (40 square meters), and a takeoff weight of 1,170 pounds (530 kilograms). Construction was mainly of ash and mahogany, covered with rubberized linen.

One of the reasons the Wrights were still ahead of their European rivals, even though they hadn't flown in many months, was that their transatlantic counterparts had not yet caught on to the vital need for full control of their airplanes. So far, the Europeans were content to build airplanes that were supposed to glide through the air much as a boat glides through the water. Whereas a boat usually rights itself after being tipped by wind or waves, an airplane does so in only a limited manner, since it is not truly floating. Most early flights by Europeans actually were struggles to keep their frail craft from crashing when upset by rough air or the pilot's lack of skill.

When, in 1908, the Wrights emerged from their self-imposed period of non flying, they did so in their Model A Flyer. After some warm-up flying, during which they carried the first airplane passengers, the brothers took two great steps on the road to practical flight. While Orville demonstrated an airplane to the U.S. Army at Fort Myer, in Virginia, Wilbur threw European aviation into something resembling a state of shock.

On August 8, 1908, at a racetrack near Le Mans, France, Wilbur made what was for him a relatively short flight of slightly less than two minutes. The gathered aeronauts, suspicious at first, were astonished by the ease with which he took off, flew under obviously total control, and landed with no apparent concern for a possible crash. Doubt about the mysterious American brothers was replaced by awe. A few days later, Wilbur and a small crew moved their demonstration a few miles to a large military training area and surpassed every recorded standard for speed, distance, and duration. On September 16, he flew for almost 40 minutes, and five days later flew more than an hour and a half, covering 42 miles (67.6 kilometers).

French and English aviators, taking note of what they had seen, prepared for what now seemed an inevitable revolution in the art and science of aerial locomotion. Now effective flight controls and more efficient propellers would have to be developed; then aviators would have to really learn to fly, rather than being content to meander along at the mercy of the elements.

There was no record-setting in 1908. The Europeans had been so thoroughly upstaged by Wilbur Wright that to challenge him was, for the time being, unthinkable. Meanwhile, Wilbur was more interested in touring the Continent to instruct pilots and sell airplanes than he was in setting records. Europeans were soon convinced that Wright airplanes were the easiest route to better flying, and that a single lesson from Wilbur was worth years of self-instruction.

The first pupil at Wilbur Wright's temporary flying school in the south of France was Paul Tissandier. Tissandier served as treasurer of the FAI for many years, becoming secretary-general in 1919. He learned quickly and well from the master, bought one of the first Wright Model A Flyers to be assembled in Europe (from parts made in Dayton, Ohio), and only three and a half months after his first flying lesson broke the French air speed record.

On May 20, at Pont-Long, near the Wright school at Pau, Tissandier made a flight that lasted one hour and two minutes. He covered 35.7 miles (57.5 kilometers) while being observed by officials of the Aero Club of France. His speed works out to 34.6 mph (55.7 km/h), though FAI records of the precomputer-era show it as 34.0 mph (54.7 km/h).

Tissandier's Wright Model A Flyer was a standard machine with no known modifications, as they weren't needed for record-setting. The airplane, built of spruce and ash and covered with unbleached cotton fabric, had a wingspan of 41 feet (12.5 meters), a length of 29 feet (8.4 meters), and a wing area of 510 square feet (47.4 square meters). Empty, it weighed 800 pounds (362 kilograms) and ready for flight, 1,000 pounds (453 kilograms). The Model A was powered by a 30-horsepower, four-cylinder, water-cooled, in-line Wright engine driving, by means of bicycle chains, a pair of 8.5-foot (2.6-meter) wood propellers.

Until the summer of 1909, speed flying was very much an individual matter, with competition between a pilot and a stopwatch. Because any sort of flying was a crowd-stopper, there was little need to add to the novelty. But that changed forever in August 1909. At Betheny flying field, near Reims, in the heart of the French Champagne country, the first air meet was held. Over a full week, thousands of spectators watched pilots push themselves and their airplanes to new levels of speed, altitude, and duration. For the first time, several airplanes were in the air at the same time, racing around a course marked by brightly colored towers, or pylons, much as they do today. Also for the first time, constraints were placed on aviators. At Reims, the already great demands applied by undependable engines, none-too-strong wings, badly designed controls, and rudimentary flying skills would not be enough. To them were added the precise course to be flown, a schedule to be met, and a throng of paying spectators to be pleased. Success — and failure — would be in full view of everyone.

The "Great Week of Aviation of the Champagne" opened August 22, 1909. Europe was still excited by Louis Bleriot's conquest of the English Channel in a fragile monoplane four weeks earlier. Bleriot, who made the first significant international flight (from Les Baraques, France, to Dover, England), was at Reims with two new airplanes to show off. He intended to demonstrate to the world that he was no one-flight wonder.

It seemed that almost everyone in aviation was at Reims, aside from the Wrights who were busy at home and Santos-Dumont, who was expected but failed to show up. Among those present were Henry Farman and Leon Delagrange, the leading pilots of Voisin airplanes, and Glenn Curtiss, the only other American then flying. Bleriot's unsuccessful rival for the cross-Channel flight, Hubert Latham, was also there with two Antoinette monoplanes. The fliers were at Reims for the prestige, for the opportunity to show their skills in this first air show, and for the not inconsequential trophies and prizes of 175,000 francs (about $35,000 then). In addition, the air show was a rare opportunity to share ideas, theories, and dreams with other top people in aviation.

The main event of the week was the "Grand Prix de la Champagne et de la Ville de Reims" (Grand Prize of the Champagne and of the City of Reims) for the longest nonstop flight of the meet. The "Prix de la Vitesse" (Prize for Speed) would go to the pilot who flew the fastest three consecutive laps around the 6-mile (10-kilometer) course immediately in front of the grandstand. The "Prix du Tour de Piste" (Prize for a Circuit of the Course) was for the fastest single lap, and the "Coupe d'Aviation Gordon Bennett" (Gordon Bennett Aviation Cup), for the fastest two laps, was sponsored by the newspaper magnate James Gordon Bennett.

A night of heavy rain had turned the dirt roads and grassy flying area into a quagmire of mud. Late in the morning of opening day, the first airplane tried unsuccessfully to take off for the elimination trials of the Gordon Bennett Race. Next it was the turn of the recordholder for speed, Paul Tissandier, who got his Wright Model A into the air for a flight that lasted only one minute. Bleriot followed and got less than halfway around the course before he had to land. If the crowd had not been enthralled by the sight of airplanes in action, they might have walked out. Around five o'clock, a heavy storm broke that forced spectators to run for cover and mechanics to shove their airplanes into hangars. When the brief storm had passed, it was as though an invisible obstruction had been removed, leaving the air more conducive to flight. In short order, there were seven airplanes above the field at the same time, something that had never before been seen.

Of five pilots who flew three times around the 10-kilometer course that day, the fastest was Tissandier in his Wright biplane. By flying the 30 kilometers (18.6 miles) in 28:29.2, he unofficially broke his own French speed record with an average of 38.6 mph (62.1 km/h), which was about as fast as the Wrights' best times. Of all the individual laps of the day, the single fastest was by Eugene Lefebvre, also in a Wright Model A, who was clocked at 41.5 mph (66.8 km/h). This was true speed flying, yet it would be bettered so soon that neither performance was submitted as a record. Two weeks later, Lefebvre died in the crash of his plane, the first pilot to lose his life in that manner.

On the second day of the Reims air races Glenn Curtiss flew his specially built "Reims Racer" around the course at 43.4 mph (69.8 km/h). The

50-horsepower engine drove the aircraft faster than the 30-horsepower Wright engines of Tissandier's or Lefebvre's planes, though the myriad struts and wires of these and other 1909 biplanes would appear impossibly clumsy and unstreamlined today. But Curtiss's performance was for the moment supreme, replacing Tissandier's three-month-old record.

Curtiss got his start in aviation in 1904, when Capt. Thomas Baldwin bought one of Curtiss's highly regarded motorcycle engines for an airship. By 1908, Curtiss was a member of the Aerial Experiment Association, along with Alexander Graham Bell, and had designed and built several airplanes. Only two months after his first flight, Curtiss won the *Scientific American* magazine trophy for the first public flight in the United States of more than one kilometer. Despite the controversy surrounding his long patent fight with the Wrights over ownership of an invention for lateral control of an airplane, Curtiss's reputation was established by his development of water-borne aircraft. A company bearing his name built thousands of military and civilian airplanes, including the major American contribution to World War I aviation, the "Jenny" trainer.

Curtiss's "Reims Racer" was a direct descendant of his earlier machines, "June Bug" and "Golden Flyer"; but in the "Racer" greater emphasis was placed on speed. The aircraft had a wingspan of 30 feet (9.1 meters), a length of 31.1 feet (9.5 meters), and a wing area of 270 square feet (25 square meters). Power was supplied by a newly designed Curtiss water-cooled V8 engine of 50 horsepower that drove a single wood propellor. The airframe was of bamboo and spruce with some steel tubing. The wings and tail were covered with rubberized fabric, whereas the fuselage was uncovered.

On the third day of Reims, a monoplane entered the speed contest. Louis Bleriot flew his latest design, the one-of-a-kind Type XII, with a 50-horsepower engine and a geared-down propellor, to another record. Bleriot's one lap around the course was completed in 8:04.4, or 46.2 mph (74.3 km/h). In only three days, four pilots had exceeded the existing Absolute French Air Speed Record and had raised the original mark by more than 10 mph (16 km/h). Both the crowd and the press loved it.

At midweek, speed flying briefly took a back seat while pilots attacked distance and duration records. On August 25, going for the most prestigious prize of the meet, Louis Paulhan flew his Voisin biplane around the course more than 13 times (81 miles, 130 kilometers), breaking Wilbur Wright's official distance record. The next day, Hubert Latham, in the Antoinette VI, repaired since ditching in the English Channel four weeks earlier, flew 96 miles (154.5 kilometers) and stayed aloft for two hours 13 minutes. The following day, Henry Farman stayed up more than three hours and covered 112 miles (180.2 kilometers). This assault on distance and duration records produced flying which topped even that of the Wright brothers.

With one day left in the world's first air meet, Bleriot once again surpassed the single-lap record with a clocking of 7:47.8, to set a new French Air Speed Record of 47.84 mph (76.97 km/h). Curtiss, his main rival, came close to matching the mark when he completed two laps of the course, winning the Gordon Bennett Race trophy with a mark of 47.1 mph (75.8 km/h). While Curtiss was acclaimed the champion speed pilot of Reims, he held the official

French Air Speed Record for a mere 24 hours. When the meet ended, Bleriot's 47.84 mph was official.

It was obvious to everyone at Reims that whatever speed record was set, it would soon be broken; the pressure of competition was rapidly replacing the calmer atmosphere of research. Sadly, Bleriot's record-setting plane was destroyed by fire on the final day of Reims; Bleriot escaped with minor injuries. The aircraft was considerably larger than the Type XI in which he had crossed the Channel and which had became a favorite among American and European pilots. The Type XII had a wingspan of 32.9 feet (10 meters) and a wing area of 237 square feet (22 square meters), compared with the Type XI's wing area of 151 square feet (14 square meters). The Type XII had a takeoff weight of 1,365 pounds (618 kilograms) and was powered by a 50-horsepower, eight-cylinder, water-cooled E.N.V. engine. Construction was the usual Bleriot mixture of steel tubing, ash, and bamboo covered with rubberized fabric. The propellor was an eight-foot (2.4-meter) two-bladed, wood Chauviere.

Despite the growing desire of pilots with little training and experience to fly faster, higher, and farther, there was not a single serious injury at Reims in 1909. There were crashes, to be sure: some well-known pilots were involved in accidents. The airplane of 1909 flew so slowly, however, and had so many small, breakable parts to absorb impact, that the pilot usually walked away with no more than cuts and bruises. During the "Great Week of Aviation," 22 pilots flew some 1,500 miles (2,413 kilometers), remained aloft 50 hours, and broke every existing record several times. The British weekly *Flight* (founded early in 1909 and still in existence) capped its thorough coverage of Reims by saying:

> It taxes the English tongue . . . adequately to picture the epoch-making events that have marked the progress of the flying races at Reims. Now they are matters of history, none can gainsay that journeys of over a hundred miles in length can be made by aeroplanes without pause; or that the same machine can fly to great heights, or that it can carry comparatively great weights as represented by three persons aboard.
>
> The Reims meeting . . . is the first occasion on which a wide variety of machines have been brought together, and on which one has been pitted against the other day after day, so that one day the monoplane is to the fore and the next day the biplane takes the lead; while the fact that many of the competitors have been [flying] for a few weeks only reveals that the management of [aeroplanes] can be acquired as quickly as one learns to drive a motor car. The result is that none who read can scoff any longer. The age of flight is the age we live in.

If anything was as predictable as breaking the Reims records, it was the attempts to repeat the meet's successes. Of the numerous cities that set out to duplicate both the thrills and serious impact of the Reims meet, the first to do so with anything approaching the same level of proficiency was Nice, in April 1910. The Nice meeting was neither as large nor as historic as its predecessor, but it added its share of achievements to the fast-growing history of air travel. Although no Americans took part, the French were there, along with the noted

British pilot Charles Rolls (of Rolls Royce), as well as fliers from Algeria, Denmark, Germany, Peru, and Russia.

Michael Efimoff, a Russian, was the over-all leader among the competitors, flying more than 600 miles (965 kilometers) during the meet and taking prizes for the shortest takeoff (34 feet, 10.4 meters) and the fastest five-kilometer flight. But it was Hubert Latham who captured racing honors by breaking Louis Bleriot's eight-month-old Absolute Air Speed Record. Latham flew an Antoinette monoplane similar to the one he ditched in the English Channel while trying to beat Bleriot across. Once around the 4.5-mile (7.2-kilometer) course took 5:36.8, for an average speed of 48.205 mph (77.562 km/h). This was less than a half mile per hour faster than the existing record, but there was then no minimum margin. Latham, who did more than anyone to popularize the sleek Antoinette airplane, took up flying in 1909. Thinking he had contracted tuberculosis, he preferred to die quickly in the air rather than slowly in bed. Latham, however, lived another three years, succumbing to a disease he picked up while hunting big game in Africa.

Like the Bleriot airplane it bested on the speed course, Latham's Antoinette was a monoplane; but unlike Bleriot's crude craft, Latham's was an early attempt at streamlining. In particular, the entire slim fuselage of the airplane was covered to keep the numerous wood structural members from causing drag. Due to its superior shape, the larger, less powerful Antoinette was slightly faster than the Bleriot. The standard Antoinette of 1909−10 was a high-wing design with a span of 42 feet (12.8 meters), a length of 37 feet (11.5 meters), a wing area of 538 square feet (50 square meters), and a height of 9 feet (3 meters). At takeoff it weighed 1,300 pounds (590 kilograms). The aircraft was powered by a 50-horsepower Antoinette water-cooled V8 engine driving a two-bladed propeller with a steel shaft and aluminum blades. The airframe was of ash and spruce and was covered with rubberized fabric except for the forward fuselage, which was covered with cedar. Although Latham's machine no longer exists, similar Antoinettes still exist that are in excellent condition and on display in museums in London and Paris.

The second "Great Week of Aviation" occurred in July 1910, at the same site as the inaugural event. While the novelty of seeing several airplanes flying at the same time had worn off, the impact on the future of flight was considerable. Every available record was broken: the altitude record of 508 feet (155 meters), set at Reims in 1909, was raised to more than 4,500 feet (1,375 meters); the old distance record of 112 miles (180 kilometers) was replaced by one of 245 miles (395 kilometers); and the duration record of just over three hours, set in 1909, was topped by Lt. Jan Olieslaeger, a Belgian, who remained aloft more than five hours.

The most noteworthy speed flying was by Leon Morane, an automotive engineer by training and profession who had a brief but bright flying career. His flying was limited to 1910, when he was in the employ of the Bleriot firm. After flights at Reims, Morane tried for a long-distance flying prize but was injured in a crash and retired from flying. He turned to designing airplanes. His scout and pursuit planes earned him considerable praise during World War I. In the area of speed flying at Reims in 1910, it is clear who was the top pilot;

but the actual speed achieved has dimmed with time. Flying a Bleriot monoplane, Morane received the prizes for flying the fastest 5, 10, and 20 kilometers (3.1, 6.2, and 12.4 miles). His speed for 20 kilometers is listed by the FAI as 66.18 mph (106.508 km/h); in contemporary publications the time given is 12:45.6 (a timing that works out to only 58.4 mph, or 94 km/h). Moreover, Morane's fastest speed for 5 kilometers is slower than that for his 20-kilometer speed, though both were made during the same flight. The solution to this confusion should lie in the permanent records of the supervising officials, which should be at FAI headquarters. All pre-World War II records, however, apparently were destroyed by the Nazis shortly after they occupied Paris in 1940. What remains is the published listing of records, and they consistently show Morane as having flown 20 kilometers at 66.18 mph; so there is little point in trying to redo someone's efforts of more than 70 years ago. Besides, Morane, by winning all the short-distance speed awards, showed that he was the fastest pilot at the meet. His 10-kilometer speed of 65 mph (105 km/h) puts him within reach of the official record, for which he is credited.

Up to this point, all records for speed in the air, for duration, and for distance had been supervised and declared official by the Aero Club of France rather than by the sole appropriate international body—the FAI (founded in 1905). Finally, during the regular FAI meeting of October 27-28, 1910, the representatives of several national aero clubs took under consideration the matter of world records. Count Georges de Castillon de Saint-Victor, secretary-general of the FAI, recommended adopting the system of the Aero Club of France for international records. This meant that the FAI would recognize, among other things, speed records set on closed courses over various distances: 1, 2, 5, and 10 kilometers; by tens of kilometers up to 100 kilometers, by increments of 50 kilometers up to 300 kilometers, and from there by increments of 100 kilometers. Any interest in recognizing straight-line speed records was opposed by Bleriot, who understandably was concerned lest someone break an existing record simply by waiting until he had a strong following wind, then flying with that advantage. Bleriot convinced the delegates, and they accepted his proposal. At the same meeting, the FAI adopted as world records those accepted by the Aero Club of France. The procedure whereby officials of the aero club of the country in which a record was to be attempted would provide supervision and authentication was made a permanent part of the rules.

The day after the FAI formally became involved in the establishment of world records, the first speed record was set outside France—in the first major American aviation meet. The site was the racetrack at Belmont Park, New York (Glenn Curtiss, an American, had won the inaugural Gordon Bennett Race at Reims in 1909, so it was up to the Aero Club of America to stage the 1910 race). Just why an air meet would be held on Long Island in late October, when the weather was almost certain to be cold and windy, hardly conducive to good flying, is not known; but the top pilots from England and France were there, along with a large contingent of Americans. Each day of the nine-day-long meet offered separate contests for distance, altitude, and duration, and there were special events for speed flying.

Highlight of the meet was the 20-lap race around the 3.1-mile (5-kilometer) course for the Gordon Bennett Trophy. The course, located in front of the grandstand and clubhouse, gave the spectators a close-up view of the action. Despite the proximity of the speeding planes to the crowd, there were no accidents, nor was a pilot seriously injured in the numerous accidents.

For the Gordon Bennett Race on Saturday, October 29, 1910, there were six entries: Claude Graham-White of Great Britain, in a Bleriot powered by a 100-horsepower Gnome rotary engine; Alfred Leblanc of France, in a similar plane; John Moisant of the United States, in a 50-horsepower Bleriot; Alex Ogilvie of Great Britain, in a 30-horsepower Wright (the only biplane); Hubert Latham of France, in a 100-horsepower Antoinette; and Armstrong Drexel of the United States, in a 50-horsepower Bleriot. A lack of reliable airplanes ruled out a mass start, and Graham-White crossed the starting line shortly before 8:45 A.M., followed by Leblanc and Ogilvie. The others entered the race as late as 3:30 P.M. Graham-White steadily worked his lap times down to the three-minute mark (100 km/h), easily beating the best that Bleriot and Curtiss had done a year earlier.

It was Alfred Leblanc, however, who captured the crowd's attention. His first full lap was just under 2 minutes 46 seconds, which beat the Absolute World Air Speed Record by more than 2 mph (3km/h), even though Leblanc was flying a much shorter, and thus slower, course than the course Leon Morane had followed in setting the record. On each lap, Leblanc cut into Graham-White's lead time by eight to nine seconds. Graham-White completed his 20 laps in 1:01:04.74, breaking Morane's 100-kilometer record by nearly five minutes. Leblanc, meanwhile, continued to tear along, methodically improving his speed. By the end of his nineteenth lap, he was more than five minutes ahead of Graham-White's time, well on his way to victory and several speed records.

Then Leblanc's fuel line broke. His Gnome rotary engine, which had been running so smoothly, promptly stopped. Leblanc began an urgent search for a safe place to land. While concentrating on preparations for an emergency landing, he overlooked a telegraph pole and flew squarely into it, snapping the pole in two and making a shambles of his Bleriot. Incredibly, Leblanc suffered nothing worse than cuts and bruises. He lost out to Graham-White for the Bennett Trophy but captured world speed records for every recognized distance from 5 to 90 kilometers. Leblanc's eleventh lap at 2:44.78, was his fastest (it works out to 67.876 mph, or 109.236 km/h). The official record for his achievement may have been based on a slight error in arithmetic, as the speed of 68.199 mph (109.756 km/h), which appears in the record book, requires a time exactly one second faster than the lap record shown for the race in magazines of the day. In lieu of official FAI timing charts (which no longer can be found), the time of 2:44.78 is as close as anyone today can get to accurate data. Still, there is no doubt that Leblanc, despite his near tragedy, was the fastest pilot at Belmont Park; of the three other finishers in the race, only Graham-White was within an hour of his time.

Alfred Leblanc was born in Paris in 1869 and, in 1909, earned one of the first pilot's licenses issued by the Aero Club of France. After his record-setting speed flying, he tried the airplane manufacturing business, with little success. He later rose to president of the society of the French aircraft industry.

The first important American air meet ended on a sour note. Its second most prestigious event — a race around the Statue of Liberty, back to Belmont Park — took almost two years to produce a winner. John Moisant turned in the fastest time, beating Graham-White by nearly a minute. There was considerable controversy surrounding Moisant's start, though, which occurred after the deadline for starting had passed. Apparently the rules were changed during the race. Protests were filed on Graham-White's behalf, and a separate final banquet was held by his friends, who boycotted the official ceremonies. Two years later, the prize for the race was awarded to Graham-White by an FAI protest committee. The controversy overshadowed the outstanding accomplishments of the meet, for example, Moisant's excellent flight in the Statue of Liberty Race in an airplane he was not familiar with and which he had just purchased to replace one from which he escaped uninjured after a mid-air collision (among history's first such air accidents).

Leblanc's record-setting Bleriot monoplane resembled many that were built in Europe and the United States following the cross-Channel flight and the subsequent publicity which placed the spotlight on this aircraft design. The airplane had been specially modified for racing in a way that would soon become standard. The wingspan was reduced from 28 feet (8.5 meters) to 26 feet (7.9 meters) and the power increased from the usual 50 horsepower of the 7-cylinder Gnome rotary engine to 100 horsepower in the new 14-cylinder, two-row Gnome. Using a propellor 5 inches (12.7 centimeters) greater in diameter, the engine nevertheless could turn faster by 100 revolutions per minute.

Less than six months after Leblanc set his initial records, a series of speed trials at Pau, France, on April 12, 1911, brought him new world records for the distances 5, 10, 40, 50, and 100 kilometers. His time of 2:41 for 5 kilometers replaced his best-lap speed at Belmont Park as the official World Air Speed Record, being good for 69.470 mph (111.801 km/h). A writer for the magazine *Aero* (of London) commented: "These times will doubtless be beaten again before long, but probably by a machine designed to decrease head resistance [aerodynamic drag] rather than by one simply carrying more power." It took just a month for this prediction to come true. On May 12, at Chalons, in northeastern France, Eduard de Nieport (popularly known as Edward Nieuport) broke Leblanc's records in an airplane one-third as powerful. The new plane — pure Nieuport, having both an airframe and an engine designed and built by Edward Nieuport — represented a major advancement in aeronautical science.

Having bettered Leblanc's time for 100 kilometers (62 miles) while carrying a passenger and using a 50-horsepower engine, Nieuport set out to beat all the important records. Using a mere 28 horsepower to Leblanc's 100, he flew 10 kilometers (6.2 miles) in 5 minutes 7 seconds, 24 seconds faster than the old mark. Additional records were set for 20 kilometers (12.4 mph; 118 km/h, 73.2 mph) 50 kilometers (31 mph; 119 km/h, 73.8 mph), and 100 kilometers (62 mph; 119 km/h).

Edward Nieuport eventually was recognized by the FAI for an Absolute World Air Speed Record of 74.415 mph (119.760 km/h), though for what distance is not clear, due to computational confusion. As happened in several earlier instances, the superiority of his performance over everything done previously is beyond question. The speeds were achieved while flying around a 3.1-mile (5-kilometer) course, which probably reduced his actual speed by some 10 percent because of loss of speed in the frequent turns. The key to Nieuport's amazing performance on such low power was the design of his airplane. It had the clean, simple lines that nearly all high-speed aircraft of the future would display. The fuselage was entirely enclosed, the engine was partially covered by a formed-metal cowling, and the landing gear was more streamlined, having just a few properly shaped parts instead of the bundles of sticks found on most airplanes of the day.

The 1911 Nieuport had a wingspan of 27 feet 7 inches (8.4 meters), a length of 24 feet 8 inches (7.5 meters), and an empty weight of just 496 pounds (225 kilograms). Although the plane was slightly larger than the 100-horsepower Bleriot, it had so much less wind resistance that it could demonstrate an important principle in a way few other airplanes could: everything else being equal, streamlining beats power every time.

Nieuport's surpassing Leblanc's briefly held record ignited the first true contest for speed-record honors. A month after Nieuport set his initial records, Leblanc responded. In the elimination races for selection of the French team for the upcoming third annual Gordon Bennett Race, Leblanc broke many of Nieuport's official records, his fastest being 5 kilometers in 2 minutes 24 seconds, for a speed of 77.671 mph (125.000 km/h). As it had been in the 1910 race at Belmont Park, his plane was the special 100-horsepower Bleriot, whose power had finally proved too much for the efficient little Nieuport.

But not for long. Four days later, Nieuport was off again, this time using a 70-horsepower Gnome rotary engine in what had become his Astra-Nieuport. The result: one lap of a 3-mile (5-kilometer) course in 2:18.4, for a speed of 80.814 mph (130.057 km/h). Facing the fact that there is only so much that can be accomplished with an engine of minimum power, Nieuport combined his superior airplane design with almost as much horsepower as Leblanc had used. On June 21, 1911, Nieuport made yet another attempt on the record book, even though Leblanc had not responded to Nieuport's most recent records. Again at Chalons, France, he flew the short course at 82.727 mph (133.136 km/h), putting himself a full 5 mph (8 km/h) ahead of his rival. By now, though, his Nieuport's racer was equipped with an 80-horsepower Gnome engine, which could easily be replaced by a 100-horsepower Gnome if the challenge required it. Unfortunately, Nieuport's career ended before he could set more records. Less than three months after setting his final mark, he died in the crash of one of his airplanes while on training maneuvers with his army unit. The Nieuport name lived on, however. Nieuport's manufacturing enterprise built thousands of biplane scout and pursuit airplanes for the French and American forces during World War I. After the war, his name was combined with that of Delage and appeared on new record-setting airplanes.

The 1911 Gordon Bennett Race was held July 1 at Eastchurch, on the south shore of the Thames River estuary, east of London. An airplane favored to win the 150-kilometer (93-mile) feature race and set new speed records was a highly modified Bleriot referred to by some as a "racing freak." Its wings had been reduced in size to the bare minimum. By clipping several feet at the wingtips, to cut down on the drag-producing wing area, the designers had also removed much of the part of the wing used to make the airplane bank (via the common technique of wing-warping). There was serious doubt about the ability of the remaining wing to control the airplane. On his first serious try over the course, Gustav Hamel, the pilot, could not negotiate the first pylon turn and crashed, destroying the airplane but escaping without serious injury.

The winner of the Gordon Bennett Trophy was a newcomer, Charles Weymann, an American who flew a 100-horsepower Nieuport monoplane at a top lap speed of about 80 mph (130 km/h). Experts generally agreed that the shape of the course — that of a kite with one very sharp turn — held speeds below what would otherwise have been record levels.

In 1912, new names, shapes, and techniques appeared, as well as a new urgency; the race for supremacy in speed was attracting greater attention from a rapidly growing aviation community. Some new names were Louis Bechereau (a designer), Armand Deperdussin (a manufacturer), and Jules Vedrines (a pilot) — all of France. A new shape was the superbly rounded fuselage of the Deperdussin racer, made of laminated wood. A new technique was "monocoque," in which the elaborate system of tubes, wires, and braces that formed the internal structure of other airplanes was replaced by a stream-lined, tapered tube of wood that was strong and simple. The urgency was inevitable as the rewards for greater speed grew in terms of prestige for the manufacturer, which, in turn, led to increased sales and greater pride. Some indication of the pressure competition could exert was the popularity of the technique — considered by some to be less than sporting — of using bottled oxygen injected into an engine's carburetor to increase the power of the engine. The idea had been tried and then banned in auto racing some years earlier, but it was reportedly in use, quite legally, in some of the faster racing airplanes.

Of considerably cleaner design than even the 1911 Nieuport, the 1912 Deperdussin monocoque was faster right from the start. Jules Vedrines' first attempt at the record book in a "Dep" came on January 13 at Pau, when he flew 30 laps around the 5-kilometer (3.1-mile) course. His speeds for every distance up to 150 kilometers (93 miles) were records, attributable mainly to the aircraft's streamlined design. His time for 5 kilometers was 2:06.4, or 88.5 mph (142.4 km/h), but for some reason, the speed listed officially by the FAI as the new Absolute World Air Speed Record is 90.199 mph (145.161 km/h).

For the initial assault on the record, the Deperdussin used a 100-horse-power, 14-cylinder Gnome rotary engine, although a 140-horsepower Gnome was installed for later attempts. A few weeks after his first session (February 22, 1912), on his second try, Vedrines again overturned a considerable number of records. His main achievement, however, was breaking the 100-mph barrier for the first time by an airplane under any conditions. Flying 10 kilometers (6.2 miles) in 3:43.2, he averaged 100.222 mph (161.290 km/h).

Vedrines' 1912 Deperdussin had a wingspan of 23 feet (7 meters), a length of 20.5 feet (6.25 meters), and wing area of only 108 square feet (10 square meters). The airframe was of ash and spruce and, aside from the fuselage which was laminated wood, was covered with linen.

Neither Vedrines nor the Deperdussin factory had any thoughts of resting on their laurels. On February 29, Vedrines went at it again and raised his 10-kilometer record to 100.944 mph (162.454 km/h). The next day, he broke this Absolute World Air Speed Record with a run at 103.658 mph (166.821 km/h) and on March 2 flew the same airplane 104.334 mph (167.910 km/h).

In less than a week, Jules Vedrines had broken the most important aviation speed records three times, even though no other pilot was pushing him to extract the ultimate from his airplane. It was the lure of pure speed that inspired him and the advanced design of his Deperdussin that made the records possible. Things calmed down briefly while preparations were being made for the forthcoming renewal of the Gordon Bennett Trophy Race. In the French team trials, held July 13, Vedrines again broke all the records, from 10 through 200 kilometers (6.2 through 124 miles). His best time was 10 kilometers in 3:33.0, the equivalent of 106.116 mph (170.777 km/h). This time, though, a fellow Deperdussin pilot, Maurice Prevost, was close behind him all the way.

The French Deperdussins thus were favorites to win the Gordon Bennett Trophy, at Clearing, Illinois, September 9, 1912 (near Chicago). The only threat from the Americans was an untested monoplane, sometimes called the "Defender," similar to the Deperdussins but meant to be powered by a new 160-horsepower Gnome engine.

When it was time to line up the contestants, however, only the French were ready. Vedrines and Prevost were there, along with Andre Frey in a small, powerful Hanriot monoplane. The "Defender" had not been completed, let alone tested, so the race went to the French by default. Not by default though, did they earn the trophy, for the performance of their French airplanes and pilots was of truly championship calibre.

The race consisted of 30 laps around a 4.14-mile (6.67-kilometer) course, for a total of 200 kilometers (124 miles). Although no World Air Speed Records were set during the race (no foreign pilots were pressing the French), the winning speed of 106 mph (171 km/h) far exceeded the previous year's 78 mph (125.5 km/h). After the race, Vedrines, the winner, flew a special three-lap speed test in which he was clocked for 20 kilometers (12.4 miles) in 6:55.95, for a published speed of 108.181 mph (174.100 km/h). This was Vedrines' seventh consecutive Absolute World Air Speed Record.

In anticipation of a busy year 1913, pilots, designers, builders and financiers headed home. In 1913, as it had been earlier, the attention of the world of fast flying was focused on the Gordon Bennett Race, this time to be held in France. During the French team trials at Reims, Maurice Prevost established himself as the man to beat. On June 17, 1913, he flew a new Deperdussin monoplane in setting several records, the most noteworthy being 10 kilometers in 3:20, for an Absolute World Air Speed Record of 111.735 mph (179.820 km/h). Prevost, a test pilot during World War I, held a variety of technical positions in the aircraft and related industries. His new Deperdussin racer was not merely the ultimate in streamlining for 1913; it was a mechanical achievement unequalled until some time after World War I. No airplane built during the war approached it in smoothness of line, attention to detail, and general appearance. Compared with the excellent 1912 Deperdussin, the Deperdussin racer of 1913 had 5 percent less wing area, a more extensively faired-in landing gear, and an engine cowling similar to the front end of a bullet, admitting a minimum of air to cool the 160-horsepower Gnome engine.

So obviously superior were the airplanes of the French team that the Gordon

Bennett Race was all but conceded to them. There was nothing in the United States — or in the world, for that matter — that could compete with them. On September 27, the first day of the three-day meet at Reims, the official selection trials were held for the French team. Three new Deperdussins vied with one Ponnier monoplane. All were powered by the latest 160-horsepower Gnome rotary engine. In the trials, Maurice Prevost was the winner, setting records for distance from 10 to 200 kilometers. His 10-kilometer speed was 119.239 mph (191.897 km/h), for a new Absolute World Air Speed Record, topping the old mark by 7 mph (11.3 km/h). Prevost's teammates in the race were Emile Vedrines (brother of Jules), in the Ponnier, and Eugene Gilbert, in a Deperdussin. The only non-French challenger was Crombez, of Belgium, in a "Dep."

On September 29, the last day of the meet, records were set for almost every lap of the 200-kilometer Gordon Bennett Race. When the race was over, Prevost stood alone, having covered the distance in less than an hour, making him the first aviator to travel at better than two miles per minute and more than 200 km/h (124 mph). Prevost's first lap around the 10-kilometer course was clocked at 2:56.6, for an Absolute World Air Speed Record of 126.667 mph (203.850 km/h).

The 1913 Deperdussin thus became the first of the classic speed planes. Perhaps the first true racing airplane, it survives, well preserved and protected, in the Musée l'Air. Its wingspan is 21.9 feet (6.65 meters); it is 20 feet (6.1 meters) long and 7 feet (2.1 meters) high and has a wing area of 104 square feet (9.7 square meters). At takeoff it weighs 992 pounds (450 kilograms). The fuselage is built up from strips of veneer shaped in conical form. The wings and tail are more conventional, having an ash structure and a doped linen covering. The two-bladed propellor is of laminated mahogany. The entire airplane, as it is currently displayed, is painted gold.

In little more than a year and a half, two Deperdussin pilots had raised the Absolute World Air Speed Record more than 50 percent. This increase in speed was more the result of design innovations than of any increase in horsepower, yet this lesson was not generally accepted for a long time.

The clouds of war cast a deep shadow over all peacetime activities, including speed flying. Long before plans could be made for the fifth Gordon Bennett Trophy Race, Archduke Franz Ferdinand had been shot dead. Men devoted to improving airplanes' speeds were soon absorbed in designing machines that would carry bombs and machine guns faster, higher, and farther. By the end of the war, the airplane had left its initial period of development and was well on its way to becoming a truly useful device — a device dependent for its usefulness largely on speed.

Streamlining

World War I ended, leaving Europe decimated and much of France a cemetery. National economies were shattered. The airplane, little more than a fascinating toy before the war, had in a few years become a major instrument of war. It had become more dependable, capable of carrying greater loads over greater distances, and, of particular significance, faster.

When the war had stopped the drive for pure speed, the land-speed record stood at 142 mph (228 km/h) set in 1911 by "Wild Bob" Burman in a Benz racing car at Ormond Beach, Florida. The Absolute World Air Speed Record, at 127 mph (204 km/h), wasn't far behind.

Once peace was declared, there were many matters of higher priority than resurrecting the FAI and setting new speed records. The nations of Europe first had to recover. But with thousands of newly proficient pilots coming home it was inevitable that interest in new attempts on the World Speed Record for airplanes would be rekindled. The FAI formally reopened its record book on January 6, 1920. In an effort to make each speed record more representative of the actual maximum speed of the airplane, the old system of timing a flight around a closed course was discontinued, at least for the minimum-distance/maximum-speed classifications. Henceforth, the pilot would make two runs in opposite directions over a straight, 1-kilometer (0.62-mile) course. The double runs were intended to cancel out the effects of wind, without the penalty of timed tight turns, which, in the past, had tended to reduce speed.

Despite the enormous losses suffered by France during the war, they were the first to begin work on new airplanes designed for speed. The two primary builders of French military pursuit planes – SPAD and Nieuport – immediately became rivals for speed-record honors by developing airplanes designed for action in World War I. The United States, having produced no significant combat airplanes during the war, was in no position to challenge the French. The British had built excellent, fast military airplanes, but they made no immediate effort to enter the competition. Germany was prohibited from any involvement in the production of high-performance airplanes. Italy might have moved in the direction of speed, but its interest was slow to develop. Thus it was left to SPAD and Nieuport to uphold France's reputation in the air. French airplanes held the last 17 Absolute World Air Speed Records. Nieuport made the first attempt, going after the seven-year-old mark with its new Type 29V ("V" stood for *vitesse*, or "speed"). The airplane had first been seen in October 1919, in the Coupe Deutsch de la Meurthe competition, in which pilots were challenged to fly more than 10 percent faster then the previous winner (who had flown 163 km/h [101.1 mph] in 1913) or the leader in the current year-long event. Aspirants had a year, from October 1919, to determine who, if anyone, deserved the trophy.

On October 14, Count Bernard de Romanet appeared with a Nieuport-Delage 29V. (After Edward Nieuport's death, his company was reorganized and the name of its chief designer, Gustave Delage, was added to all airplane designations). Although de Romanet failed to complete the 190-kilometer (117.8-mile) course, he showed the observers present that the Type 29V was an airplane to watch. Its main rival, the SPAD-Herbemont S.20, was also at the Coupe Deutsch starting point, but it too suffered from developmental troubles.

The Nieuport-Delage 29, designed as a military airplane, was too late for use during the war. For the Schneider Trophy Race for seaplanes, held in 1919, two 29s were equipped with twin floats, but because of a series of accidents during landings, neither plane started the race. The only pilot who started was foiled by dense fog, and the race was scrubbed. After that, the 29 got its wheels back. In addition, a dozen feet were taken off the wings and half the generous wing area was removed in an effort to boost the plane's speed sufficiently to win races and set records. The Vitesse version had the same basic fuselage as its military counterpart; such expendable items as machine guns were removed to reduce weight and wind resistance.

The first serious try for a speed record with a Type 29V came on February 1, 1920, at Villacoublay, near Versailles. Sadi Lecointe, an experienced French speed pilot, averaged 170 mph (273 km/h) over four passes along a 10-kilometer course. Even though the old record was left far behind, the new speed was never submitted to the FAI for recognition. Six days later, on February 7, it was another story. Lecointe set the first FAI-recognized postwar speed record, averaging 171.041 mph (275.264 km/h). Not only was the old record bettered by a third, the air-speed record had at last been raised above the fastest ever attained on land by an automobile. From then on, the airplane would be the standard of speed.

Lecointe's Absolute World Air Speed Record stood for only three weeks. It was broken by another French pilot flying another French airplane: Jean Casale in a SPAD-Herbemont 20bis$_4$. This aircraft was a development of the SPAD 20 two-seat pursuit plane used late in the war. In this version, major reductions had been made in the plane's wingspan and area. Casale's SPAD 20bis₄ had a wingspan of 21.7 feet (6.6 meters), a length of 24 feet (7.3 meters), a height of 9.5 feet (2.9 meters), and a wing area of 172 square feet (16 square meters). It was powered by a 275-horsepower Hispano-Suiza H-S 42 engine and weighed 1,960 pounds (888 kilograms) empty and 2,315 pounds (1,048 kilograms) fully loaded. Jean Casale, born in Corsica in 1893, learned to fly in 1915 and became a double ace in World War I before getting into speed flying. He set several altitude marks and was a pilot on the pioneering Paris-to-London route. He died in 1932 in the crash of a four-engine Bleriot, when the controls failed as he flew to pick up Louis Bleriot to take him to an air meet.

On February 28, Casale flew the 1-kilometer (0.62-mile) FAI course at Villacoublay four times in an average 12.7 seconds, or 176.136 mph (283.464 km/h). It was the first important speed record set by a SPAD airplane.

In Italy, in 1920, Francesco Brack-Papa was making speed runs with a huge Fiat ARF built for a transatlantic race planned for 1919 but canceled for reasons of safety. Brack-Papa was timed at 162 mph (261 km/h) on February 26 and then 170 mph (273 km/h) on March 3. This feat was possible in such a large airplane only because of its engine, an 800-horsepower Fiat V12.

In England, too, there was interest in speed records. Freddie Raynham was chosen to fly the unusually named Martinsyde Semiquaver, a small, trim biplane that resembled, in scaled-down form, the "Buzzard," probably the fastest airplane of World War I. On March 21, 1920, at Martlesham Heath, Raynham set a British speed record of 161 mph (259 km/h), but the mark was well below the existing Absolute World Air Speed Record. On June 17, Leslie Tait-Cox increased the national record to 166 mph (268 km/h) in a British-built Nieuport & General L.S.3 Goshawk, a one-of-a-kind racer designed by H.P. Folland. The British were gaining in speed, experience, and prestige; but the Absolute Record was still beyond their reach.

In late September 1920, the sixth James Gordon Bennett race was held at Etampes, France (since the French had won the race in 1913, they were the host this year). The entry list was perhaps the most impressive for any race up to that time, with important airplanes and pilots expected not only from France but from England and the United States. During elimination trials for the French team, held September 25, Sadi Lecointe averaged 174 mph (280 km/h) in a Nieuport 29V, Georges Kirsch did 167 mph (269 km/h) in another 29V, and Bernard de Romanet was clocked at 160 mph (258 km/h) in the SPAD 20bis₅. All were near the Absolute World Air Speed Record of 176 mph (283 km/h), which had been set on a short, fast course, with their speeds clocked for 100 kilometers (62 miles).

In the race on September 28, the French trio was scheduled to be challenged by three American airplanes — a Curtiss-Cox "Cactus Kitten" (which crashed upon arrival at Etampes); a Dayton-Wright Racer (a plane with revolutionary retractable landing gear and variable-camber wings, which dropped out during the first lap of the race); and a Verville VCP-R Army Racer (flown without testing in France and retired on the first lap with an overheated engine).

The British contingent fared no better. The Semiquaver, flown by Raynham, completed one lap at a record 178 mph (286 km/h); then its oil pump broke.

The Goshawk, flown by Jimmie James, arrived after the deadline, and the Sopwith Rainbow was withdrawn shortly before race time when its manufacturer went out of business.

Again, the French were alone. Kirsch took off first and flew an initial lap at 174 mph (279 km/h) and a slow second lap, landing on the third lap with fouled spark plugs. De Romanet was next up and turned in a pair of laps at 162 mph (260 km/h) before being forced to make a pit stop for repair of his oil system (which cut his 300-kilometer [186-mile] speed to just over 100 mph [161 km/h]). Lecointe, who was last up, won by averaging 169 mph (272 km/h) over the 300 kilometers. The French thus won the Gordon Bennett Trophy for the third time in succession and, having complied with the donor's rule, retired it permanently. They also established themselves as world leaders in speed by setting official records for 100 kilometers (62 miles) and 200 kilometers (124 miles) in a race that no other country's airplanes even finished.

The French quickly organized an air meet in their own honor, to be held two weeks later at Buc, headquarters of the SPAD company. The feature event of the meet was trials for the Absolute World Air Speed Record. The contestants were de Romanet, in a SPAD 20bis$_6$, which differed from the 20bis$_5$ mainly in having a large bowl-shaped propellor spinner that covered most of its blunt radiator; and Lecointe, in his Gordon Bennett-winning Nieuport-Delage 29V.

The rivalry was intense. On October 9, de Romanet was first up. He tore along the measured 1-kilometer course at an average 181.864 mph (292.682 km/h), breaking Casale's seven-month-old record. Lecointe accepted the challenge and went aloft, where he made a series of runs at 179 mph (288 km/h) and another at 182.6 mph (293.9 km/h), the latter being faster than de Romanet's but not by the minimum margin demanded by the FAI. Confronted with the obvious threat to his position, de Romanet made the day's fourth attempt. While he was being clocked at nearly 200 mph (320 km/h), his airplane's propellor spinner shattered; bits of it wrecked the radiator, forcing him to land immediately. De Romanet was out of the meet. The next day, Lecointe boosted his record to 184.357 mph (296.694 km/h), sufficiently faster than de Romanet's mark to qualify. With five attempts (two successful) in just five days, the French had achieved their goal: proving that their airplanes and pilots were still the fastest in the world.

Later that month, Lecointe made another attempt in the same Nieuport-Delage 29V, this time at Villacoublay, and became the first man officially to travel faster than 300 km/h (186 mph). His speed of 187.983 mph (302.529 km/h) erased his previous Absolute World Air Speed Record, thus posing an irresistible challenge to de Romanet and the SPAD team.

The Nieuport-Delage 29V had a wingspan of 19.9 feet (6 meters), a length of 20.4 feet (6.2 meters), a height of 7.8 feet (2.4 meters), and wing area of 142 square feet (13.2 square meters). Empty it weighed 1,366 pounds (620 kilograms) and loaded, 1,838 pounds (834 kilograms). Power for the 29V was supplied by a 12-cylinder Hispano-Suiza H-S 42 engine displacing 1,127 cubic inches (18.47 liters) and producing 275 horsepower.

Two weeks after Lecointe's successful run, the challenge was taken up by de Romanet in the SPAD 20bis$_6$. His airplane had a wingspan of 21.3 feet (6.5 meters), a length of 24.6 feet (7.5 meters), a height of 9 feet (2.7 meters), and a wing area of 164 square feet (15.3 square meters); it had an empty weight of 1,960 pounds (890 kilograms) and a gross of 2,315 (1,050 kilograms). The aircraft was powered by a Hispano-Suiza V12 rated at 300 horsepower. The Marquis de Romanet's brief but successful career in speed flying ended abruptly September 23, 1921, when he crashed to his death while testing a new Lumiere-de Monge Racer. At the time it was thought that the stitching holding the fabric cover to the wing was inadequate for the plane's speed, estimated at more than 185 mph (300 km/h), but it later became apparent that wing flutter caused the wing to fail.

Despite heavy fog at Buc, September 4, 1920, the Frenchman took off and sped over the course only a few feet above the ground. His fastest timed pass was made at exactly 200 mph (320 km/h); his average speed was 192.011 mph (309.012 km/h), for an Absolute World Air Speed Record barely sufficient to satisfy the FAI. De Romanet's mark was the sixth record set in 1920.

All the speed-record activity so far had been in Europe. Now, the United States was awaking to the possibilities of the sport. America's fruitless attempt in 1920 to win the Gordon Bennett Trophy had at least had the effect of stimulating interest in speed flying. The focus of this interest was the newly established Pulitzer Trophy Race, backed by Joseph Pulitzer, publisher of the *St. Louis Post-Dispatch* newspaper. The first race, held November 25, 1920, at Mitchell Field, on Long Island, was open to both civilian and military airplanes and pilots. The race drew 38 starters, and was run in seven heats, each heat consisting of four laps around a 29-mile (47-kilometer) triangular course.

Most of the pilots flew leftover World War I airplanes, such as British deHavilland deH.4 bombers and S.E.5 pursuit planes. One airplane stood out, however: the Verville VCP-R Army racer that had been forced by an overheated engine to drop out of the last Gordon Bennett Race. This time the plane was flown by U.S. Army test pilot Corliss Moseley. The plane was the brainchild of Fred Verville, who was inspired by the French pursuit planes of World War I to create a biplane with a plywood fuselage and unusually clean lines. By the time the Pulitzer Trophy Race arrived, his VCP-R was powered by a 600-horsepower, water-cooled Packard V12 engine.

Moseley and the Verville racer won the Pulitzer Trophy Race of 1920 by a margin of several minutes over the runner-up, averaging 157 mph (252 km/h) for the 116 miles (187 kilometers). With this evidence of the airplane's potential speed, plans were immediately made for an attempt on the Absolute World Air Speed Record, which hadn't been held by an American since Glenn Curtiss held it for one day in 1909. On November 27, Moseley made six tries, each time encountering carburetor trouble that kept his maximum engine speed well below its potential. Nevertheless, he achieved an estimated 186 mph (300 km/h), not far off the existing record of 192 mph (309 km/h).

Once the Americans failed, the French rubbed it in. On December 12, Sadi Lecointe, in his Nieuport-Delage 29Vbis, which had been modified by removing the windshield and cockpit opening, went for the record held by de Romanet. The windshield and opening were replaced by a flush cover and a small teardrop-shaped window in either side of the fuselage (the pilot's visibility was severely limited). These radical, and potentially dangerous, changes provided just enough reduction in wind resistance to enable Lecointe to boost the record to 194.516 mph (313.043 km/h). The 29Vbis had an upper wingspan of 17.9 feet (5.46 meters), a lower wingspan of 19.7 feet (6 meters), a length of 20.3 feet (6.2 meters), and a height of 8.2 feet (2.5 meters). Its wing area was 132 square feet (12.3 square meters). The empty weight was 1,520 pounds (690 kilograms); maximum weight was 2,063 pounds (935 kilograms). Power was the same as for the 29V — a 275-horsepower Hispano-Suiza 42 engine. After a long, productive career, Nieuport-Delage 29Vbis number 11 was seen no more in races or attempts at records, for it was destroyed during a test flight the following summer.

The 29V was replaced by the Nieuport-Delage sesquiplane. Exactly why it was called a "sesquiplane" is not clear, since that is a type of biplane in which one wing is substantially smaller than the other, though still definitely a wing. The Nieuport-Delage was actually a parasol type of monoplane with an airfoil-shaped fairing around the axle between the wheels, similar to some German Fokker pursuit planes of World War I. Regardless of its name, the sesquiplane was an impressive airplane that deserved all the attention it got. The new French racer was of approximately the same length as its predecessor (20 feet; 6.1 meters). Although its top wing was much longer (26.3 feet; 8 meters), the lack of a full-size lower wing cut the total wing area to a mere 118 square feet (11 square meters). Considerably heavier, it weighed 1,632 pounds (740 kilograms) empty and 2,160 pounds (980 kilograms) fully loaded. Both the 29V and the sesquiplane were powered by a Hispano-Suiza V12 engine, though the latter plane's engine developed an additional 25 horsepower. The real difference in design lay in streamlining. The "sesqui" had a fuselage that was an almost perfect teardrop, as well as a more carefully faired-in, tight, engine cowling, wing struts, and low windshield. It *looked* fast.

During trials before a new series of races for the Coupe Deutsch de la Meurthe, one of the two sesquiplanes was wheeled out so Lecointe could attack his own record, which had stood at 195 mph (314) km/h) for almost a year. On September 25, 1921, after having been timed unofficially at 218 mph (350 km/h), he flew the required four passes over the 1-kilometer course at an average speed of 205.223 mph (330.275 km/h). This mark broke not only Lecointe's Absolute World Air Speed Record but the 200-mph (320-km/h) barrier as well — an impressive debut for an airplane — and made Lecointe the favorite in the upcoming Coupe Deutsch Race.

On race day, October 1, Lecointe was joined by his teammate, Georges Kirsch, in an identical airplane, and by Fernand Lasne, who would be flying the Nieuport-Delage 29V that won the Gordon Bennett in 1920; Jimmie James, from England, in a Gloster Mars I; and Francesco Brack-Papa, from Italy, in a Fiat R.700. Lecointe tore off at terrific speed. Then his plane seemed to explode! Somehow he came out of the crash with only minor injuries, but the sesquiplane was ruined. At first, it was thought a collision with birds had caused the crash; later, the possibility of control surface flutter, then barely suspected even by aeronautical scientists, was suggested.

Kirsch then took off in an attempt to salvage something from a day that had been disastrous so far. He won the race, setting a World Speed Record for 200 kilometers (124 miles) of 173 mph (278 km/h). Lasne, the only other pilot to finish the race, was 20 km/h (12 mph) slower.

No attempts on the Absolute World Air Speed Record, already held by Lecointe, were made after the Coupe Deutsch Race. Instead, the scene shifted to the United States. The Pulitzer Trophy Race of 1921, scheduled for November 3 at Omaha, Nebraska, would be a much different affair from the race of 1920. Gone was the long, unwieldly entry list crowded with aging military planes. Of the dozen speedsters originally entered, only five started, of which four finished the five laps of the 31-mile (50-kilometer) course. The winner, by only two minutes, was Bert Acosta in a new Curtiss CR-1 Racer, at 177 mph (285 km/h).

Acosta's plane was something new in American aviation; powerful and aerodynamically clean, it was designed to be both pleasing to fly and easy to land at reasonable speeds (the ability to fly a *complete* race had become as important as all-out speed). The CR-1, built almost entirely of wood, had a smoothly polished surface that contributed to streamlining. For power, it used a 420-horsepower Curtiss CD-12, a water-cooled V12 that represented the first of several steps in building American aircraft engines superior to any built in Europe. Acosta, born in 1895, became a flamboyant character in the aviation world of the 1920s. He was as well known for his exploits with fast women as for his ability to fly airplanes. After setting records in flying, Acosta headed for skid row, recovered briefly in 1927 when he helped set an endurance record. Next, he made a transatlantic flight with Admiral Richard Byrd that was almost successful. Acosta flew for the Loyalists in the Spanish Civil War, then vanished from the aviation scene.

Several weeks after winning the Pulitzer Trophy Race, Acosta made his first try at the Absolute World Air Speed Record. He flew eight times over the 1-kilometer course at Curtiss Field, on Long Island. His fastest run was made at 198 mph (319 km/h), and his best four consecutive runs averaged 184.8 mph (297 km/h). Although this was almost 20 mph (32 km/h) slower than Lecointe's world record, at least it was an American record, a strong indication that the combination of Curtiss airframe and Curtiss engine might be just what was needed to make the Americans known in speed flying.

A few days after Acosta's effort in the Curtiss CR-1, the British made another attempt at the Absolute Speed Record. The Gloster Mars I, which had flown half the 1921 Coupe Deutsch Race before landing with suspected structural problems, was brought out again on December 19, 1921, to be flown by the veteran Jimmie James. An unusually small biplane, with wings spanning just over 20 feet (6 meters), it had a 530-horsepower Napier Lion engine which had its 12 cylinders arranged in what was known as the "broad arrow" form, with one bank of four cylinders sticking straight up between a widespread V8. James's attempt was made at Martlesham Heath, over the official Royal Air Force speed course, where he averaged 197 mph (316 km/h) for a British Air Speed Record but fell short of the standing World Record of 205 mph (330 km/h). Like the Americans, the British were moving closer to serious contention for the French-held record.

One last attempt was made before the winter of 1921-2. On December 25,

1921, Lecointe flew a Nieuport-Delage sesquiplane to a speed of 210.6 mph (339.0 km/h). It is not known why there was no effort to declare this speed official.

In 1922, Italy made its only serious attempt to capture the Absolute World Air Speed Record with a land plane. As a member of the victorious Allies in World War I, Italy had produced a variety of effective combat airplanes, and this ultimately led its aircraft industry to look to speed for international recognition. The airplane chosen for the speed-record attempt was the Fiat R.700, designed by Celestino Rosatelli.

As had become common practice by the early 1920s, the R.700 was built with an eye toward extracting every last mile per hour from its potential, with neat fairings at every intersection of two or more parts, a low windshield (though open cockpits were still in vogue), and a tightly cowled engine. The engine was the airplane's most unusual feature. It was a huge Fiat A.14 V12 rated at a maximum 825 horsepower. That such a power was necessary can be deduced from the aircraft in which it was installed. The R.700 was much larger than any of its rivals, having a wingspan of 35 feet (10.7 meters) and an empty weight sometimes exceeding 4,000 pounds (1,812 kilograms).

The key to the plane's performance was its engine, and that, in turn, dictated a large, hefty airframe. Rosatelli believed that power was what he needed to demonstrate that Italian airplanes were the fastest in the world. On August 22, 1922, Francesco Brack-Papa, who had flown the R.700 in the 1921 Coupe Deutsch Race, prepared himself for the flight. At Mirafiori Airport, near Turin, Italy, the runs were made before a group of timers holding stopwatches, a technique increasingly suspect as speeds rose and times shrunk. His speed for the four 1-kilometer passes averaged 208.9 mph (336.1 km/h), fast enough to qualify for FAI recognition.

The Italians made no move, however, to submit the required paperwork to the FAI, reportedly because they were satisfied they had broken the World Air Speed Record and would be duly recognized. There was also some suspicion that the Italians may not have wanted to take a chance that the French, who staffed FAI headquarters in Paris, might find some excuse to disallow the record for reasons of nationalism. Regardless of the justification (or lack of it) for holding back, no data were submitted; thus the achievement remains unofficial but highly impressive.

Attention turned once more to the Coupe Deutsch Race, to be held September 30, 1922, at Etampes, France, over the same 100-kilometer out-and-return course as had been used for the previous year's race. The "mystery racer" of the event was the fat, teardrop-shaped Nieuport-Delage Type 37, rumored to have superior streamlining and power. Other serious contenders were a Gloster Mars I and a Bristol 72, both from Great Britain.

Sadi Lecointe once more prepared for an assault on a series of speed records. His Nieuport-Delage sesquiplane was now equipped with a new wing having a symmetrical airfoil (similar curves on the upper and lower surfaces) for reduced drag. On September 10, at Villesauvage, he was timed unofficially for 1 kilometer at 222 mph (358 km/h), and on September 21 he did it officially, this time at a speed of 211.902 mph (341.023 km/h), thus adding almost seven miles per hour to the Absolute World Air Speed Record.

When the time came for the Coupe Deutsch, however, the intriguing, streamlined Nieuport-Delage Type 37 was nowhere to be seen. The plane had failed to take off on its first test flight and was quietly retired. This left the French with the sesquiplane (hardly a come-down, in view of its recent record performance) and the Nieuport-Delage 29V, which had won the Gordon Bennett Race two years earlier.

The only foreign racers entered were Jimmie James in the Gloster Mars I and the Fiat R.700 piloted by Brack-Papa. James got off to a good start but was forced to drop out when his map of the course blew out of the open cockpit and James was unable to find his way. The Italian entry turned in an excellent speed of 179 mph (288 km/h) but was disqualified for having made an incorrect start; a second try ended when the Fiat's carburetor began leaking.

This left only the French. Lecointe, fresh from his recent record, did his first lap at 202 mph (325 km/h) but was forced to land when a spark plug blew completely out of his engine. While landing, he hit a rut and flipped over, doing considerable damage to the plane but little to himself. Now the French pinned their hopes on the shoulders of Fernand Lasne, in his Nieuport-Delage 29V. Lasne did not let them down. His average speed for the 300 kilometers (186 miles) was 180 mph (290 km/h) — hardly a record pace but more than enough to win, for Lasne was the only pilot to complete the course officially.

Racing and speed records remained in French hands, but it wasn't because others weren't trying. Over the next few days, there was a flurry of speed-record activity. The American hope for record-setting was the Curtiss R-6, an outgrowth of the Curtiss CR-1 Racer, winner of the 1921 Pulitzer Trophy Race. The new aircraft was a better design — from propellor spinner to tail skid — thanks to awakened interest in air racing as a means of acquiring knowledge and experience for the military air services. The key to the new design was, once again, the powerplant. Starting with the marginally successful Curtiss CD-12 engine of 1921, the manufacturer had developed the D-12, which, though of almost the same overall dimensions, had more power and, more important, greater durability. Like the CD-12, the D-12 was a water-cooled V12 displacing 1,145 cubic inches (18.8 liters). By operating at considerably higher revolutions per minute, it produced 10 percent more power initially and eventually 20 percent more. The D-12, with its soon-to-be famous ear-piercing scream at maximum power, was squeezed into the tight nose cowling of the Curtiss R-6. All that showed was a row of short exhaust stacks on either side. Everything else was hidden inside, thus reducing wind resistance to a minimum. At first, the D-12 was used to turn a conventional wood propellor (the rules of the Pulitzer Trophy Race demanded it); but it was soon fitted with one of the first Curtiss-Reed metal propellors, a propellor far more efficient than the best wood ones, since it could be made much thinner and did not need to be thick for structural strength, as does a wood propellor. To cool the engine, Curtiss engineers developed a system of skin radiators which covered upper and lower surfaces of both wings from their centers out almost to the I-shaped interplane struts. The drag produced by these radiators was considerably less than that of earlier configurations, particularly the awkward barrel-shaped Lamblin radiators hung from struts of many other racers. Skin radiators were useful, however, only in airplanes designed for speed; they were too fragile for military or commercial purposes.

The R-6 was somewhat smaller than the CR-1, with wings of just 19 feet (5.8

meters), a length of 18 feet (5.75 meters), a wing area of 135.9 square feet (12.6 square meters). Empty, the plane weighed 1,616 pounds (732 kilograms) and loaded, 2,121 pounds (961 kilograms). Two R-6s were built in less than three months at a cost (to the U.S. Army) of about $35,000 apiece.

The first flight of an R-6 came in late September 1922. Not wishing to waste time telling interested parties why he thought the airplane was a winner, Army test pilot Lester Maitland immediately made a half-dozen passes over a speed course, clocking an unofficial 211 mph (340 km/h), equaling the existing Absolute World Air Speed Record—a startling feat for the first flight of a new design.

There wasn't enough time to get the airplane to France for the September 30 running of the Coupe Deutsch Race, no matter how good its chances were. Instead, the Army and Curtiss set aim on the Pulitzer Trophy Race, to be held two weeks later at Selfridge Field, Michigan. The second R-6 flew on October 2. Piloted by Russell Maughan, it was clocked at an unofficial 219 mph (353 km/h). Engine and airframe performed beautifully. Thanks to government funds and encouragement, the outlook for American speed airplanes had improved greatly.

Meanwhile, in England, Jimmie James determined to grab a share of the limelight with his Gloster Mars I, after an abortive try for the Coupe Deutsch. Three days after that race, at Etampes, France, James made three sets of four passes over the official 1-kilometer course. His best average speed was 210.7 mph (339 km/h), only 1 mph slower than Lecointe's record, proof that the Mars I was a fast airplane. The next day he made four more runs, averaging 212.7 mph (342.4 km/h), topping the official record but not sufficiently to satisfy the FAI. Still, the Mars I was now the world's fastest airplane, the first British flying machine to hold the title.

On October 8, it was once again the turn of Russell Maughan, in the second Curtiss R-6. In his four-pass practice run he averaged 220 mph (355 km/h), more than 8 mph over the record. Both R-6s were now ready for the Pulitzer Race and, despite limited test flying, were the heavy favorites to sweep the event, with Maughan the predicted winner.

The 1922 Pulitzer Trophy Race, held October 14, 1922, was as imposing a public debut as an airplane ever received. Maughan went quickly through five laps of the 31-mile (50-kilometer) triangular course at 205 mph (330 km/h). His average speed of 205.9 mph (331.4 km/h) was only slightly slower than the Absolute World Air Speed Record. And the Curtiss R-6 had been flying less than two weeks. In second place was Maughan's colleague, Lieutenant Maitland, who averaged 199 mph (320 km/h) in the other R-6. The next two pilots in the final standings flew Curtiss CR-1s, which had been modernized with D-12 engines and wing-skin radiators. Navy Lt. Harold J. Brow flew one of the CR-1s to third place, at 194 mph (312 km/h), while the other plane was flown by Lt. Al Williams, who took fourth place with a speed of 188 mph (303 km/h). No manufacturer up to that time had experienced a better day of air racing than had Curtiss. The company's engines and airframes had been proved world-class.

Clearly, the sequel to the highly successful introduction of the R-6 was an assault on the Absolute World Air Speed Record, which the French had held for the last 12 years. First, however, would be an attempt to break the record with an airplane of even greater innovation than the Curtiss R-6. Fred Verville's R-3 Army Racer was a low-wing monoplane of clean lines with a set of the then novel retractable landing gear. Had it been equipped with a Curtiss CD-12 engine, wing-skin radiators, and a Curtiss-Reed metal propellor, as planned, it would have been a worthy contender for the Pulitzer Race Trophy and the speed record; but Curtiss had a proprietary commercial interest in its engine, radiator, and propellor and refused to allow their use on the rival R-3 Racer. As a result, the best that could be attained during 1-kilometer speed tests on October 16-17 was 191 mph (307 km/h). It was a sad ending for a revolutionary airplane.

The day after the Verville R-3 speed runs, Curtiss and the Army were ready to show the world what their new plane could do. In place of Pulitzer Trophy winner Maughan (who had gone on leave after the race to be with his wife and baby son, born during the Pulitzer) and runner-up Maitland was a new pilot: Gen. Billy Mitchell was famous as commander of the Army bomber squadron that sank several large warships in a 1921 demonstration of air power, of which Mitchell was the most outspoken proponent. His was the strongest voice for air power in the period from World War I to 1930. He was court-martialed by the Army in 1925 for his opposition to official policy. Following a Far Eastern trip in 1924, Mitchell predicted a Japanese attack on Pearl Harbor but was ignored.

That the R-6 was capable of breaking the Absolute World Air Speed Record wasn't in doubt. On October 16, while the Verville R-3 was struggling to reach 200 mph (320 km/h), Russell Maughan flew several practice passes over a 1-kilometer course at 229 mph (368 km/h). Because the flight was not made in a set of four passes, there was no way to submit the achievement to the FAI as a record. Nevertheless, it was clear that the days of Lecointe's 212 mph (341 km/h) mark were numbered.

On October 18, it was General Mitchell's turn. Without even a practice flight in a Curtiss R-6, Mitchell made two sets of four runs in the space of an hour. The fastest set was done in Maughan's Pulitzer-Race-winner, at 222.970 mph (358.836 km/h). The Absolute World Air Speed Record was finally in American hands. Not since Glenn Curtiss had held it for one day in 1909 (at 43 mph [70 km/h]) had the prize been out of European hands. The money, time, hard work, and creativity that had gone into the R-6 and its D-12 engine had paid off.

The Curtiss R-6 had a wingspan of 19 feet (5.79 meters); length of 18 feet, 10½ inches (5.8 meters), a height of 7.6 feet (2.3 meters), and a wing area of 135.9 square feet (12.6 square meters); empty, it weighed 1,615.5 pounds (731.8 kilograms), loaded, 2,121 pounds (961 kilograms). The Curtiss D-12 engine developed 450 horsepower at 2,200 rpm.

Just as the Americans were thrilled with the success of their R-6, the French were equally unhappy, for they had held the Absolute World Air Speed Record for almost the entire 16 years of speed records. Regaining the record was immediately placed at the top of their agenda. The airplane chosen for this mission was a Nieuport-Delage sesquiplane christened the "Eugene Gilbert." The pilot chosen was the veteran Sadi Lecointe, who had already broken the speed record three times. The "sesqui" was brought out of storage and refurbished in preparation for its next flat-out runs, at Istres, a French military flight test center near Marseilles, where the usual problems encountered in winter flying would not be a factor. On December 31, 1922, Lecointe went at it. His average of 216 mph (348 km/h) was considerably slower than Mitchell's official mark, and Lecointe could do no better in another attempt on January 2.

If the standard "sesqui" couldn't meet the test, changes would have to be made. The clumsy "lobster pot" Lamblin radiators were replaced by thin sheet-metal radiators that covered the underside of the wings. The well-worn Hispano-Suiza engine was replaced by a 400-horsepower, water-cooled Wright V8.

On February 15, 1923, Lecointe was ready to try again for the Absolute World Air Speed Record. His airplane was much improved over the version that had failed him six weeks earlier. This time, the "Eugene Gilbert" was up to the challenge; it carried Lecointe four times along the short 1-kilometer course at Istres at an average speed of 233.014 mph (375.000 km/h) adding 10 mph (16 km/h) to Mitchell's best. Once again, French aviation was supreme.

This time, the Americans viewed Lecointe's flight as no more than a signal to fly faster; they had tasted victory, and they liked it. They were convinced the Curtiss R-6 had far greater potential than the older, more developed Nieuport-Delage sesquiplane. A few little changes here and there, and they should be able to reclaim the title.

Several weeks later, U.S. Army lieutenants Maughan and Maitland began a series of speed runs at Wright Field, near Dayton, Ohio, where some of the Wright brothers' earliest flights were made. Appropriately, the chief official of the National Aeronautic Association (NAA, which had just replaced the old Aero Club of America as the U.S. representative to the FAI) was Orville Wright, secretary of NAA's Contest and Records Board.

On March 26, 1923, Russell Maughan became the first to try the 1-kilometer course. He made a dozen runs, the fastest four consecutive being at 234 mph (376 km/h). Only marginally faster than the standing record, the mark failed to exceed the official mark by the required 4 km/h (2.5 mph). Maitland's best try was even slower: 219 mph (352 km/h). The Army colonels and generals were getting nervous. Their R-6 was supposed to have beaten the French record with speed to spare; it just couldn't seem to do it. On the twenty-ninth, all stops were pulled out. From an altitude of 7,000 feet (2,130 meters), Maitland dived his R-6 at the speed course, leveling out shortly before he entered the timed section. Over and over he attacked the kilometer, straining the airplane and himself, trying to eke out every extra bit of speed. His fastest four passes averaged 240 mph (386.2 km/h), far enough past the record to qualify him.

The NAA officials, however, would not allow the mark, claiming Maitland had failed to fly level through the course. According to Maitland, there was "nothing to it except which one is the biggest fool and takes the highest dive. That's where I got most of my speed." Diving to increase speed had long been tacitly accepted as a legitimate tactic in the sport, even though everyone was aware that it artificially distorted an airplane's performance. In an attempt to control the diving, the FAI insisted that an airplane be flown level for a specified distance before entering the timed portion of the course, as well as throughout the remainder of the course. That way, any speed gained during a dive should be dissipated before the official timing began. Once speeds exceeded 200 mph (320 km/h), however, this requirement was inadequate. In the heyday of the Curtiss R-6, the rules did not forbid steep dives. Later in the day following Maitland's attempt, Maughan went up for his turn, being careful to hold his altitude where required – but only after a long dive. He made more than 20 runs over the course, with the fastest four a fraction slower than Maitland's mark but fast enough to establish an Absolute World Air Speed Record: 236.588 mph (380.751 km/h). For some reason, the speed was calculated by averaging the four fastest *times* instead of the four fastest *speeds,* as required by FAI rules. The difference is slight, but it prevented Maughan from being recognized as the first to officially fly faster than four miles per minute. Had his speed runs been calculated properly, the result would have been 240.01 mph (386.26 km/h). Still, the U.S. Army had the record, and this time there was no fear the French would grab it back right away.

As an indication of the technological advances made in the years following Maughan's runs, his speed was equaled in 1982 – 59 years later – by a biplane with an engine that developed one-third the power. On May 2, of that year, Dan Mortensen, a race pilot, flew his 850-pound (387-kilogram) Amsoil-Rutan Racer to a 3-kilometer (1.9-mile) record for the FAI's Class C.1.b. With a mere 150 horsepower, Mortensen averaged 234.64 mph (377.61 km/h) with no speed-boosting dive.

Two days after Maughan brought the Absolute World Air Speed Record back to the United States, the FAI made a change aimed at improving the accuracy of timing for record. No longer would a pilot be permitted to make runs over a 1-kilometer course, for it had become obvious that with such runs now taking less than 10 seconds, an error of even 0.1 second would amount to more than 1 percent, too much to be tolerated. Henceforth, the shortest distance for speed records would be 3 kilometers (1.86 miles). Errors in timing would, at least in theory, be reduced 66 percent.

As 1923 wore on, speed flying again focused on the Pulitzer Trophy Race, this year to be held in early October in Dayton, Ohio. With the Army content to stick with its eminently successful Curtiss R-6, the Navy suddenly became excited about the race and decided to back two Curtiss R2Cs and two Wright F2W Racers.

Considered "mystery racers," the Wright biplanes were built around the new, powerful Wright T-3 "Tornado" V12 engine, which developed nearly 800 horsepower at 2,200 rpm, half again as much as the Curtiss D-12 in the Army's R-6 racers. Then, too, the F2W was substantially larger than the R-6 with wings 2.5 feet (0.8 meter) longer and an area almost 30 percent greater. Empty, the F2W weighed 50 percent more than the R-6, although its overall wind resistance was only slightly greater.

The other Navy racer – the Curtiss R2C – represented an evolution from the R-6. Compared with the R-6, the new aircraft had a slightly greater wingspan (22 feet, or 6.7 meters, for the upper wing, and 19.3 feet or 5.9 meters, for the lower) and a wing area of 144.25 square feet (13.4 square meters). By lowering the top wing onto the fuselage, to eliminate drag from the cabane struts between the wing and fuselage, the R2C-1's drag was not only reduced, but its pilot was provided with better visibility, since he could now look forward both above the upper wing or below it. The nose of the R2C-1 was longer and slimmer than that of its predecessor, resulting in a somewhat longer fuselage of 19.7 feet (6 meters). The airplane weighed slightly more than an R-6 — 1,692 pounds (766.5 kilograms) empty and 2,112 pounds (956.7 kilograms) loaded — but this was more than compensated for by the greater power of its Curtiss D-12A engine. By increasing the piston displacement from 1,145 to 1,210 cubic inches (18.8 to 19.8 liters) and boosting the compression ratio, the engineers raised the power output from 465 to 520 horsepower.

With the Pulitzer Trophy Race less than a month away, the two Wright F2Ws and two Curtiss R2C-1s were prepared for speed trials. On September 10, 1923, Lt. W. H. Sanderson took the first F2W up for some runs over a 2-mile (3.2-kilometer) test course at Mitchell Field, on Long Island. Although he could set only an unofficial record on a course of such odd length, his 238 mph (383 km/h) was an indication that the racer was capable of challenging the Absolute World Air Speed Record set six months earlier. Three days after Sanderson's practice runs, and just three days after its initial flight, Navy Lt. Harold J. Brow gave a Curtiss R2C-1 its first chance to show some speed. Over the same course at Mitchell Field, he averaged 244 mph (393 km/h) with a wood propellor, thus unofficially breaking the present record by 7 mph (11.3 km/h). Even though his airplane had 200 horsepower less than the F2W, its superior streamlining gave it greater speed.

Three days passed, and again it was Sanderson's turn in the Wright Racer. With maximum power from his roaring Wright engine, Sanderson averaged close to 248 mph (399 km/h) over the course, which was slightly longer than regulation. This was 11 mph (17.7 km/h) faster than the current record and somewhat better than the rival Curtiss had done so far. It was becoming a classic contest between two of the oldest and proudest names in American aviation: Curtiss and Wright. Also on September 16, Al Williams got his first chance at a speed record. Flying an R2C-1, he promptly turned in a speed of 255 mph (410 km/h) in tests over the 2-mile (3.2-kilometer) course, becoming the first to reach both the 250-mph and the 400-km/h frontiers. For Williams, it was the start of a colorful public career in aviation.

The 1923 Pulitzer Trophy Race, held at Lambert Field, near St. Louis, was one of aviation history's great air races. The hoped-for foreign contingent consisting of Brack-Papa (Italy) in a Fiat R.700, Larry Carter (Great Britain) in a Gloster Mars I, and Sadi Lecointe (France) in a Nieuport-Delage sesquiplane, withdrew shortly before the race, but the Americans made up for their absence, and then some. The Pulitzer Race was unquestionably the highlight of the air meet. It was run in three heats of four laps around the 31-mile (50-kilometer) triangular course. In the first heat, Sanderson, in a Wright F2W, won with a mark of 230 mph (370 km/h), not much slower than Maughan's 3-kilometer sprint record of 237 mph (381 km/h) in the R-6.

In heat number three, Harold Brow, in an R2C-1, was pitted against Lt. Steven Calloway, in the other F2W, and Lt. Walter Miller in an R-6 used the preceding year. The R-6 performed credibly, averaging 219 mph (353 km/h), while the F2W's speed was almost exactly the same as its stable-mate in the first heat. Brow, however, flew the 200 kilometers (124 miles) in the R2C-1 at 241.8 mph (389 km/h). While deserving of praise, Brow's speed was overshadowed by Williams' winning performance in the second heat. Flying the other Curtiss R2C-1, Williams set an official Absolute World Air Speed Record for 200 kilometers of 244 mph (392 km/h). Williams got the headlines, and Curtiss was the most prestigious name in the aviation world.

No one doubted Brow's and Williams' ability, or that of their R2C-1s to break the Absolute World Air Speed Record; it was merely a question of who would do it, and by what margin. On November 2, the stage was set. The attempt would be made between Mineola and Garden City, on Long Island. Less than 20 miles from downtown Manhattan, two of the world's fastest aircraft would go for the record.

Brow got first crack at the 3-kilometer course. Born in Fall River, Massachusetts, in 1894, Brow became a career Navy officer after learning to fly in 1918. His fastest four runs — of many he made during a half hour of trying, tense flying — averaged 257 mph (414 km/h), more than 20 mph (32 km/h) faster than the old record and enough to satisfy almost anyone, including the official timers from the NAA. Everyone, that is, except Al Williams. He went up in the other R2C-1 and immediately broke Brow's record, with an average speed of 258.5 mph (416 km/h). Brow then went back up and boosted the mark to 259.148 mph (417.059 km/h), a mark that stood and was submitted to the FAI as the first 400-plus km/h speed officially recorded.

The record stood for only two days, however, primarily because of high winds on November 3 which prevented all flying. On the fourth, the duel began again. This time, Williams was allowed to fly first, and he acknowledged the honor with a set of runs at 263 mph (424 km/h), which exceeded the previous mark by a wide enough margin to warrant consideration by the FAI had it remained for any length of time. Just as Williams was getting ready to leave for the day, though, Brow took up the challenge laid down by Williams and raised his mark to 265.7 mph (427 km/h). Williams couldn't very well leave after having been dethroned, so he got back into his flying clothes and had a go at it again. He climbed to an altitude of almost two miles (3.2 kilometers) and put the sleek racer in a steep dive, leveling out a mere few yards above the ground. Time after time, Williams charged over the course, quitting only after he almost collided with a formation of Army bombers. The speed of Williams' dangerous flight averaged out to 266.584 mph (429.025 km/h). For the third time in two hours, the Absolute World Air Speed Record had fallen; it now stood a full 30 mph (48 km/h) above its level only three days earlier.

While heaping praise on its pilots, the Navy, concerned for the lives of its pilots and about the impact the death of a pilot would have on the Navy's image, promptly ordered an end to the aerial jousting matches.

That ended such flying for 1923. It wasn't until the middle of 1924 that anyone tried to break Williams' speed record. This time it was Lecointe, in a new airplane, the Nieuport-Delage Type 42, which had been built for the upcoming Coupe Beaumont Race and for recapturing the Absolute World Air Speed Record, whose residence in America had made the French unhappy. The layout of the Type 42 was similar, overall to the older sesquiplane, but it was larger and heavier. With more than 500 horsepower from its Hispano-Suiza V12 engine, compared with the older design's 400 horsepower, the Type 42 expected to attain greater speeds.

Lecointe attacked the speed course in late June 1924 but was unable to match, let alone exceed, Williams' 267 mph (429 km/h). He won the 1924 Coupe Beaumont Race, however, and set a 500-kilometer (310-mile) record of 191 mph (306 km/h), but that was little consolation for Lecointe. After winning the Coupe Beaumont in 1925 by default, when the only other starter dropped out, Lecointe left speed flying for good. He served for 15 years as chief test pilot for Nieuport-Astra, then went to Africa, where he commanded French forces allied with Gen. Charles de Gaulle. He returned to Paris in July 1944 and died there a few weeks before Allied armies liberated the French capital.

The Nieuport-Delage Type 42 had failed even to threaten the American-held record. Nothing further happened until October 1924, when the Pulitzer Trophy Race was held at Wright Field, in Dayton, Ohio. Two Curtiss R-6s were entered, to be flown by Army pilots Burt Skeel and Wendell Brookley, along with a Verville R-3, piloted by Harry Mills, and a Curtiss PW-8A pursuit plane, flown by Rex Stoner. Skeel's racer disintegrated during the diving start, killing him. Mills won the race at an uninspiring 217 mph (349 km/h) in the R-3, followed by Brookley at 214 mph (345 km/h). Of the two great Curtiss R2C-1s, one had been wrecked the previous September and the other was converted into a seaplane by the addition of twin floats. A substantial lead in airplane design and construction was being frittered away.

A few weeks after the disappointing Pulitzer Race, the French introduced a surprising airplane from a manufacturer with only limited experience in producing racing planes. The Bernard V.2 was a sleek, midwing monoplane with a 500-plus-horsepower Hispano-Suiza broad-arrow engine tightly cowled within three slender, teardrop-shaped "cheeks." Developed from the V.1 which flew poorly and crashed on its first landing, the V.2 was far from ideal to fly—it had little control in the roll axis even before a vital part of its aileron area was clipped off—but the V.2 had clean lines and it was powerful. It should therefore be fast. To fly it, the firm of Avions Bernard chose Florentin Bonnett, a military pilot with considerable experience in long-distance racing. Bonnett, born in 1894, became a career officer in the French Army and was credited with 10 aerial victories in World War I. He continued flying high-performance airplanes after his record flight in 1924, and died in a takeoff accident in August 1929. Bonnett's first try for the Absolute World Air Speed Record came on November 8, at Istres; but he could do no better than 244 mph (393 km/h). It was then that 8 inches (20 centimeters) was snipped off each wingtip, to reduce wind resistance and, in a calculated risk, controllability. Bonnett's second try in the Bernard V.2 took place December 11. This time, the airplane was ready. The fastest four (of six) runs averaged out to 278.481 mph (448.171 km/h), a record. After a year and a half, world honors had been returned to the French. The Absolute Speed Record had been returned to the monoplane as well.

The Bernard V.2 had a wingspan of 29.8 feet (9.1 meters), a length of 22.3 feet (6.8 meters), a height of 7.6 feet (2.3 meters), and a wing area of 116.3

square feet (10.8 square meters). Its empty weight was 2,127 pounds (964 kilograms) and its gross weight 2,621 pounds (1,187 kilograms). The Hispano-Suiza Type 50 engine displaced 1,691 cubic inches (27.7 liters) and developed 620 horsepower at 2,200 revolutions per minute.

In view of the frantic speed-record activity of the early 1920s, few imagined that Bonnett and the Bernard V.2 would hold the land-plane record into the next decade; but the situation had changed radically in many countries. Priorities had to be reordered, with the result that land-plane speed simply wasn't as important as it had been. In the United States and Great Britain in 1925, however, there was still some interest, though not as much as had been evident until recently. The British were now concentrating their speed efforts on the Schneider Trophy Race for seaplanes. Among the series of marvelous racing seaplanes to emerge from Britain were the Gloster Type II through VI. Two Gloster IIs built in 1924 closely resembled the Curtiss R2C-1 seaplane, but their 600-horsepower Napier Lion engines were more powerful. When the first of the pair sank upon landing after its first flight, the second was equipped as a land plane for test purposes. On June 11, 1925, Larry Carter made a speed-record attempt as part of a plan to enter the 1925 Pulitzer Trophy Race. As Carter streaked over the 3-kilometer (1.9-mile) course at Cranwell, England, at a speed estimated in excess of 250 mph (400 km/h), the tail began to flutter, threatening to throw the plane out of control. Carter tried to hang on, but the wildly gyrating "Bluebird" hit the ground at high speed and was demolished. He survived the accident despite severe injuries but died from meningitis a year later.

With the Pulitzer Trophy Race still the premier event on the American aviation calendar, the Navy and the Army pooled their resources and built three Curtiss R3C racers, to be flown in the Pulitzer and Schneider Trophy races. At the heart of the new design was the experimental Curtiss V-1400 engine, whose severe oil consumption made it of little value for military airplanes but could be coped with in short races. The first flight of an R3C came September 11, 1925, just a month before the Pulitzer Race but hardly unusual for a racing program, as last-minute rushes had long been an accepted part of the sport. A week later, Jimmy Doolittle and Al Williams began speed tests with a prototype R3C. Doolittle turned an unofficial of about 250 mph (400 km/h) around the Pulitzer Race course; then Williams was timed at an estimated 285 mph (460 km/h) for a series of passes on the 3-kilometer course. The latter series was significantly faster than Bonnett's Absolute World Air Speed Record and made the R3C the clear favorite in the upcoming race.

On October 12, 1925, the sixth and last of the colorful and productive Pulitzer Races was held at Mitchell Field, on Long Island. All five starters were Curtiss aircraft: two R3C racers, two PW-8B Army pursuits, and a P-1 pursuit. To the surprise of no one, the R3Cs walked away with the race. Cyrus Bettis was first in an Army-sponsored airplane, with 249 mph (401 km/h), and Al Williams, of the Navy, was close behind, with 242 mph (389 km/h). Doolittle, as alternate pilot for Bettis, was not needed. Two weeks later, the two R3Cs and a third, now equipped with twin floats, were in Baltimore for the annual Schneider Trophy Race. Bettis's Pulitzer Trophy winner was taken over by Doolittle, who proceeded to win at a Schneider Race and seaplane record pace of 233 mph (374 km/h), thus demonstrating that properly designed water-landing gear cost surprisingly little speed. The other two R3Cs developed mechanical trouble and had to drop out. The second-place winner — Hubert Broad, in a British Gloster III-A — averaged less than 200 mph (320 km/h).

The day after the race, October 25, Doolittle set a World Air Speed Record for seaplanes over a 3-kilometer course at Bay Shore Park, Maryland, flying 245.7 mph (395.4 km/h) in his biplane. With military interest focused on the Schneider Trophy Race, however, there was no move to convert the R3C back to wheels for a try at Bonnett's record.

Of three R3Cs built, one was converted into the R3C-4, with a Curtiss V-1550 engine. After failing to complete the 1926 Schneider Trophy Race, the plane vanished. Another became the R3C-3, with a geared Packard V12 engine which permitted a nearly perfect engine cowling; it crashed while landing, the day before the 1926 Schneider Trophy Race. That left one airplane — the winner of the 1925 Pulitzer and Schneider Races.* Nothing else is known to exist of the wonderful Curtiss Racers other than a lower wing panel from an Army R-6, which today hangs in the U.S. Air Force Museum at Wright-Patterson AF Base, near Dayton, Ohio.

The basic Curtiss R3C-1 had an upper wingspan of 22 feet (6.7 meters) and a lower wingspan of 20 feet (6.1 meters), a length of 20.12 feet (6.13 meters), a height of 6.8 feet (2.1 meters), and a wing area of 144 square feet (13.4 square meters); its empty weight was 1,792 pounds (812 kilograms) and its gross weight was 2,181 pounds (988 kilograms). The airplane was powered by a Curtiss V-1400 engine displacing 1,400 cubic inches (22.9 liters) that developed 565 horsepower at 2,400 rpm.

With the end of formal involvement of the U.S. military in seaplane racing in 1926, it was left to Al Williams to carry the flag, with some quiet Navy support. His Kirkham-Williams Racer was designed for both land-plane and seaplane racing. If its experimental Packard X-2775 engine, consisting of two V-12s joined at the crankcase in an "X" shape, had worked well enough to produce anything like the projected 1,250 horsepower, some records might have fallen; but the engine was plagued by mechanical trouble throughout its brief life. In 1927, shortly after Williams' failure to attend the Schneider Trophy Race, in Italy, with his new machine, he reportedly clocked himself with a stopwatch at 325 mph (523 km/h) — hardly a precise measurement but still indicative of the speed the Kirkham-Williams was capable of. In 1928, the racer was converted from a biplane to the Mercury Racer, a midwing monoplane in which little more than the engine and fuselage center section were carried over from the original. In August 1929, Williams tried to test fly the aircraft off the water at Annapolis, but, because it was too heavy by several hundred pounds, it refused to lift. Any hope of taking it to England for the 1929 Schneider Trophy Race vanished.

Williams, who flew for both the U.S. Navy and the Marine Corps, is credited with some of the earliest serious research in the causes and prevention

---

*On exhibit in the National Air & Space Museum, in Washington, D.C.

of crashes resulting from spins. An apprentice pitcher for the old New York Giants baseball team, he earned a law degree in 1925 and in 1930 began to practice law. From 1933 to 1951, Williams was aviation manager for the Gulf Oil Corporation, and during much of that period, he was one of the best-known air-show pilots in the United States.

Magnificent Seaplanes

The justification for racing is supposed to be improvement of the breed. No doubt, today there are finer horses roaming the pastures of horse farms because of efforts to win the Kentucky Derby than there might have been without that stimulus. By the same token, an automobile's efficient and dependable tires, engine, brakes, and fuel owe much to the response of inspired men to the special demands of Grand Prix and Indianapolis car racing.

The clearest example of the contributions of airplane racing to the development of flight technology is the long series of Schneider Trophy Races held from 1913 to 1931. Enormous advances were made in engines and streamlining as a direct result of the emotion-laden desire — need — for more speed in the air.

All this is logical; but what at first does not seem to make much sense is that the progress resulted from a trophy offered for seaplane racing! Throughout the period of the Schneider Trophy Race, some of aviation's finest pilots devoted their efforts to aircraft which, by definition, paid a great penalty to operate from the water. Whereas, today it may seem obvious that any aircraft will fly faster without wind resistance from a boat-shaped underside or from multiple pontoons, in the era of the Schneider Trophy other design problems were confronted, problems that took precedence over the need for aerodynamic efficiency. The main such problem was a lack of long runways for specialized high-speed airplanes to take off from.

For any airplane to operate effectively at high speed, it must sacrifice some performance at low speed, though the need for drastic compromise has decreased since the days of the Schneider Trophy Race, mainly by means of elaborate systems of wing flaps. In the 1920s and 30s, however, the only long runways were of water; to use them, aircraft designers had no choice but to create airplanes that were part boat.

When, in 1913, Jacques Schneider offered his trophy (and a substantial cash prize) for the winner of a seaplane race, his goal was to improve seaplane technology and thus advance what then seemed a segment of aviation with a bright future. The Schneider Trophy was permanently retired by the British in 1931, but not before it had stimulated considerable advances in several areas. The event, however, had led to little of value for waterborne flying machines. Initially, the Schneider Trophy Race attracted land planes that had been converted into seaplanes simply by adding floats. The race attracted modified standard flying boats, craft whose fuselages had been adapted to boat shape so they would float and taxi on water. As the competitiveness of the event increased, highly specialized aircraft were developed and came into their own, first with creative streamlining and then with great strides of power. National governments soon saw the opportunity for international prestige, often under the guise of military-oriented research.

The first truly streamlined Schneider Trophy seaplane was the British Supermarine S.4, a midwing monoplane inspired by the United States' highly successful racing biplanes, which, in turn, were derived from the Curtiss R series of land planes that dominated the Absolute World Air Speed Record in the early 1920s. The brainchild of Reginald Mitchell, who later designed the Spitfire fighter plane, the S.4 had a cantilever wing (a wing with no external bracing), a slim fuselage, highly streamlined floats, and a Napier Lion engine that generated 680 horsepower. The engine developed so many problems that neither it nor the S.4 were ever fully developed; still, Henry Biard flew the plane to a World Seaplane Speed Record in 1925, at 227 mph (365.2 km/h) — only 50 mph (80 km/h) slower than Bonnett had flown the Bernard V.2 land plane in setting an Absolute World Air Speed Record in 1924.

In late 1926, Mario de Bernardi set a Schneider Trophy Race record of 246 mph (395.8 km/h) around a 31-mile (50-kilometer) closed course (which suggests a straightaway speed of well over 250 mph [400 km/h]). His Italian Macchi M.39 Racer had a liquid-cooled 800-horsepower Fiat V12 engine. Because the Supermarine S.4 had experienced difficulties, possibly related to the wing's structural design, the Macchi's designers went back to a wire-braced wing. Such a wing design was stronger than an internally braced one, and it could be made thinner (and thus more streamlined), since not all the structural support had to be inside.

A few days after winning the 1926 Schneider Trophy Race, de Bernardi set a World Seaplane Speed Record of 259 mph (417 km/h), further narrowing the gap between seaplanes and land planes. By this time, it was clear that it was the land plane that was handicapped in the speed record race; it was the latter that had to fly with a wing designed to lift it from the extremely short runways of the day. Such an airplane needs a wing designed to lift the aircraft's weight at a lower air speed than does a seaplane, since short runways offer less opportunity to accelerate to high speed. A seaplane, at least in theory, can use runways of great length and can accelerate gradually to much higher speeds, where the wings, designed to perform best at high speed, can produce enough lift to raise the craft from the surface. While most of the effort of the world's governments and airplane designers went into creating seaplanes with which to test designs and capture public attention, the high-speed land plane was virtually ignored. Air racing and speed records had become, at least on the international level, the preserve of watercraft.

In 1927, it appeared that the effort was about to pay off. In September, Sidney Webster, of the British High Speed Flight, won the Schneider Trophy Race, held in Venice, with a speed of 282 mph (454 km/h). Although Webster had to fly around a 31-mile (50-kilometer) course with two speed-killing hair-pin turns on each of the seven laps, he exceeded the highest speed any land plane had yet achieved on a short, straight course. His Supermarine S.5 had 875 horsepower, whereas the Bernard V.2 flown by Bonnett had only 600.

It had become something of a tradition for the Schneider Trophy winner to go immediately for an official FAI speed record; but this time the British, for some reason, did not. Seeing an opportunity for their Macchi M.52 (all three of which had failed to complete the 1927 Schneider Trophy Race because of engine trouble), the Italians went after the record. On October 22, just four weeks after the Schneider Race, Mario de Bernardi, who already held the World Seaplane Speed Record, made Italy's second serious try for the Absolute World Air Speed Record. His four passes over the 3-kilometer course at Venice averaged 484.304 km/h, which was announced to the public as 298 mph but actually was almost 301 mph. Had the Italians realized this was the first time an airplane of any type had exceeded 300 mph, they might have submitted the mark to the FAI for official recognition. The set of runs, however, was considered inferior to what the Italians perceived as the Macchi's ultimate; so a later attempt was scheduled, at which time foreign air attachés would be invited to witness the historic event. It was a calculated risk.

On November 5, de Bernardi again fired up the Macchi M.52's 1,000-horse-power Fiat AS.3 V12 engine. Low over the course at the Lido, just offshore at Venice, he roared four times while officials of the Italian Aero Club clicked their stopwatches. De Bernardi's average speed of 297.817 mph (479.290 km/h) was the fastest official speed to date by anyone in a human-carrying vehicle, but it was several miles per hour slower than de Bernardi's unofficial speed and just under the significant 300-mph (480-km/h) barrier at which pilots and designers had long aimed. Still, it was an Absolute World Air Speed Record—the first by an aircraft other than a land plane. That a seaplane hampered by pontoons almost as large as its fuselage could achieve such speed was a tribute to Schneider and his trophy. Without the impetus of the prestigious award, the advances needed to overcome the handicap inherent in seaplanes would not have been made.

The Macchi M.52 had a wingspan of 29.4 feet (9.0 meters), a length of 23.4 feet (7.1 meters), and a wing area of 151 square feet (14 square meters). It weighed 2,625 pounds (1,189 kilograms) empty and 3,340 pounds (1,513 kilograms) fully loaded. Power was supplied by a Fiat AS.3 engine of 2,150 cubic inches (35.2 liters) displacement driving a ground-adjustable, two-bladed, metal propellor.

The Italians were elated by winning the Absolute World Air Speed Record. The Italian aircraft industry had shown that it was capable of taking on the best aircraft in the world and beating them. The increasingly militant fascist government of Benito Mussolini took advantage of the opportunity for touting Italian nationalism. Still, it could not be denied that when the British passed up the chance at a record with their Supermarine S.5, the Italians effectively filled the gap.

Just as the Italians were pleased with their historic record, the British were chagrined; the record should have been theirs. Plans were quickly laid for recapturing the lead in speed. The S.5, which had won the Schneider Trophy Race with a speed of 282 mph (454 km/h), clearly had the power to approach 300 mph (480 km/h), though whether it could beat the Macchi M.52 by the required margin of 1 percent was less clear. Even before the Schneider Trophy Race of 1927, an S.5 had made an unofficial set of four passes over a 3-kilometer (1.86-mile) course at 284 mph (457 km/h). Why the mark wasn't submitted to the FAI is not known.

The Supermarine S.5 had a wingspan of 26.7 feet (8.1 meters), a length of 24.2 feet (7.4 meters), and a wing area of 115 square feet (10.7 square meters). Its gross weight was about 3,250 pounds (1,472 kilograms). The engine was a 1,464-cubic-inch (24-liter) Napier Lion VII B V12 rated at 875 horsepower at 3,300 rpm driving a two-bladed metal propellor.

It was March 12, 1928, and the British were finally ready. Flight lieutenant S.M. Kinkead, a South African with the RAF, who was trying for second place in the 1927 Schneider Trophy Race when his seaplane's spinner broke, was selected for the attempt. He was to fly the third S.5, which had been held in reserve for the race. Kinkead's first flight in any S.5 had been made just the day before, yet everything seemed in order. It took him two tries to get the racer off the water; but that wasn't surprising: the floats tended to submerge when power was applied, so care must be taken. Kinkead made a wide, sweeping turn to build up speed and get lined up for his first run at the course, which began off Calshot and went up Southampton Water toward the seaport on England's southern coast.

As Kinkead neared the Calshot Light, his S.5 suddenly dived into the water, at an estimated 300 mph (480 km/h), destroying the craft and killing the pilot. Although the exact cause of the accident was never released, it was reported that Kinkead had felt ill the previous day while flying and that he was not up to par on the morning of the fatal flight. Add to this the fact that he began his run with a dive from 1,000 feet (305 meters) toward a flat sea he could see only indistinctly through the haze, and it becomes apparent that the attempt should have been put off until a better time.

The British mourned the loss of their pilot and wondered about the future. Meanwhile, the Italians were busy. Less than three weeks after the crash, de Bernardi set out to improve his existing mark of 298 mph (479 km/h) in a highly modified version of the seaplane in which he set the Absolute World Air Speed Record. To convert the Macchi M.52 into the M.52R, the wings were shortened from 29.5 feet (9. meters) to 25.8 feet (7.9 meters), reducing the wing area almost 30 percent. Some minor changes were made in the floats, but the all-important engine remained basically the same.

On March 30, 1928, de Bernardi flew the required four passes along a

3-kilometer (1.86-mile) straight course at the Lido. He averaged 318.624 mph (512.776 km/h), breaking — in slightly more than 40 seconds flying time — both the 300 mph and the 500 km/h barriers.

De Bernardi, pilot of the Macchi M.52 and the M.52R, was born in 1893 and flew in both world wars. He died of a heart attack in 1959 after completing an aerobatic flying demonstration in a light airplane at an air show near Rome.

The contest for speed-record honors was now between the British High Speed Flight (of the Royal Air Force) and a similarly named group in Italy's Reggia Aeronautica. The prize was the national prestige that would accrue from demonstrations of superior technology and flying skill. The British effort remained focused on the Schneider Trophy Race. For the 1929 running of the event, there would be two brand-new Supermarine S-6s. The heart of the aircraft was its Rolls Royce "R" (for racing) engine, a liquid-cooled V12 that soon enabled the British to take the lead in engine design.

Installed in the S.6, the R engine was considerably more powerful than the Napier Lion in the S.5 (1,900 horsepower versus 875). It was also larger and heavier, which necessitated a larger airplane. Thus the S.6 had a wingspan of 30 feet (9.1 meters), a length of 28.6 feet (8.7 meters), a wing area of 145 square feet (13.5 square meters), an empty weight of 4,540 pounds (2,057 kilograms) and a gross weight of 5,775 pounds (2,616 kilograms).

The 1929 Schneider Trophy Race was held September 7, 1929, at Spithead, in the Solent between Portsmouth and the Isle of Wight, near the site of the 1927 race. Pitted against the two S.6s and the 1927-winning S.5 were the Italians' record-holding Macchi M.52R and the two remaining, new M.67s, the third having crashed two weeks earlier, killing the pilot, Guiseppe Motta. As an indication of the effectiveness of the work that went into improving racing seaplanes in the two years since the last Schneider Trophy Race, all six starters flew faster than the old race record, though some of them did not fly that fast very long. By the end of the second lap (out of seven), both Macchi M.62s had dropped out because the hot blast of their exhaust was being blown directly back into their open cockpits, where it threatened to cook and/or poison the pilot. The airplanes had been averaging 282 to 284 mph (454 to 457 km/h).

The two Supermarine S.6s finished with speeds of 329 mph (529.4 km/h) for the winner, Henry Waghorn, and 326 mph (525 km/h) for Richard Atcherly, who cut inside a turn-marking pylon and was penalized. (Atcherly's racer, N248, is now on public display in the R.J. Mitchell Hall, in Southampton, England.) The only Italian to finish the race was Tomaso Dal Molin, who averaged 284 mph (457 km/h) in an M.52R. The third British pilot, D'Arcy Greig, flew a Supermarine S.5 to third place, at 282 mph (454 km/h).

The event clearly showed that any number of seaplanes were capable of breaking the Absolute World Air Speed Record. Having missed their opportunity two years earlier, the British now lost no time in attacking de Bernardi's record of 319 mph (513 km/h) with their successful racers.

Three days after the Schneider Trophy Race, two high-powered seaplanes were rolled out on their handling cradles at Calshot. A Gloster-Napier VI, an airplane held in reserve for the Schneider Race, would be flown by George Stainforth if needed. The Supermarine S.6 Waghorn had flown in winning the Schneider Trophy at record speed would be flown by A.H. Orlebar, a test pilot. Stainforth, born in 1899, began his military career in 1918 and started flying in 1923. By 1942 he had become, at age 43, the oldest active pilot in the RAF's Middle East Command, leading a night-fighter squadron. He was killed in action in September 1942.

Stainforth was the first to try for the record. He completed four runs along the 3-kilometer, over-water course at calculated speeds of 351.3, 328.3, 336.2, and 329.3 mph (565.2, 528.2, and 529.8 km/h). His average speed of 336 mph (541 km/h) was almost 18 mph (29 km/h) faster than the record, but it was not immediately submitted for FAI recognition, since more flying was yet to come. Orlebar, the next to try, was a combat pilot in World War I, later becoming captain of the Schneider teams of 1929 and 1931. Orlebar headed off in the victorious S.6 with slightly better visibility prevailing during Stainforth's flight. His four runs, made as low as conditions permitted, were 368.8, 345.3, 365.5, and 343.7 mph (593.4, 555.6, 588.1, and 553 km/h). His average speed of 356 mph (573 km/h) was 20 mph (32 km/h) faster than Stainforth's and more than 37 mph (60 km/h) faster than that of the Italian record-holder, de Bernardi. But because the British felt they could do better, the paperwork was held back until another attempt could be made.

On September 12, Orlebar got his second crack at the course. A day-long wait for the haze to dissipate was rewarded at 4 P.M. The water was calm and the wind down as he shoved his throttle forward and the coarse-pitch propellor began to bite the air. After a run over the water of about 40 seconds, the S.6 lifted off. Orlebar made six runs over the course, of which the middle four were the fastest. His average speed of 357.723 mph (575.700 km/h) was an increase of almost 2 mph (3 km/h) over his previous best in the Supermarine S.6. Stainforth went up for another turn in the Gloster VI, but engine trouble forced him to return. Orlebar was thus the man of the hour, for the record was submitted to the FAI and quickly accepted. He and the designers, builders, mechanics, and leaders of the High Speed Flight had added 12 percent to the old record. The years of disappointment for the RAF were soon forgotten.

Early in 1930, as Italy was preparing its challenge to the British in next year's Schneider Trophy Race, its High Speed Flight was struck by a fourth fatal accident. While testing the unusual Savoia-Marchetti S.65 over Lake Garda, at the edge of the Italian Alps, Tomaso Dal Molin dived into the water at high speed. The cause of the crash has never been revealed.

It had been Italy's plan to attempt to win back the Absolute World Air Speed Record and the Schneider Trophy with the S.65 as part of an overall program to develop a series of racing seaplanes. Because the winning of air races often seems to be done by carrying conventional design theory to its limit, the motivation to head off on a tangent frequently attracts support. Unfortunately, the colorful story of air racing is strewn with truly different airplanes whose superior performance did not extend beyond their originators' imaginations. In the case of the S.65, the plan was to add power without adding wind resistance — in itself, a conventional goal. The designers did it by placing one engine at each end of the central pod housing the pilot. Rather than extend the fuselage all the way to the tail, as is done in most airplanes, the pod ended just aft of the trailing edge of the wing. The tail, in turn, was held on by a pair of slim booms running back from the wings, located directly above the twin floats. The tail booms necessitated more external bracing struts and wires than a conventional layout; but by combining the two engines in one unit, total drag was supposed to be less than if the two engines had been in individual nacelles. The engines were souped-up versions of the standard Isotta-Fraschini V12, which was rated at 1,000 horsepower and displaced 1,690 cubic inches (27.7 liters).

The estimated dimensions of the S.65 were: length, 33.5 feet (10.2 meters); wing area, 194 square feet (18 square meters); empty weight, 5,060 pounds (2,292 kilograms) and gross weight, 6,160 pounds (2,790 kilograms). No official performance figures were ever released, but the airplane's top speed was estimated at over 350 mph (563.2 km/h).

If the design of the S.65 in which Dal Molin was killed is considered radical, the Piaggio/Pegna P.c.7 being developed at the same time is downright wild. If the design had worked, the course of seaplane design might have been changed forever; it was not merely a different arrangement of familiar parts, as was the S.65, but an entirely new way of doing things. Gone were the ponderous floats that had proved such a handicap. Gone was the boat hull meant for speeds of less than 100 km/h (62 mph) in the water but not for 500 km/h (310 mph) in the air. What remained was the most streamlined aircraft of the era. Its fuselage was long and thin, with an unusually streamlined nose ending in a sharply pointed spinner.

When it was in the water, the P.c.7 floated with its fuselage partly submerged. To move forward, power from its V12 engine was routed to a small water propellor at the rear of the plane, under the tail. When this propellor began to move the seaplane forward like a motorboat, its most unusual feature became evident: a pair of "water wings," what would later be called "hydrofoils." The water wings were about 4 feet (1.2 meters) in span and 2 feet (0.6 meters) long. Compared with a typical set of 20-foot (6.1-meter) racing floats, they were insignificant. The foils were designed to react to the water as wings do to air—lifting as the rate of flow increases. Once sufficient lift was generated, the seaplane should rise from the water, to be supported by its small racing wings, which would not have to carry extra area to provide lift at lower speed. As the seaplane began to lift off, its engine power would be rerouted to the main propellor, and the "boat" would become an airplane. Once in the air, its much lower wind resistance would prove a major advantage when pitted against other racers, with their larger wings and bulky floats. The fascinating little Piaggio had a wingspan of 22.2 feet (6.8 meters), a length of 29 feet (8.8 meters), and a wing area of only 106 square feet (9.9 square meters). Apparently, no estimates of its weight or intended performance exist. Sadly, as was the case with numerous radical racing designs, the P.c.7 never flew; therefore, its innovative design was never tested.

The speed-record scene was quiet for more than a year and a half as preparations went ahead for the 1931 Schneider Trophy Race. Entries were expected not only from Great Britain, the defending champion, but from Italy and France as well. Italy was working hard on the Macchi MC.72, while France had at least two designs in the works. Shortly before the race, two MC.72s were lost in training crashes, which killed the test pilots Giovanni Monti on

August 2, and Stanislao Bellini. Clearly, the racer wasn't ready; so it was withdrawn. The French airplanes, even further from ready, were also scratched.

That left the British the only nation prepared to race. Aware that a third consecutive victory would give them permanent possession of the Schneider Trophy, they nevertheless declined to postpone the race until at least one rival was ready, as had the Americans in 1924. To their credit, the British did not simply parade to victory but put on a brilliant display of fast flying. John Boothman streaked alone around the Calshot course at a record 340 mph (547 km/h). Pride was at stake — Boothman's pride, as well as the pride of the RAF's High Speed Flight and the British aircraft industry. Actually, the British came close to failing. Faced with the great cost of preparing for the 1931 Schneider Trophy Race, the British government declined to participate, and without government financing, there seemed no way the race could be held. At the last minute, Lady Houston, a patriotic philanthropist, contributed the equivalent of $500,000, and the Supermarine S.6B became a reality.

When, in 1927, the Italians were quick to grab the Absolute World Air Speed Record after the British won the Schneider Trophy Race, the lesson was well learned. In 1931, while Britain was still celebrating its Schneider Race triumph, the country lost no time in going for the Absolute Record, which then stood at 358 mph (576 km/h). On the same day the Schneider Race was run, an alternate Supermarine S.6B was prepared for the 3-kilometer (1.86-mile) dashes. Mechanics emptied most of the fuel from number S.1596; far less of it would be needed for the short course than would have been needed for the approximately 40 minutes the Schneider course took. The timers and altitude observers were positioned, and the pilot, George Stainforth, was launched.

Stainforth made four runs along the coastal route that extends north from Lee-on-Solent and is directly across the water from the famous boating center at Cowes. He was timed at an average speed of 379 mph (610 km/h). Although that was more than 20 mph (32 km/h) faster than Orlebar's two-year-old record, it was seen as merely a warm-up for the faster runs the British were convinced were possible.

On September 13, Stainforth was testing a shorter propellor which he thought might give greater thrust. After a flight showing that the propellor tended to make the engine overspeed, Stainforth set number S.1596 down smoothly on the water. The seaplane slowed to a low speed — then suddenly swerved sharply to the side and turned upside down. Stainforth got out safely, but the seaplane sank. Although the aircraft was recovered by divers, and though little damage was done, it never flew again.

If another attempt was to be made on the Absolute World Air Speed Record, there was no time for major changes to the airframe or the engine, especially since efforts by Rolls Royce to boost engine power had not produced the desired results. Experiments with propellors had so far led to little of value; fuel was about the only way left to increase power. Since only a few minutes of fuel (for running at top speed), was needed, it might be possible to use an extremely hot mixture. F. R. Banks, the fuels expert for the British team, devised a special mixture for the maximum-speed effort that contained no petroleum products. It was 30 percent benzole (a form of benzene used in solvents), 60 percent methanol (wood alcohol), 10 percent acetone (a paint solvent), and 0.1 percent tetraethyl lead. Use of the volatile fuel for anything but a brief dash was unthinkable.

Late in the day, September 29, the weather cleared, and the leaders of the High Speed Flight decided to try. The troublesome sea mist persisted, cutting visibility, but the British had long since learned that to wait for ideal weather could mean they would never fly. The Rolls Royce engine was warmed up carefully, then shut down and covered to retain its heat. Stainforth was buckled into the cramped cockpit, and the engine was restarted. He quickly taxied away from the mooring pontoon. His takeoff, nearly obscured by the spray from the Supermarine's floats, was somewhat slower than usual. Once he was in the air, though, the seaplane accelerated rapidly. Stainforth made one pass by the observers at top speed, to make sure that everything was working properly. Satisfied that all was well, he made a wide turn and headed back for the start of his first official run, at an altitude of about 100 feet (30.5 meters).

Stainforth began each run with a maximum allowable dive, which had to be ended well before he entered the 3-kilometer portion of the measured course but which would still add somewhat to the airplane's speed. Each of the five runs was made straight and true, near the maximum altitude of 165 feet (50 meters). With only 100 gallons (378.5 liters) of fuel on board (to keep the weight to a minimum), Stainforth knew he could fly no longer than 29 minutes. When he landed, he had only three or four minutes' flying time remaining.

It wasn't until 4:00 the next morning that the computations were complete. According to officials from the Royal Aero Club, Stainforth had made runs at 415.2, 405.1, 409.5, 405.4, and 404.5 mph (668.1, 651.8, 658.9, 652.3, and 650.8 km/h). Averaging the first four gave a speed of 408.8 mph (658 km/h), but the FAI eventually came up with an official speed of 407.0 mph (655.0 km/h). Whichever computation was accepted, the Supermarine S.6B number S.1596 had demonstrated its superiority over other flying machines. The Absolute World Air Speed Record has been boosted from 358 to 407 mph (576 to 655 km/h). Never before had such an increase been achieved. More important, never before had anyone traveled faster than 400 mph (644 km/h). The combination of Mitchell's airframe, Rolls Royce's R engine, and Banks' fuel had shown just how much could be achieved.

The Supermarine S.6B never flew again. Its purpose had been to win the Schneider Trophy and the Absolute World Air Speed Record. Its engine, however, was used again, though neither in the air nor on the water. In 1937 it was installed, along with a second, similar engine, in the "Thunderbolt," a sleek car with a triangular rudder. George Eyston drove the "Thunderbolt" to a World Land Speed Record of 311 mph (501 km/h). Then the engine was retired.

The S.6B has a wingspan of 30 feet (9.1 meters), a length of 28.8 feet (8.8 meters), and a wing area of 158.2 square feet (14.7 square meters). Empty, its weight is 4,585 pounds (2,077 kilograms) and the gross weight is 6,085 pounds (2,757 kilograms). At 3,200 rpm, and using the special fuel, the Rolls Royce R engine developed 2,650 horsepower. Today, the S.6B is on display in the

Aeronautical Hall of the Science Museum, in London. With it are the R engine and the small bronze Schneider Trophy.

Although the Schneider Trophy Race series ended in September 1931, the drive to extract ever more speed from racing seaplanes did not. The Italians, in particular, had invested too much time and money in propaganda to let it die, especially since the British now had the trophy. All the seaplanes tested by Reggia Aeronautica at Lake Garda in the early 1930s were in some way radical — and troublesome. The tandem-engined Savoia-Marchetti S.65 had crashed, and the floatless Piaggio/Pegna P.c.7 would not fly. All that was left was a Macchi-Castoldi MC.72; three of the original five were moving slowly through the development program.

Called the "Bolide Rosso" or the "Red Meteor," the MC.72 looked, at first glance, merely like a variation on the Supermarine. It had a long fuselage, two huge floats, a tiny open cockpit, and a tail at the rear. At the extreme front was the first clue to its novelty: a pair of two-bladed propellors, one behind the other, in a long, pointed spinner. Each propellor was attached to an engine, and one engine was placed directly behind the other in the unusually long nose. Two sets of exhaust stacks on each side of the engine cowling was another clue. The aim was to achieve the advantage of two engines without the usual penalty of drag from two separate engine nacelles.

Streamlining, though of major importance in such a racing machine, wasn't the only reason for adopting the tandem-engine arrangement. Another was torque, or the tendency of an airplane to twist in the opposite direction its propellor turns. In all airplanes, this is a problem. In powerful seaplanes, however, torque is capable of forcing one float deeper in the water and raising the other, with the result that anything can happen, from a swing to one side to capsizing.

In the MC.72, the front engine turned its propellor in one direction while the rear engine, facing back-to-front, turned its propellor in the opposite direction. Thus the torque of one propellor cancelled out the torque of the other propellor. It was the first time the concept had been tried in a powerful airplane.

The first flight of an MC.72 occurred in June 1931. By early September, both prototypes had been lost when explosions occurred in air-intake ducts that had not been tested sufficiently in the laboratory. When the Schneider Races ended later that year, however, urgency was no longer a factor.

In 1932, speed-record activity was at a bare minimum. The U.S. and the British governments, convinced that further expenditure would not bring the required return, had bowed out. The Germans were busy secretly rebuilding their air force and industry. The French were working on a couple of Schneider Race designs that looked good — until the discontinuance of the race killed their enthusiasm. About the only movement was in the United States, where civilian air racing was booming, with scores of racers being custom built. Although land planes were the object of interest for attempts on the World Air Speed Record, privately financed airplanes stood no chance of challenging the records set by the Supermarine racing seaplanes.

Finally, on April 10, 1933, Francesco Agello, a second lieutenant in the Italian Air Force, took control of one of the three remaining MC.72s. Over

Lake Garda, he made the requisite four passes over a 3-kilometer course, averaging 423.824 mph (682.403 km/h) and adding almost 17 mph (27 km/h) to Stainforth's Absolute World Air Speed Record, set in 1931, and boosting the record for seaplanes to 130 mph (219.2 km/h) over the record for land planes. The tradition of the Schneider Trophy Race was being continued.

When the Italian's achievement became known in the aeronautical and political worlds, there was a sudden rush of acclaim for the Italian Air Force and for the industry that had created such an aircraft. No one denied that the MC.72 was an outstanding flying machine. To reinforce the point, on October 8, 1933, Guglielmo Cassinelli set a World Speed Record for a 100-kilometer (62-mile) course in an MC.72 of 391 mph (629 km/h). Two weeks later, Pietro Scapinelli flew another MC.72 at 385 mph (620 km/h) for a half hour, thus becoming the first winner of the Bleriot Cup.

Flushed with success, Italy's High Speed Flight set out to improve its Absolute World Air Speed Record. Another MC.72 was chosen and was fitted with smaller floats designed to carry the smaller load of fuel needed for a brief dash. Colonel Bernasconi, the leader of the unit, made some practice runs at 435 mph (700 km/h), then signaled that the airplane was ready.

Shortly before 3:00 P.M., October 23, 1934, Agello took off from Lake Garda for the short series of speed runs. Flying conditions were nearly ideal; visibility was excellent, with little or no wind. Agello went back and forth, driving the airplane and its 3,000-horsepower engine as though they were a racehorse. In a few minutes it was all over. Agello's average speed in the spectacular floatplane was announced as 440.678 mph (709.202 km/h). He had added more than 15 mph (24 km/h) to his record and become the first human to travel faster than 700 km/h (434 mph).

The MC.72's core was, of course, its engines. Two Fiat AS.5 liquid-cooled V12s were combined to produce the most powerful reciprocating powerplant yet seen in an airplane. With a combined displacement of 3,063 cubic inches (50.2 liters), the engine developed 3,000 to 3,100 horsepower at 3,300 rpm. Excluding its elaborate cooling system, the AS.6 weighed only 2,050 pounds (929 kilograms), making it the first aircraft engine to develop more than one horsepower per cubic inch of displacement.

The front engine, placed conventionally, drove a two-bladed metal propellor. The rear engine drove a similar propellor via a long shaft that turned inside the hollow drive shaft of the front engine. A turbosupercharger driven by the rear engine boosted the engines' power. The entire system had taken years to perfect, but the effort had paid off, at least for speed records (the configuration was never used in another aircraft). The water that cooled the engines was, in turn, cooled by passing through a long series of copper tubes under the surface of the wings; this eliminated the need for drag-producing radiators. The oil was cooled by routing through tubes that covered much of the upper surfaces of the floats, the float struts, and the sides of the fuselage.

The MC.72 had a wingspan of 31.2 feet (9.5 meters), a length of 27.6 feet (8.4 meters), and a wing area of 165.8 square feet (15.4 square meters). The empty weight of the final version was 5,510 pounds (2,496 kilograms) and its gross weight was 6,667 pounds (3,020 kilograms).

The MC.72, which holds the speed record for piston-engine seaplanes, survives, though the two not destroyed in accidents in 1931 vanished, probably during World War II. The remaining copy is in the national aircraft collection and is occasionally displayed. Francesco Agello was the sole survivor of the original team of high-speed pilots who trained for the Schneider Trophy Races and the record flights. An aviator since 1924, he received Italy's Gold Medal for Aeronautical Valor for his MC.72 flying. Agello died in a flying accident in 1942.

While Britain was winning the Schneider Trophy and Italy the Absolute World Air Speed Record, France continued to hold out hope of perfecting its competition seaplanes. Two sleek racers were developed, the Bernard H.V.220 and the Dewoitine D.450. Both airplanes were intended to be powered by the 2,200-horsepower Lorraine "Radium" inverted V12 engine. Whereas both looked as though they were in the same class as the S.6B and the MC.72, neither plane was fully developed, because the financial backing necessary vanished along with the Schneider Trophy Race series.

The technological advances spawned by the racing seaplanes gradually emerged as a major influence on military aviation. In the United States, the work done on the Curtiss D-12 racing engine led to development of the Allison V-1710 engine, which powered the early P-51 Mustangs, most Curtiss P-40s, and the Lockheed P-38 Lightning. The impact of the Schneider Race and of speed-record efforts was even more pronounced in Great Britain. Rolls Royce's R engine led to development of the Merlin V12, built for Spitfire, Hurricane, and Mustang fighter planes and for Mosquito and Lancaster bombers. The Spitfire, Reginald Mitchell's supreme creation, is today regarded as the direct descendant of his racing seaplanes.

Only Italy, of the major competing nations, failed to take advantage of the knowledge acquired in its speed-related efforts. Its Fiat and Alfa Romeo V12 engines were used in military airplanes of only limited production, while German Daimler-Benz engines built under license powered many Italian airplanes in World War II. Aerodynamic progress as well was in limited evidence among Italian airplanes of the era. Except for the development of high-speed, water-borne aircraft, the great surge of activity in the 1920s and early 30s had a minor long-term effect. With the advent of jet engines after the war, there was a brief resurgence of interest in fast seaplanes. The British introduced a prototype Short SR.A1 flying boat fighter, while the U.S. Navy experimented with its single-seat Convair Sea Dart. Both aircraft flew reasonably well and fast, but neither was practical.

As for large seaplanes, the furtherance of which was certainly a goal of Jacques Schneider, the advanced designs of the 1930s were soon replaced by land-based airplanes. Once long, hard-surface runways became common during and after World War II, it was no longer necessary for heavily laden aircraft to be designed to operate from the water. The concurrent development of sophisticated wing flaps so reduced takeoff and landing speeds that airplanes could now lift great loads from runways and cruise at relatively high speed.

Seaplane construction continued into the 1950s, however. The giant Martin Mars and Saro Princess flying boats were among the largest and most majestic airplanes that ever flew. Despite the application of modern technology, they could not match the performance of land planes and soon faded from the scene. A few flying boats can still be seen in such specialized areas as fighting forest fires, search-and-rescue missions, and sport flying. Technological advances, however, have all but eliminated them from commercial and military aviation. The record set in 1934 by Francesco Agello in a Macchi-Castoldi MC.72 may turn out to be the most durable of the hundreds of entries in the FAI record book.

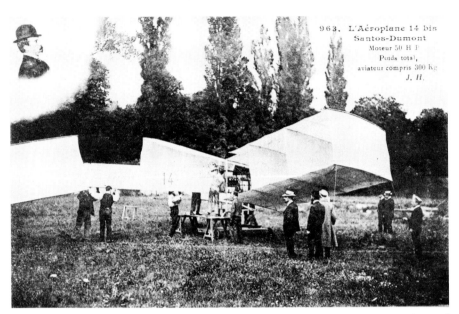

963. L'Aéroplane 14 bis
Santos-Dumont
Moteur 50 H P
Poids total,
aviateur compris 300 kg
J. H.

November 12, 1906. Alberto Santos-Dumont of Brazil set the first recognized speed record in his Type 14-bis, at Bagatelle, France; his speed was 25.66 mph (41.292 km/h). (SMITHSONIAN INSTITUTION)

August 23, 1909. Glenn Curtiss won history's first major air race at Reims, France, setting a record of 43.385 mph (69.82 km/h) in his Reims Racer. (SMITHSONIAN INSTITUTION)

GRANDE SEMAINE D'AVIATION DE CHAMPAGNE (Journée du 22 Août)
L'américain Curtiss et son biplan
Phototypie J. Bienaimé, Reims   Librairie L. Michaud, Reims

1913. All three records this year were set by Marcel Prevost in this improved Deperdussin. His best speed was 126.667 mph (203.850 km/h), set at Reims, France, September 29. (SMITHSONIAN INSTITUTION)

1920. Bernard de Romanet, the pilot of this SPAD-Herbemont 20bis, set two records: 181.864 mph (292.682 km/h), October 9, and 192.011 mph (309.012 km/h), November 4. (MUSÉE DE L'AIR, PARIS)

1922, 1923. A Curtiss R-6 like the one in which Billy Mitchell set a record of 222.970 mph (358.836 km/h) in 1922. In 1923, Russell Maughan set a record of 236.588 mph (380.751 km/h) in another R-6. (SMITHSONIAN INSTITUTION)

September 29, 1931. The first flight over 400 mph (644 km/h) was made in this Supermarine S.6B (S1595) flown by George Stainforth at Lee-on-Solent, England: 407.001 mph (655 km/h). (VICKERS)

December 11, 1924. Adj. Florentin Bonnet set a record of 278.481 mph (448.171 km/h) in this Bernard V.2, at Istres, France. (MUSÉE DE L'AIR, PARIS)

1933, 1934. The world's fastest propellor-driven seaplane: Italy's Macchi-Castoldi MC.72. The aircraft set records of 423.827 mph (682.078 km/h) in 1933, and 440.485 mph (709.209 km/h) in 1934. Both flights were by Francesco Agello. (AERONAUTICA MACCHI)

Left: *September 5, 1932. Jimmy Doolittle flew this GeeBee R-1 (NR-2100) to a land-plane speed record of 294.420 mph (473.820 km/h) at Cleveland, Ohio. (TRUMAN WEAVER COLLECTION)*

Right: *September 13, 1935. Howard Hughes flew his own Hughes H-1 Racer (NR-258Y) to a land-plane speed record of 352.391 mph (567.115 km/h), at Santa Ana, California. (SMITHSONIAN INSTITUTION)*

December 25, 1934. Raymonde Delmotte flew the Caudron C.460 at 314.321 mph (505.848 km/h), for a land-plane speed record, at Istres, France. (TRUMAN WEAVER COLLECTION)

November 11, 1937, Hermann Wurster flew this prototype Messerschmitt Bf-109V-13 (D-IPKY) to a land-plane record of 379.629 mph (610.950 km/h), at Augsburg, Germany. (MESSERSCHMITT ARCHIV)

April 26, 1939. The Messerschmitt Me-209V-1 (D-INJR) prototype in which Fritz Wendell set a record for propellor-driven airplanes that lasted 30 years. (MESSERSCHMITT ARCHIV)

The High-Speed Spitfire (N.17) that might have set a record for land-planes but was rendered obsolete by Germany's well-financed efforts. (VICKERS)

June 12, 1940. This powerful and superbly streamlined Napier-Heston Racer was destroyed on its first test flight, long before anyone knew if it could reach its 485 (776 km/h) mph design speed. (THE SCIENCE MUSEUM, LONDON)

September 27, 1946. Geofferey deHavilland Jr. died in the crash of this deHavilland deH. 108 Swallow research airplane as it was preparing for a record attempt. (DEHAVILLAND PHOTO)

November 7, 1945. RAF Group Capt. H. J. Wilson set history's first jet speed record at 606.260 mph (970.0 km/h) in this Gloster Meteor IV. (RAF MUSEUM, HENDON, ENGLAND)

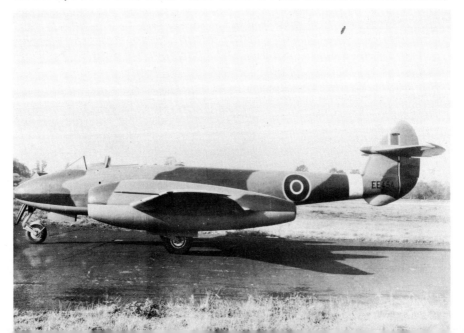

June 19, 1947. The Lockheed P-80R Shooting Star (44-85200) brought the World Absolute Air Speed Record back to the United States after 22 years, when Col. Al Boyd flew it 623.73 mph (1,003.60 km/h) at Muroc Army Air Field, California. (LOCKHEED AIRCRAFT CORPORATION)

August 20 and 25, 1947. The Douglas D-558-1 Skystreak set two Absolute records: 640.66 mph (1,030.95 km/h) by Cdr. Turner Caldwell, then 650.796 mph (1,047.356 km/h) by Maj. Marion Carl. (MCDONNELL DOUGLAS CORPORATION)

July 16, 1953. Lt.Col. William Barns set a record of 715.751 mph (1,151.883 km/h) in this North American F-86D-35 at the Salton Sea, in California. (ROCKWELL INTERNATIONAL CORPORATION)

September 7, 1953. This Hawker Hunter Mark III was flown by Sqd.Ldr. Neville Duke to a record of 727.60 mph (1,170.76 km/h) at Littlehampton, England. (HAWKER SIDDELEY AVIATION LIMITED)

Left: *Timing equipment used on the Nash and Barns flights. The operator of the camera follows the speeding airplane and photographs it as it passes behind the vertical wire strung from the post, indicating one end of the course. The camera simultaneously films a clock. (ROCKWELL INTERNATIONAL CORPORATION)*

Right: *September 25, 1953. A Supermarine Swift streaks low across the North African desert at better than 700 mph (1,126 km/h). (VICKERS)*

October 3, 1953. Lt.Cdr. James Verdin brought the record back to America with a set of runs at 752.949 mph (1,211.746 km/h) in a prototype Douglas XF4D-1 Skyray, at the Salton Sea, in California. (DOUGLAS AIRCRAFT CO.)

October 29, 1953. The last subsonic record is timed by high-speed cameras along the shore of the Salton Sea. The cameraman is at right, while a communications van to his left is used to coordinate the logistics of Everest's runs. (ROCKWELL INTERNATIONAL CORPORATION)

October 29, 1953. The final subsonic record and the first at the 15/25-kilometer distance was set by Lt.Col. Frank Everest in this North American YF-100A Super Saber, at the Salton Sea, in California. (U.S. AIR FORCE)

August 20, 1955. The first supersonic speed record was set by Col. Horace Hanes in this North American F-100C Super Saber, at Palmdale, California. (ROCKWELL INTERNATIONAL CORPORATION)

August 20, 1955. The special timing camera used for the first high-altitude record runs. Operators sight in with two telescopes attached to the telescopic camera. (ROCKWELL INTERNATIONAL CORPORATION)

March 10, 1956. Peter Twiss flew the Fairey Delta 2 (WG774) to set a record of 1,132.13 mph (1,821.6 km/h) over Chichester, England. (FAIREY, LTD.)

December 12, 1957. The McDonnell F-101A Voodoo (53-2426) was flown at 1,207.6 mph (1,943.5 km/h) by Maj. Adrian Drew at Edwards AF Base, California. (MCDONNELL AIRCRAFT CORPORATION)

May 16, 1958. This Lockheed F-104A Starfighter (55-2969) set a record of 1,404.09 mph (2,259.65 km/h) at Edwards AF Base, California, flown by Capt. Walter Irwin. (LOCKHEED AIRCRAFT CORPORATION)

December 15, 1959. Maj. Joseph Rogers flew this Convair F-106A Delta Dart (56-0459) 1,525.965 mph (2,455.736 km/h) at Edwards AF Base, California. (GENERAL DYNAMICS CORPORATION)

August 28, 1961. USN Lt. Hunt Hardisty sets a 3-km record at 902.77 mph in this McDonnell F4H-1 Phantom II, barely 50 feet above the ground in "Project Sageburner." (*MCDONNELL DOUGLAS CORPORATON)*

July 6, 1962. This rare experimental E-166 set a record of 1,665.89 mph (2,680.97 km/h) at Podmoskovnoe, USSR, flown by Col. Georgi Mossolov. (AEROFAX INC.)

May 1, 1965. Robert Stephens flew this Lockheed YF-12A Blackbird (60-6936) at 2,070.115 mph (3,331.507 km/h) above Edwards AF Base, California. (LOCKHEED AIRCRAFT CORPORATION)

July 27, 1976. A Lockheed SR-71A Blackbird (71-7958) similar to this one was flown by Col. Eldon Joersz to a record of 2,193.64 mph (3,529.56 km/h) at Edwards AF Base, California. (LOCKHEED AIRCRAFT CORPORATION)

December 10, 1947. Jackie Cochran set an Absolute World Air Speed Record for propeller-driven airplanes when she turned 100 kilometers at 469.549 mph (755.668 km/h) in this converted North American F-6C Mustang (N5528N, 43-6859) photo plane. (AL CHUTE)

August 16, 1969. Darryl Greenamyer set a piston-engine record of 482.462 mph (776.449 km/h) in this highly modified Grumman F8F-2 Bearcat (N1111L, #121646) at Edwards AF Base, California. (JIM LARSEN)

August 14, 1979. The Red Baron RB-51 Mustang (N7715C, 44-84961A) flown by Steve Hinton at 499.059 mph (803.152 km/h) at Tonopah, Nevada. (AL CHUTE)

October 24, 1977. Darryl Greenamyer's one-of-a-kind Lockheed F-104 Starfighter (N104RB) in which he set a low-altitude speed record of 988.260 mph (1,590.45 km/h) at Tonopah, Nevada. (HARRY GANN PHOTO, VIA DUSTY CARTER)

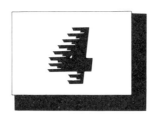

Pylon Racers

It was called simply "Event #26" on the program of the Cleveland National Air Races, held in 1929. Billed as a "Free for All," the event was open to any type of airplane regardless of design, power, or ownership. With a total purse of only $1,500, the race was a minor event in the nine-day aerial extravaganza; but it drew a rare mixture of civilian and military airplanes and thus attracted more interest than it might have otherwise.

By the time the ten pilots completed the required five laps around the 10-mile (16.1-kilometer) course, history had been made. For the first time in any major, closed-course pylon race, a civilian (Doug Davis) flying a civilian airplane (Travel Air "Mystery S") beat every military entry. By applying the latest aeronautical technology—single wing, a scientifically designed engine cowling, tight-fitting wheel covers—the builders came up with a racer capable of outrunning the best U.S. Army pursuit plane, a Curtiss P-3A. For his achievement in flying 195 mph (314 km/h), compared with the 187 mph (301 km/h) posted by R.G. Breene in an Army plane, Davis received a cup and a cash prize of $750. His airplane was soon copied and improved on, and the Travel Air "Mystery S" became a favorite among fans of air racing. Its impact on the small group of private race-plane builders was tremendous; at last, one of their own had shown his mettle. No longer was it necessary for "backyard mechanics," looked down on by professional aviators, to keep a low profile. They finally had the freedom to apply their knowledge of practical aeronautics to airplanes on the frontiers of aviation. For those who used their heads (and whose heads contained ideas based on knowledge), the way was now open to set records and even found industries. Their inspiration was the red-and-black

Travel Air, built by a team in Wichita, Kansas, who later became famous for the Beechcraft airplane. The first Travel Air Racer (of several built) was hardly a radical departure from contemporary practice; rather it was a significantly improved arrangement of ideas and components. For pylon racing, the Travel Air had a wingspan of 27.7 feet (8.4 meters), a length of 20.2 feet (6.2 meters), and an empty weight of 1,475 pounds (668 kilograms). With at least 400 horsepower from its nine-cylinder Wright J6-9 radial engine, the aircraft was capable of an estimated 235 mph (380 km/h), considerably better than anything the U.S. military was flying at the time.

The Travel Air had a brief life, even by the standards of the day. In 1931, as Doug Davis was test flying the plane before the National Air Races, it caught fire, forcing Davis to bail out and let the airplane crash. Davis, one of the most successful racing pilots of the era, died when his Wedell-Williams Racer crashed while leading the Thompson Trophy Race in 1934.

Despite the violent nature of 1930s air racing, two of the five Travel Air Racers have survived. One is intended for restoration in California; the other is on display in Chicago's Museum of Science and Industry. Moreover, a fine reproduction of the historic 1929 Travel Air has been flying since 1979.

In September 1930, the active participation of the U.S. military in air races ended after several years of diminishing interest. When Capt. Arthur Page, of the Marine Corps, crashed fatally during the 1930 Thompson Trophy Race, the negative publicity ended whatever enthusiasm remained among the military. Page was flying one of the most highly modified military racers ever, the Curtiss XF6C-6, when he was overcome by carbon monoxide from the exhaust.

With the decline in racing activity by the government came a decline in the quality of American airplanes. International prestige deteriorated into mediocrity; while the major countries in Europe built better and faster pursuit planes, the United States made do with what it had.

The Travel Air "Mystery" demonstrated what could be achieved by a custom-built airplane with minimal financial backing, and other racers soon followed. The best known U.S. plane built in the 1930s was the GeeBee, a racer that emerged from a tiny factory in West Springfield, Massachusetts, operated by the Granville brothers. The hallmark of the brothers' plane was maximum power combined with a minimum of airplane. They built a reputation for small, blazing fast speedsters that were so difficult to fly that they rarely lasted long enough to finish a race. Every GeeBee built solely for racing was destroyed in a crash, but at least some of the accidents were blamed on problems not directly connected to the planes' novel design.

While it was obvious that the relatively low-powered GeeBees were hardly in the same class as the Schneider Trophy racing seaplanes that held the Absolute World Air Speed Record, they were capable of challenging the land-plane record, then held by Bonnett in a Bernard V.2, at 278 mph (448 km/h). In 1931, this mark became a goal of the Granville brothers, in the form of the GeeBee Model Z. The "City of Springfield" was a stubby little craft, with a hefty Pratt & Whitney Wasp Jr. radial engine of 535 horsepower crammed in its bulbous nose and prominent, streamlined wheel pants jutting from underneath the wings. The Model Z, at a length of just 15.1 feet (4.6 meters), had a wingspan of 23.5 feet (7.2 meters) and a wing area of 75 square feet (7 square meters). At 1,400 pounds (634.2 kilograms) empty, and 2,280 pounds (1,033 kilograms) loaded, it was easily the smallest powerful airplane yet built.

The Shell Speed Dash was part of an extensive program for the Cleveland National Air Races to be held over Labor Day 1931. It would be a series of straight dashes over a 3-kilometer (1.86-mile) measured course, and the results might become national or world records. On September 1, Lowell Bayles made two trial runs in a GeeBee Z, averaging 267 mph (430 km/h), an American Air Speed Record and not far behind the land-plane record. No one doubted that the yellow-and-black racer had still more speed in it. On September 7, Bayles won the Thompson Trophy Race ten laps around a 10-mile course at an average speed of 236 mph (380 km/h). He made other runs that day, of which his best was 257 mph (414 km/h) — nearly as fast as de Bernardi's speed set in 1926 in the more powerful Macchi M.39 seaplane. The next day, after the crowds had left, Jimmy Wedell tried his luck. In a Wedell-Williams Racer of his own design, he could get no more than 243 mph (392 km/h) out of the 975-cubic-inch (16-liter) Pratt & Whitney Wasp Jr.

While American pylon racers were struggling to reach 300 mph (482.7 km/h) in their home-built speedsters, George Stainforth, in England, topped 400 mph (650 km/h) in a 2,650-horsepower Supermarine S.6B seaplane. The Absolute World Air Speed Record was steadily receding from the reach of ordinary pilots. Still, they at least had each other to do battle with. Bonnett's land-speed record had stood for seven years when Bayles began another series of attempts on it at Detroit City Airport in early December 1931. This time, the GeeBee Z NR-77V was ready. On December 1, Bayles showed the officials of the NAA that he meant business. Bayles made a run at 314 mph (505 km/h), then a series of four at 281.1 mph (452.4 km/h). Though it was the highest speed yet recorded by a land plane, it failed by a vital 0.17 mile per hour of topping the existing mark by the required margin of 1 percent. Another try would be needed.

On December 5, Bayles went up again in the GeeBee Z. Diving toward the course from 1,000 feet (300 meters), he leveled off at 50 meters (165 feet) and sped along at nearly 300 mph (480 km/h). During the pass, the GeeBee suddenly nosed up. Its right wing broke off and it snap-rolled into the ground. Bayles died instantly, and fire destroyed the airplane. An inspection of newsreel footage suggested that the gas cap, located just forward of the windshield, came loose and hit the windshield, shattering it and sending pieces flying back into Bayles's face. Such a momentary loss of vision could well have caused Bayles to pull back hard on his control stick, forcing the airplane upward so suddenly that a wing broke off. At that speed and altitude, the pilot had no chance to regain control, and in a split second, his fate was sealed.

The crash and the dramatic film of it became world famous, unfortunately bringing the Granville brothers a reputation for building dangerous airplanes; it is a black mark that remains to this day. That isn't to say that the GeeBee was not a hot airplane, only, apparently, that it could be flown only by above-average pilots. Years after the event, a group of aeronautical engineers studied the film of Bayles's accident frame by frame, to determine whether anything more could be learned about the cause or causes. Detecting a deformation in the right wing before the racer pitched upward, they concluded that there is a strong chance that wing flutter set in motion the sequence of events that led to the crash. In 1931, wing flutter was hardly suspected, let alone understood.

A year later, in the Cleveland National Air Races of 1932, the Shell Speed Dash was raised to the status of a fully competitive event on the program. Nine pilots entered, hoping for a share of the $3,500 purse and, of course, a significant speed record. The man of the hour was Jimmy Doolittle, until recently in the U.S. Army and already famous for his 1925 Schneider Trophy Race win and subsequent seaplane-speed record in a Curtiss R3C-2. Doolittle had as good a reputation for flying skill as anyone in the United States; so he was chosen to fly the new GeeBee Model R "Super Sportster," a barrel-shaped airplane with an 800-horsepower Pratt & Whitney engine in a fat nose that dwindled to a tiny canopy directly in front of a minuscule tail. The Model R had the look of speed; it was a single-purpose airplane whose design had not been compromised for the sake of practicality or comfort. With its red-and-white scalloped paint scheme, the Model R soon became a symbol of speed.

Doolittle and his GeeBee R-1 number 11 warmed up with a run on August 31 of 293 mph (472 km/h). The mark could not be recognized, however, because Doolittle had failed to carry a barograph to confirm that he maintained the proper altitude. He made more runs on September 1, averaging 283 mph (455 km/h). Finally, on September 3, he tore up the course with an average (according to the "official" results published by the Air Races) of 296 mph (477 km/h). When the FAI in Paris finished processing the data, the mark came out somewhat less — 294.418 mph (473.820 km/h) — but still enough for an Absolute World Air Speed Record for land planes. The eight-year-old mark set by Florentin Bonnett had at last been broken by a true racing airplane.

Doolittle quickly followed with a record-shattering win in the Thompson Trophy Race, clocking almost 253 mph (407 km/h) for ten laps around the 5-mile (8-kilometer) pylon race course. Not far behind him, in both the record run and the Thompson Trophy Race, was Jimmy Wedell in his steadily improving Wedell-Williams #44. Wedell recorded 277 mph (445.7 km/h) in the Shell Speed Dash and 242 mph (390 km/h) in the Thompson Race.

The substantial jumps in maximum speed again demonstrated that few things push competitors to innovation and excellence more effectively than trophies and recognition — and prize money. The total purse at Cleveland in 1932 exceeded $65,000. While members of the American air racing fraternity were patting themselves on the back for boosting the old French-held land-plane speed record to almost 300 mph (480 km/h), the Italians were pushing the Absolute World Air Speed Record further out of reach. Francesco Agello achieved 424 mph (682 km/h) in a Macchi-Castoldi MC.72. Seaplanes were now so far ahead that it seemed to be two separate contests.

On Labor Day 1933, the International Air Races at Glenview, Illinois, near Chicago, was the setting for more Shell Speed Dashes. This time, it was a Wedell-Williams monopoly, with three racers piloted by Jimmy Wedell, Roscoe Turner, and Lee Gehlbach. Wedell's number 44, in which he had already tried unsuccessfully to set a land-plane record, was given a better shot at the record, because of the new 1,340-cubic-inch (22-liter) Pratt & Whitney Wasp Sr. engine that had been installed. Wedell-Williams Racer NR-278V was black with red trim and silver lettering. The wings, of spruce spars and ribs, were covered with plywood, which, in turn, was covered with fabric. The tail was welded steel tubing covered with fabric; the fuselage was also welded steel tubing covered with a combination fabric and sheet aluminum. The airplane had a wingspan of 26.2 feet (8 meters), a length of 21.3 feet (6.5 meters), and a wing area of 130.4 square feet (12.1 square meters). It weighed 1,510 pounds (684 kilograms) empty and 2,216 pounds (1,004 kilograms) loaded.

Wedell's four passes on an official course worked out to 311 and 317 mph (500.4 and 510.1 km/h) downwind and 294 and 299 mph upwind (473 and 481.1 km/h), for an average speed of 304.522 mph (490.080 km/h). Wedell thus became the first pilot to top 300 mph (482.7 km/h) in a land plane — a nice accompaniment for his 1933 Thompson Trophy Race in the same airplane. Wedell, one of the steadiest and most talented of the top race pilots of the 1930s, died in June 1934, when a student he was instructing froze at the controls and their airplane crashed.

Shortly before Wedell was killed, Turner tried for the land-plane speed record in the gold Wedell-Williams number 57. According to unofficial sources, he averaged 299.5 mph (482 km/h), 7 miles per hour short of the speed needed for a record. Turner later became the world's most famous racing pilot, known equally for his flamboyant flying and his flying skill. His record of three Thompson Trophy Race wins suggests that he had what it took to win air races.

In the Labor Day 1934 Cleveland National Air Races, the Wedell-Williams racers were again out in force, two powered by a 650-horsepower Pratt & Whitney Wasp Sr. engine and one (flown by Turner) with an even more powerful Pratt & Whitney Hornet engine. In the Shell Speed Dash, J.A. Worthen turned 302 mph (486 km/h) in a prototype of the Wedell-Williams P-34 Army pursuit plane (which was never developed). Doug Davis, who had beaten the military in 1929, to launch the "Golden Age of Air Racing," was then timed at 306.215 mph (492.802 km/h) in his racer, topping Wedell's mark, though not by a wide enough margin for recognition as an official record. It was in the final event of that year's air races that Davis crashed to his death; at the time, he was leading the Thompson Trophy Race at better than 250 mph (400 km/h). Of seven Wedell-Williams racers built, only one remains; the gold number 57 usually flown by Roscoe Turner is on display in the Western Reserve Museum, in Cleveland, Ohio.

The racing of specially designed, custom-built airplanes wasn't a purely American sport, though few Americans were aware of its European counterpart. While GeeBees and Wedell-Williamses and many other exciting airplanes were tearing around checkered pylons at Cleveland, some equally innovative racing planes were touring France for the Coupe Deutsch de la Meurthe. Unlike the Thompson Trophy Race, which was a slam-bang affair tailored to the emotions of cheering crowds, the Coupe Deutsch was conducted over an intercity course, and thus had few witnesses. The airplanes that took part in it, however, were unquestionably racers.

Actually, there were three series of Coupe Deutsch races: 1912-19; 1921-22; and 1933-36. It was the last series that produced a truly great line of speed airplanes — the Caudron Racers. The long, slim, blue, French airplanes, built by an old firm credited with the first twin-engined bombers, a series of splendidly awkward contraptions of World War I, probably got more speed from a given power output than any airplane built before the Formula One racers of the 1960s. While American designers were forced to build their racers around bulky radial engines—the only type that met the power requirements of the early 1930s—the French had the good fortune to use in-line and "V" airplane engines developed by Renault, one of the first auto manufacturers. These engines could be fit into more streamlined engine cowlings than could the radials, thus lowering the wind resistance significantly. The improved streamlining helped increase speed more than the planes' somewhat lower power hindered it.

The Coupe Deutsch race was held in May 1933 over a 100-kilometer (62-mile) course—Etamps to Chartres to Bonce and back to Etampes—in two heats of ten laps, or 1,000 kilometers (620 miles), each. Of 13 airplanes entered, one was a small British Comper Swift sport racer; the other 12 entries were French machines.

Among the racers were a Caudron C.366 and two C.360s. A C.360 was destroyed in a crash a week before the race, and the C.336 was damaged on the ground and could not start. This left one C.360, which, despite having half the power of the winning Potez 53, averaged 181 mph (291 km/h) compared with the winner's 201 mph (323 km/h). In comparison with the 600 horsepower or more used by American racers, the Caudron had only 140 and the Potez about 270. This was the best demonstration that Marcel Riffard, chief designer of the Caudron racers, knew what he was doing. The Absolute World Air Speed Record for land planes of 305 mph (390 km/h) may have been well beyond the reach of the first Caudron racer, but with more power, improved streamlining, and retractable landing gear, who could tell what might be accomplished?

In October 1934, the French speed pilot Raymond Delmotte set a French Air Speed Record of 298 mph (480 km/h) in a Caudron C.460 powered by a 310-horsepower Renault six-cylinder, in-line engine of 580 cubic inches (9.5 liters) displacement. The slender, pointy-nosed airplane was little larger than the smallest airplanes of the period. It had a wing span of 22.1 feet (6.7 meters), a length of 23.3 feet (7.1 meters), and a wing area of 75 square feet (7 square meters); empty, it weighed 1,300 pounds (589 kilograms). The following December, Delmotte reportedly flew the airplane at 343 mph (552 km/h); but no convincing evidence of this has been found.

On December 25, 1934, Delmotte finally did what all of France had wanted to do ever since Jimmy Doolittle captured the land-plane speed record with his GeeBee. At Istres, Delmotte flew a Caudron C.460 with an improved Renault engine of 380 horsepower to an official Absolute World Air Speed Record for land planes of 314.321 mph (505.848 km/h), making him the first pilot of any but a seaplane to exceed 500 km/h (310 mph). In the Coupe Deutsch Race of May 1935, Delmotte enhanced his reputation, as well as that of the Caudron C.460, by leading a pair of them to a sweep of the race. Delmotte's average speed in the four-and-a-half-hour grind—276 mph (444 km/h)—was far beyond anything previously achieved by an airplane of that power. And off to the side sat the shiny new Caudron C.560, with its 475-horsepower Renault V12, unable to race because of insufficient testing.

Before the French could make another attempt, however, a new personality emerged: the eccentric American millionaire Howard Hughes. Having made his fortune as head of the Hughes Tool Company, Hughes was in a position to indulge his fantasies, for example, by producing *Hell's Angels,* one of the great aviation epics. In early 1934, Hughes hired a small staff of talented engineers and set out to build the world's fastest land plane. He had gotten a taste of speed by winning an air race in a souped-up version of a Boeing P-12 Army pursuit plane. By late summer 1935, the Hughes Racer was ready. A marked advancement in aeronautical technology, the racer was cleaner and more powerful than any plane yet seen. In its nose was the latest Pratt & Whitney Twin Wasp Jr. — a two-row, 14-cylinder, radial, air-cooled engine generating 1,000 horsepower; yet, in overall size it was smaller than the Wasp engine used by the GeeBees and Wedell-Williamses.

A two-bladed, metal, constant-speed propellor converted power from the engine into thrust, while an unusually close-fitting cowl reduced the drag of the engine to little more than that of an in-line engine. Fuselage and tail were entirely of aluminum; the wings were of wood. All rivets were machined flush with the aluminum skin, a novel technique that soon became standard practice. Unlike almost every other airplane then flying, the cockpit of the Hughes Racer was completely enclosed. The landing gear retraction system was designed and built so efficiently that even today it is difficult to detect the line that separates the fixed portion of the wing from the metal covers that move with the landing gear, enclosing it when the wheels are retracted. The wingspan of the Hughes Racer, as it was prepared for the 3-kilometer speed record, was 25 feet (7.6 meters), its length was 27 feet (8.2 meters), and the wing area 138 square feet (12.8 square meters). The plane's takeoff weight was about 5,500 pounds (2,492 kilograms) giving it an unusually high (for the 1930s) wing loading of 39.8 pounds per square foot (194 kilograms per square meter).

On September 12, 1935, the Hughes Racer — with a dark-blue fuselage, aluminum wings and tail, and yellow lettering — was wheeled out of the factory for its first assault on the 314-mph (506 km/h) record which had been held by Raymond Delmotte since the previous December. Three passes over the short course yielded an average speed of 345 mph (555 km/h) — not as fast as Hughes expected, so the first effort was canceled. The next day, Hughes went at it again, after some finetuning of the airframe and engine. Among the official timers from the NAA was Amelia Earhart. The first run was made at 335 mph (539 km/h) and the second at "only" 339 mph (546 km/h). The next five were considerably faster, and the eighth began even better but ended abruptly when the engine quit because a wad of steel wool got caught in the main fuel line. Hughes landed the airplane on its belly in a plowed fiield, doing surprisingly little damage.

Hughes was elated with the timers' calculations. By averaging 352.391 mph (567.115 km/h), he had added an amazing 38 mph (61 km/h) to the nine-month-old French record. NAA records show the fastest four consecutive runs to have been numbers three through six, which average out to 348.8 mph (561.2 km/h); but the faster speed has long been accepted as official.

The only jump in the land-plane speed record that was greater followed the major scientific advancements of World War I. In January 1937, Hughes again fired up the racer—now with longer wings and additional navigational equipment and designated the H-1. He proceeded to set a California-to-New York record of just under seven and a half hours, two hours faster than his existing record set in a Northrop Gamma. Today the H-1 is the centerpiece in the National Air & Space Museum's Hall of Flight Technology.

Hughes went on to earn several more fortunes as head of the Hughes Tool Company and the Hughes Aircraft Company (a major builder of helicopters). He died in 1976, his accomplishments in aviation overshadowed by an eccentricity that had turned him into a recluse. His name, however, remains a part of the American aviation legend, thanks to his racer, to his enormous, eight-engine flying boat christened "Spruce Goose," and to *The Outlaw,* a film starring then unknown actress Jane Russell.

American pylon racers had done well with limited resources in setting speed-record land planes, but they couldn't keep up the pace. The need for large-scale financing, for procuring ever more powerful engines, was the ultimate barrier. The speeds achieved by Thompson Trophy Race airplanes actually dropped during the mid-1930s as the GeeBees were reduced to scrap by a series of accidents. In addition, much of the enthusiasm for the Wedell-Williams vanished with the death of Jimmy Wedell. When Howard Hughes boosted the record past 350 mph (563 km/h) in 1935, it became clear that no home-built, self-financed racer could match such performance. The "pylon polishers" went back to what they knew best: racing at breakneck speed around short courses, close to the ground where paying customers could see them.

Further proof, if such were needed, of the futility of trying to break speed records on a shoestring came at the National Air Races, held in Los Angeles in 1936. One of the French Caudron C.460s visiting the United States took every event Michel Detroyat, its pilot, entered. With significantly less horsepower than many of his rivals, but with clearly superior streamlining, the factory-built Caudron so shocked the Professional Race Pilots Association that its members voted to refuse to race against any more airplanes built with government money, as was then assumed concerning the Caudron Racers. Since that time, most American pylon racing rules have included a clause restricting entry to airplanes built by "private enterprise." (Not long after the C.460's display of speed at Los Angeles, the French Caudron racers was lost during an attempt on the Women's World Speed Record by Maryse Hilsz, at Istres.)

Still, the French had proven their point, and they went home from Los Angeles content. By the time a purely American racer broke the Caudron's competitive records, in 1938 (Roscoe Turner, in his "Meteor," won that year's Thompson Trophy Race with a speed of 283 mph [455 km/h]), the speed record for land planes was almost 100 mph (161 km/h) faster. The French had shown that their formula of a minimum airplane built around an in-line air-cooled engine was superior to other airplanes with comparable power. They intended to pursue that line of development. After the C.460 came the C.560, with its flush (nonprotruding) canopy and 475-horsepower Renault V12. As imposing as the C.560 was, its record was insignificant. Two C.560s were entered in the 1935 Coupe Deutsch Race but were not ready in time. The next year, an attempt on the record by Raymond Delmotte in a C.560, had to be canceled.

Enthusiasm at the Caudron factory was not dimmed much by the failure of the C.560, and Marcel Riffard, the technical director, moved ahead with his next project: the land-plane record, using the C.712. Like its predecessors, and even the Caudron military airplanes, the C.712 was built primarily of wood and with the finest craftsmanship—a technique that works well for custom aircraft but which is time-consuming for mass production. While developing the C.712, Riffard considered a C.711, which was to have been a lightweight C.710 fighter plane with retractable landing gear and greater power. The design was soon dropped in favor of the C.712, which was to use the fuselage of a C.710 intended for the Soviet Union but never delivered. The fuselage would be combined with the wings, landing gear, and horizontal tail from a C.560 racer. The power of the C.710 V12 was increased and the size of the rounded vertical tail was reduced.

Test flights of the C.712 began at the military test base of Istres in December 1936 and proceeded well. Engineering estimates had predicted a top speed for the airplane of 421 mph (677 km/h) at sea level, which would have placed the C.712 well ahead of anything the Hughes Racer could do. On the first attempt at the record, however, the pilot, Delmotte, lost elevator control while flying at an estimated 385 mph (620 km/h) and had to bail out. He parachuted safely, but the C.712 crashed. Caudron's attempt to dethrone Howard Hughes had failed.

Piston-engine Propaganda

For years, most attempts on the Absolute World Air Speed Record were tied to national goals. The prestige to be gained by demonstrating that one's country had the fastest airplanes was considered of great value, both diplomatically and financially. Never, though, had the world seen anything like the program of Nazi Germany in the middle and late 1930s, when vast sums of money and aggressive propaganda were used to "prove" that National Socialism was capable of technical achievements beyond those of the democracies. It was muscle-flexing to a degree never before seen in aviation, in which peacetime aviation technology was used to frighten potential enemies.

Paradoxically, Germany's entry into the age of aviation was made using a Rolls Royce Kestrel engine, the mainstay of British fighters and bombers since the late 1920s and a direct descendant of the engines developed by Rolls Royce for Supermarine's racing seaplanes. In the summer of 1934, the German Air Ministry announced a competition to design a replacement for the biplane fighters with which Germany had secretly been building an air force, despite the Treaty of Versailles, which forbade such rearming. Among the entries were designs for two airplanes that later played a role in the story of the Absolute World Air Speed Record. One of the designs became the most widely produced military airplane in history. Comparison flight tests of the four entries were conducted in October 1935, and the winner was announced: the Bf-109, designed by Willy Messerschmitt and built by the Bavarian Aircraft Works. Like the rival Heinkel He-112, which had equal performance, the Bf-109 was a modern, all-metal, low-wing monoplane powered by a 695-horsepower Kestrel engine (both of the losers had German engines).

The Bf-109 was unveiled during the 1936 Berlin Olympic Games. They were the only games that included an appreciable amount of flying, even though it wasn't part of the formal competition. The prototype Bf-109, proclaimed a "wonder fighter" by the German Ministry of Propaganda, flew demonstrations. To demonstrate that its new fighter was a superior airplane, the Germans entered a team of four Bf-109s in the International Flying Meeting, held at Zurich, Switzerland in July 1937. Three production Bf-109Bs, powered by Junkers engines, were joined by the Bf-109V-13 (the thirteenth test model), the first "ringer" — an airplane palmed off as standard but in reality replete with special features designed to improve the aircraft's performance.

The Messerschmitts dominated the air meet, winning the Circuit of the Alps Race, the Alpenflug, and the dive-and-climb race (in which the experimental airplane climbed to almost 10,000 feet [3,000 meters] and dived to 1,000 feet [300 meters] in just over two minutes). Had this performance been achieved by a production military fighter, the world would have been justified in being impressed, for no other military airplane of the time could come even close to matching the Messerschmitts. The Bf-109V-13, however, was far from standard, as information uncovered after World War II revealed. In place of the usual Daimler Benz V12 engine of about 950 horsepower, used in other prototypes, this aircraft had a specially modified engine that could produce 1,600 horsepower, or more, for short periods. It had a three-blade propellor rather than the standard two-blade and a pointed propellor spinner that blended smoothly with the carefully fitted cowling. The cockpit canopy was lower and more streamlined, and the tail and wings had been reduced in size.

Neither the press nor the public were told of these changes at the time, as the Germans had embarked on a carefully orchestrated program of deception. The conquest of Europe was being planned, and a large part of the effort would depend on the Germans' ability to overawe their future opponents. Long before the Nazis possessed superior air power, the world was convinced they had it, and responded accordingly.

On November 11, 1937, the Germans ended Howard Hughes' reign as the world's fastest land-plane pilot. At Bavarian Aircraft Works headquarters in Augsburg, Dr. Hermann Wurster, the company's chief pilot, averaged 379.629 mph (610.950 km/h) in the special Bf-109V-13, setting an official 3-kilometer (1.86-mile) Absolute World Air Speed Record for land planes. For the attempt, the airplane had been given a special smooth finish to reduce wind resistance, in the manner of earlier racing and record airplanes. Such finishing, however, was infeasible for a production aircraft — which the Germans insisted it was. Strangely, they told the FAI the record was set by a Bf-113R, a fictitious airplane.

With other speed-record airplanes being developed in several countries, the mark set by the Bf-109V-13 was expected to be short-lived. For one thing, a bitter rivalry was developing between Willy Messerschmitt and Ernst Heinkel, whose design had lost to Messerschmitt's in the 1937 fighter competition.

Unbeknownst to the two manufacturers, they were aiming at the Absolute World Air Speed Record with highly specialized airplanes. Each manufacturer's goal was a production contract for thousands of fighter planes. Heinkel got into the air first with his He-100, an imposing airplane with an aerodynamic cleanliness superior to anything else then being flown. The first flight of the

He-100V-1 was made January 22, 1938, and by June the second prototype had captured the Absolute World Speed Record for 100 kilometers (62 miles) over a closed course, at 394 mph (634 km/h), even faster than Messerschmitt's best had done in a short, straight sprint. The He-100 was a prototype fighter, though some of its features were hardly ordinary. For one thing, surface radiators were used similar to those on the Curtiss, Supermarine, and Macchi racing seaplanes. While effective for short flights, the radiators could not absorb even minor battle damage and continue to function. The airplane's wing loading (its weight in relation to the area of its wings) was higher than anything yet experienced by military pilots, and some handling qualities had been sacrificed to achieve speed. After three prototypes had been built in this configuration, common sense prevailed and some major changes were made. The wingspan was increased from 26.9 feet (8.2 meters) to 30.9 feet (9.4 meters) and the surface-evaporation cooling system was replaced by a partially retractable belly radiator. Three more such prototypes were built, along with a dozen production airplanes, called the He-100D.

Heinkel was left with his three racerlike prototypes, and it was with one of them — the He-100V-3 — that an attempt on the 3-kilometer record was planned for September 1938. Years later, the pilot, Hans Dieterle, described the He-100V-3 and its operation to the author:

> In order to reduce unnecessary aerodynamic drag, all irregularities on the body and wings were smoothed and the whole airplane was polished. Furthermore, the engine power of 1,000 horsepower was increased to 1,800 by increasing manifold pressure in connection with higher revolutions per minute. The high thermic stresses of such a tuned motor could be mastered only with a special fuel. This fuel had the capacity to absorb heat from the engine [for cooling] and to function at high compression ratios without preigniting. Special heat-resistant spark plugs were necessary; however, they fouled at low engine performance.
>
> It is obvious that these extremely strained engines had a rather short life. The engine builder estimated a 30-minute running life.
>
> As a last measure, this plane was fitted with a special propellor which was very effective at high speeds; [it] showed rather low acceleration at takeoff, [however].
>
> Due to the many modifications, the plane was very sensitive, and so difficult to fly that it had to be handled like a raw egg. I had been given the order to undertake the necessary test flights. At that time I was only a young company pilot; therefore the chief pilot of the Heinkel-Werke was supposed to do the last test flight and the actual record flight. Unfortunately, this never happened. During the last test flight, in September 1938, the landing gear jammed, and when the engine suddenly seized, the pilot was forced to leave the plane by parachute. The real reasons for that disaster were never found out.
>
> The loss of his beloved [airplane] came as a shock to Dr. Heinkel, but he did not give up his plans, and had another He-100 built as a new record-breaker — the He-100V-8. He now ordered that I should be the record pilot.

Heinkel's He-100V-8 had even less wingspan than the early prototypes — down to a mere 24.9 feet (7.6 meters) — but the German Air Ministry continued to refer to it as a standard, production He-100 fighter.

Dieterle continued:

By the end of February 1939, the V-8 was finished. The record trials were now done at the Heinkel subsidiary at Oranienburg, near Berlin, . . . because there was a longer runway and . . . less disturbance for our team, consisting of about 25 people. I looked around for an appropriate racing line and found one that went along a railway track. With a standard He-100, which I had been given for that purpose, I made as many trial runs as possible.

After each run, I reduced engine power somewhat and at about 400 meters [1,300 feet] altitude I directed myself to the turning point which was at a distance of 20 to 25 kilometers [12 to 16 miles]. From the turning point I [turned] at full power to the race course and reduced my altitude to below 75 meters [245 feet]. It was [very important] that I [know] the landscape offhand, since the . . . plane allowed only limited view, due to the cockpit modifications.

The "V-8" was first flown with a standard motor in order to define the last-minute modifications. To minimize the risk for the plane, only necessary flights were made. After the plane had received its special engine, it started for its first attack on the existing record; [but] it had to be stopped short at the approach to the race course because the engine started to vibrate and did not develop its full power. We found out later that the carburetor [could] not . . . provide the quantity of fuel which this engine needed. This motor was very "thirsty" and needed up to 300 gallons [1,135 liters] per hour.

After the existing fuel pump was replaced by a higher-capacity one, I started my second try, which was unsuccessful also. I had already passed the racing distance twice* when I was forced to land due to high oil temperature [that was too high] and [to] low oil pressure. This He-100 had none of the conventional oil coolers because they could have created aerodynamic disturbance. The hot oil ran through a heat exchanger, [located] in the fuselage behind the pilot's seat. [It] was cooled by methyl alcohol, which has a very low evaporation temperature. When the oil reached 65°C (150°F), the methyl alcohol evaporated and thus cooled off the oil by dissipating heat. The alcohol vapors were cooled in the wings and condensed back to liquid alcohol which was then pumped back by little pumps to the heat exchanger. . . . this cooling system could not handle the extreme heat that developed when the engine ran at full power.

The two trials and the different, standard runs already accounted for a running time of the engine of about half an hour. Therefore, there was a high risk that the engine might fail very soon. The good news from these trials was that our measurements taken showed the He-100V-8 was fast enough to break the speed record of the Italian, Agello.

On March 30, 1939, the weather was okay, and I decided to make another takeoff. However, my "taking off" was not as easy as the words sound. For every takeoff, my "ballerina" needed a great deal of preparation. She was hauled to the runway; there she was [faced into] the wind and warmed up [using] normal spark plugs. [When] the running temperature was reached, the engine was shut off. Specialists of the engine builder exchanged, as quickly as possible, the standard

---

*Apparently, Dieterle means he completed two passes over the course.

plugs with so-called racing plugs. This had to be done extremely fast in order to prevent the motor from cooling off too much.

In the meantime, I had taken my cockpit seat, buckled myself in, and started the engine again. Because of the sensitive spark plugs, the motor could run only at high speed. Since the motor did not run smoothly, I had no way to control it by feel. This was done by the engineers of the engine-builder, who checked the exhaust flames of the twelve cylinders and only let the plane take off when this analysis was to their satisfaction.

The wheel chocks were taken away, and the bird started rolling. My big problem was to get up speed, since I had only moderate acceleration with the special propellor. At the end of the runway, a large colored flag was posted to serve for direction.

Time after time, I directed my plane to the "racing track," with the firm intention to risk more than usual. Within thirteen minutes between takeoff and landing, I flew the racing distance four times, each time pushing the throttle to maximum and not being as critical with the temperature control as before.

Dieterle and the He-100V-8 averaged 463.921 mph (746.604 km/h), setting the first official Absolute World Air Speed Record in more than four years. At long last, after more than eleven years of domination by seaplanes, the record was held by a land plane. The Heinkel crew rejoiced and the German Ministry of Propaganda cranked out reams of adulatory prose about Germany's "standard fighter plane" that could outrun anyone else's by at least 100 mph (160 km/h). It didn't matter that the airplane which set the record was not, as the Ministry claimed, a Heinkel He-112U, or that it was about as combat-ready as a GeeBee Super Sportster, or that it took a top test pilot to keep the airplane from crashing. All that mattered was convincing potential enemies that it would be futile to try to beat the Luftwaffe in the skies.

Ernst Heinkel's plan to use the He-100V-8 to go for another record, this time at a higher elevation, was prevented by the Air Ministry, for political reasons, and the airplane was retired to a museum. Its exact travels are unknown, but apparently it was in Munich's Deutsches Museum when the technical exhibition was demolished during an air raid in July 1944 by the U.S. 8th Air Force. There is reason to believe its fuselage was replaced by that of the static test airframe. Although the museum was rebuilt, no trace of the airplane is known to have survived.

The He-100V-8 was built of aluminum except for the rudder and elevators, which were covered with fabric. During the record runs it was the natural color of aluminum, but on display in the museum afterward, the airplane was painted light blue with black numbers and the red-white-and-black Nazi flag was on its rudder. The wingspan was 24.9 feet (7.6 meters), the length was 26.8 feet (8.2 meters), and its height was 8.2 feet (2.5 meters). It had a gross weight of about 5,600 pounds (2,537 kilograms).

The dozen He-100D "production" airplanes served Goebbel's Propaganda Ministry well. Photographs of them—in various imaginary squadron markings—appeared in various publications, giving the impression that combat units were equipped with them. For some reason, they were designated "He-113," and recognition handbooks showed the silhouette of such an airplane; but Allied pilots searched in vain for the fighter plane. Of eight prototypes built, one was destroyed in a test, one went to the Deutsches Museum, and the other six were sold to the Soviet Union (while it was still an ally of Germany). Three preproduction He-100D-0s were built and eventually sold to Japan, where it might have gone into production had not Heinkel failed to supply tools and jigs.

The closest an He-100D/He-113 came to active service was in a special squadron formed by Heinkel test pilots to defend Heinkel's main plant at Rostock, Germany. That this potentially fine airplane was never used can be blamed on Willy Messerschmitt, whose distaste for anything connected with Heinkel was a factor in numerous Air Ministry decisions. The He-100 was probably superior to the Bf-109, but the production run of the Bf-109 was more than 30,000, whereas the He-100D was little more than a curiosity. Messerschmitt's efforts to freeze Heinkel out of government work were not limited to using political influence. Along with the development of the "109" came his own speed-record contender. It was built with government money, whereas Heinkel's was built in secret with private financing.

Messerschmitt's airplane began life in late 1937 as project P-1059. While there was some thought of basing a production airplane on it, the main purpose was to recapture the Absolute World Air Speed Record from Italy, which, though an ally, was held in contempt by the Germans. For years, most people accepted the German pronouncements that the airplane, called the Me-109R, was a modified version of an early production fighter plane, probably the Bf-109E. In reality, it was a vastly different design that had little in common with the military craft.

The first flight of the Me-209V-1 (the true designation of the record aspirant) came on August 1, 1938. The pilot was Hermann Wurster, Messerschmitt's chief test pilot. It was Wurster who, in 1937, set the record for land planes of 379 mph (610 km/h) in a genuine Bf-109. His report on the seven-minute test, discovered after the war among captured documents, was so damning that Messerschmitt could easily have used it to justify canceling the program, had it actually been aimed at developing a useful airplane:

(1) The engine runs unevenly; (2) the high temperature reached by the coolant fluid results in unsatisfactory cooling; (3) cockpit ventilation is inadequate and engine gases penetrate the cockpit, necessitating the constant use of an oxygen mask; (4) the undercarriage cannot be extended at speeds in excess of 250 km/h [155 mph]; (5) the main wheels tend to drop out of their wheel wells during high-speed maneuvers; (6) the fuel filler caps tend to lift off at high speed; (7) the undercarriage hydraulic oil escapes from its reservoir and sprays the windscreen; (8) the takeoff run is excessive and the takeoff characteristics vicious; (9) visibility from the cockpit is severely limited; (10) marked instability manifests itself during the climb; (11) the rudder is inadequate to control the plane in a bank, and the plane tends to nose down with any divergence from course; (12) when banking at full throttle, the plane rolls over on its back; (13) stick forces are excessive and tiring; (14) at speeds in the vicinity of 160-170 km/h [100-105 mph] the controls soften up; (15) landing characteristics are extremely dangerous except under windless conditions; (16) on touching down, the plane swerves violently; (17) it is

impossible to employ the brakes during the landing run, as immediately they are applied, the aircraft swerves from the runway.

It might make an amusing parlor game for experienced flyers to search for some aspect of the Me-209V-1 that did not pose a threat to the test pilot's life. Some problems were solved in time to be incorporated in the second prototype, which flew in February 1939. This machine was soon destroyed, however, when the engine failed during a landing and the plane dropped like a rock, with the test pilot, Fritz Wendel, somehow escaping with only minor injuries.

Messerschmitt having just learned of his rival's successful speed runs, it was his plan to go for the record in the second Me-209. Because the third and fourth prototypes were unfinished, Messerschmitt had no choice but to put the new, souped-up Daimler Benz DB 601ARJ engine in the original Me-209V-1 and see how fast the airplane would go. Although the homely Messerschmitt lacked the Heinkel's clean lines, it did have two important advantages: an engine that developed 2,300 horsepower in short bursts (500 more than the Heinkel's engine), and a speed course more than 400 meters (1,323 feet) higher than his rival's, where the thinner air was more conducive to high speed.

Five days after Dieterle set the record in the Heinkel, Fritz Wendel, Messerschmitt's test pilot, set out to break it. The weather finally cleared on April 26, and Wendel made four screaming runs near the Augsburg headquarters of the manufacturer, averaging 469.224 mph (755.138 km/h). The FAI required that the old mark be surpassed by at least 1 percent; the Me-209V-1 came through with barely 1 km/h (0.6 mph) to spare, but it was enough to satisfy the FAI, Messerschmitt, and the Propaganda and Air ministries. Having decided to gamble everything on the Bf-109 fighter plane, the Air Ministry desperately wanted the Absolute World Air Speed Record to be held by an airplane it could claim was ready for combat. Had Heinkel held the record, the embarrassment would have been considerable, since its fighter had already been rejected.

Like the He-100, the Me-209V-1 was all-aluminum. Painted dark blue for the record attempt (the few available photographs show no numbers or other markings), it had a wingspan of 25.6 feet (7.8 meters), a length of 23.8 feet (7.3 meters), a wing area of 114.1 square feet (10.6 square meters), and a gross weight of 5,545 pounds (2,512 kilograms).

As soon as Heinkel heard about the Messerschmitt record, he began making plans to take it back, calculating that his airplane could hit at least 478 mph (769 km/h) if allowed to fly at the same altitude the Messerschmitt had flown at. The Air Ministry promptly clamped down on Heinkel, though, making it clear that the Ministry was content with the record set by Messerschmitt and that it wanted no public rivalry.

With war imminent, the Germans were pleased with possessing the Absolute World Air Speed Record with an airplane the world had been led to believe was ready to fight. The third and fourth Me-209 prototypes were completed as more modest machines, apparently with the intention of actually trying to develop a combat fighter plane from them. A radically changed wing was designed, with a span of 32.9 feet (10 meters), and fitted, along with conventional radiators. As each change was made, however, the airplane's performance deteriorated, until it was inferior to the standard Bf-109F; meanwhile, the handling characteristics remained difficult. Understandably, the Air Ministry lost interest in the design, and finally dropped it.

In 1943, Messerschmitt began testing the first of its Me-209-II fighter prototypes, an airplane with no connection to the original Me-209. By the time tests on the aircraft had reached the point of military-acceptance trials, however, the airplane was outclassed by such jet aircraft as the Messerschmitt Me-262, and the project was discarded.

The record-setting Me-209V-1 was sent to the mysterious Berlin Air Museum, where it was treated with great sensitivity. No photographs of it on display are known to exist. In 1943, an RAF raid on Berlin destroyed much of the museum and most of its contents — but not all. Some of the rare airplanes and engines were dragged out of the burning building and shipped east for safekeeping. Sometime later, a Polish Army officer reportedly found them and, realizing their historic value, had them shipped south. Then, in 1967, Norman Wiltshire, an Australian member of Air Britain, the International Association of Aviation Historians, discovered the remains of the Me-209V-1 while exploring the National Museum of Air and Space, in Kracow, Poland. A subsequent article by Wiltshire in the *Air Britain News* led to the author visiting the Polish Museum, where he saw for himself what was left of the airplane: the fuselage aft of the firewall. After decades of "nonexistence," at least part of the famous airplane had been found, though there seems little chance that it will ever be restored to display condition.

On June 20, 1939, the first flight of one of the world's most radical and most advanced airplanes took place under tight secrecy. At Peenemünde, a test base on the Baltic coast, the Heinkel He-176, the first true rocket-powered airplane, flew. The tiny craft had a wingspan of only 13 feet (4 meters) and a wing area of 54 square feet (5 square meters). With a Walter rocket motor capable of generating 1,100 pounds (498 kilograms) of thrust, the He-176 flew 500 mph (805 km/h). Its designer, Heinkel, hoped to use it to make a speed-record attempt, as well as to conduct research. Lack of interest on the part of the German high command doomed the project, and it was retired to the Berlin Air Museum, where it was destroyed in the same bombing raid that badly damaged the Me-209V-1.

Fascinating Failures

The 1930s were the most active years in the history of the Absolute World Air Speed Record. More separate efforts were made at the record than were made before or since. While most of the attempts failed, the creativity and individuality evident even in the failures marked the decade as special. While the major industrial nations prepared to launch themselves into the jet age, others were trying to squeeze the last few miles per hour from propellor-driven airplanes. Had World War II not intervened, at least some experimental speed airplanes probably would have made serious attempts on the Absolute World Air Speed Record, and at least one might have broken it. The war, however, changed everything, including the sport of speed flying. Still, the decade was a time of grand experimentation. Ideas were tried that once would have brought only laughter. More horsepower was extracted from a few cubic inches than had been thought possible.

American speed-record aspirants ranged from overly ambitious pylon racers to scientific dreamers. While the Granville brothers, with their GeeBees, and the men of Wedell-Williams used pylon racing planes to push the land-plane mark over the 300 mph (480 km/h) barrier, one of their compatriots set out to design an airplane expressly for the 3-kilometer (1.86-mile) record, using knowledge gained in building several highly successful, limited-displacement-class racers.

Keith Rider built his first racer, the R-1, in 1931, with a 260-horsepower engine that drove it to an estimated top speed of 235 mph (378 km/h). A later plane, the R-2, with a smaller, 200-horsepower engine, achieved 210 mph (338 km/h). Both were minimal airplanes with slim lines, low canopies, and (a rarity then) retractable landing gear. They were unusually fast for their size and power, strong evidence that Rider knew what he was doing. His design for the Absolute World Air Speed Record, revealed in 1934, bore a superficial resemblance to earlier Rider Racers. It was built around a supercharged V16 rated at 2,500 horsepower, using a steam cooling system. The engine, said to be the brainchild of Harry Miller, a famous builder of racing cars, would have been more than twice as powerful as anything used so far in a land plane, though shy of the 3,000-horsepower dual engine built by Fiat for the Italian Macchi-Castoldi MC.72 seaplane recordholder.

Rider's airplane was designed as a low-wing monoplane with the landing gear retracting into slight bulges beneath the wings. Its wingspan was to be 26.7 feet (8.1 meters), its length 27.8 feet (8.5 meters), and its weight about 3,000 pounds (1,359 kilograms). The cockpit canopy was a minimal affair offering little wind resistance (or visibility); unlike canopies on other high-speed airplanes of the day, it could be completely closed by a sliding partition while in flight. Rider estimated that, by holding down the frontal area of the "Super-Speed Racer" to a mere 31 by 18 inches (79 by 46 centimeters), he could achieve a top speed of 465 mph (750 km/h) long enough to make four 3-kilometer runs. A major limitation would be the airplane's fuel capacity; Rider estimated that at maximum power, the engine would burn 240 gallons (908 liters) of gasoline per hour.

There is no evidence that the design ever got off the drawing board, though Rider was capable of building such an airframe. Possibly, lack of a 2,500-horsepower engine killed the project.

An even more theoretical study of a speed-record airplane was made by John Stack, a top aerodynamicist at Langley Field, Virginia, the facility of the National Advisory Committee for Aeronautics (NACA) and predecessor of the National Aeronautics and Space Administration (NASA). In January 1934, Stack published a paper in the *Journal of the Aeronautical Sciences* entitled "Effects of Compressibility on High Speed Flight." The article was both an early discussion of the anticipated effects on airplanes approaching the speed of sound and the design of a hypothetical speed-record airplane. Stack proposed a land plane to be powered by a 2,300-horsepower Rolls Royce R engine similar to the one that drove the Supermarine S.6B seaplane at more than 400 mph (650 km/h). His airplane would have a fuselage diameter of only 40 inches (102 centimeters), a wingspan of 29.1 feet (8.9 meters), and a wing area of 141 square feet (13.1 square meters). The wing airfoil cross section would be perfectly symmetrical, with a thickness ranging from 18 percent at the wing root to 9 percent at the tip.

Stack theorized that such an airplane, using every known technique for reducing drag, would be able to fly at a top speed of 566 mph (911 km/h). He did not actually suggest building the airplane, though it might have proved a valuable tool for research, in the same way the X series of rocket airplanes did for NASA later. In 1934, however, there was no money for such a project, nor was it certain an "R" engine could have been obtained from the British.

A speed plane that not only was built but flown was "Time Flies," closely tied to Frank Hawks, a well-known American speed pilot, and sponsored by the Gruen Watch Company (hence the name). It had the misfortune to be under construction when Howard Hughes raised the land-plane speed record from 314 mph (505 km/h), which "Time Flies" might have beaten, to 352 mph (566.4 km/h), which it probably could not have equaled. "Time Flies" was meant to break records, in particular, long-distance records. The airplane's heritage included the GeeBee Super Sportster, in which the designer, Howell Miller, played an important role. It had a minimal fuselage with almost no protrusions – the shape designer-purists find most desirable. The landing gear was fully retractable and, once the airplane was in the air, its windshield folded down flush with the fuselage.

Power was from an 825-horsepower Pratt & Whitney R-1830 Twin Wasp Jr., which the Army and Navy had given Hawks and Miller permission to install in their speedster even though it was supposed to be limited to military use. It used a newly designed three-blade, constant-speed propellor on loan from the Hamilton Standard Propellor Company. Incorporating the latest technological advances, the airplane caught the public's fancy. It first left the ground in October 1936, and the following April flew from Washington to New York City at 300 mph (480 km/h). Upon landing, Hawks announced plans to break both the American transcontinental speed record and the Absolute World Air Speed Record for land planes. A few days later, however, at the end of a 230-mph (370-km/h) run from Miami to Newark, New Jersey, Hawks made an unusually hard landing and cracked one of the main wing spars. Major repairs were needed, repairs Hawks could not afford; so the airplane sat idle while other planes broke records.

Eventually, "Time Flies" was converted into a two-seat prototype of a planned military fighter plane. Flown by Leigh Wade, the airplane, rechristened "Hawks Military Racer," placed fourth in the 1938 Thompson Trophy Race, in Cleveland, at 250 mph (402 km/h). Nothing came of the plan to build quantities of the plane for the military, however, and shortly before the Thompson Trophy Race, Hawks was killed in the crash of the underpowered Gwynn "safety plane." Finally, on October 3, 1938, the veteran race pilot Earl Ortman was practicing aerobatics in the Hawks Military Racer when a wing broke off and he was forced to bail out; the airplane crashed and was destroyed.

In contrast to other countries, neither the U.S. government nor American industry showed any interest in U.S. speed planes breaking the Absolute World Air Speed Record. Once Howard Hughes pushed the land-plane record past 350 mph (560 km/h), there was no move to build a fighter plane that could top Hughes' speed. In fact, American military airplanes didn't start to show much speed until 1939, when a Lockheed P-38 hit 400 mph (640 km/h) on a transcontinental run; but the aircraft was then a top-secret project and not available for attempts to set records. This was nothing like the situation prevailing in Great Britain in the late 1930s. Despite the proximity of the Continent, where war seemed increasingly imminent, the British took the luxury of planning two assaults on the Absolute World Air Speed Record. One was with a modified fighter plane, the other with a beautiful, special-purpose speed machine.

When the Germans set a land-plane speed record with what appeared to be a standard Messerschmitt Bf-109 fighter, interest was stimulated in bettering the performance with a Supermarine Spitfire, then being promoted as the world's fastest production fighter. It was thought, with reason, that a cleaned-up Spitfire Mark I with greater power could boost the record from the Messerschmitt's 379 mph (610 km/h) to around 410 mph (660 km/h). Soon after the Germans announced their record in November 1937, the Royal Air Force and the Vickers Supermarine Company set out to build a record-breaker. Construction of the "High-Speed Spitfire," as it was called, began in 1938 and was completed in January 1939. Beginning as the forty-eighth production plane, the Spitfire received a low-drag racing canopy, a special Rolls Royce Merlin engine rated at 2,160 horsepower for short periods, a four-blade wood propellor and an extremely smooth finish with flush rivets and numerous coats of high-gloss paint.

The testing, which began in late winter 1939, had not progressed far when word came that the Germans had broken not only the land-plane record but the Absolute World Air Speed Record. The 464 mph (747 km/h) achieved by Hans Dieterle in a Heinkel He-100V-8 was well beyond the capability of the special Spitfire even under the most ideal conditions. With this setback, the British abandoned the effort and returned the Spitfire to a military configuration. The airplane, its color scheme of royal blue and silver replaced by camouflage, served as the personal transport for Air Commodore Sir John Boothman throughout the war. It was scrapped in 1946.

If a modified Spitfire could not cope with the German's all-out racers, something else would have to be done. Even before the high-speed Spitfire flew, development of another airplane was under way, one that might well meet the competition on at least equal terms, and possibly emerge the victor. The Napier-Heston was a flying machine designed from the start almost solely for speed. Into its streamlined nose was jammed a Napier 24-cylinder engine that was still in the experimental stage but which could develop an estimated 2,350 horsepower and which was the forerunner of the production Napier Sabre. Its cylinders were arranged in a compact, horizontal "H" shape, giving minimum frontal area. Advanced but conventional cooling was used rather than the temperamental, radical cooling systems used in German airplanes.

The airframe was of wood except for the control surfaces, which were aluminum alloy covered with fabric; the engine cowling was of sheet aluminum. The Napier-Heston had a wingspan of 32 feet (9.8 meters), a length of 24.6 feet (7.5 meters), a height of 11.8 feet (3.6 meters), a wing area of 167.6 square feet (15.6 square meters), and a loaded weight of 7,200 pounds (3,262 kilograms). It had as much power as the 469-mph (755-km/h) Messerschmitt, as well as superior streamlining. Thus the prediction of a top speed near 485 mph (780 km/h) seemed reasonable.

The silver-and-blue Napier-Heston was still unfinished when war broke out on September 1, 1939, but its status as a flying test bed for the Napier engine was used to justify continuation of development. The engine was run in the airframe for the first time in December 1939, and taxi tests began the following March. On June 12, 1940, everything was ready for the first flight. G. L. G. Richmond, Heston's chief test pilot, prepared for takeoff, knowing he had an airplane with good handling qualities but a maximum flying duration of only 30 minutes at normal cruise power, and considerably less at maximum power.

Richmond advanced the throttle, sped across the 1,800-foot (548-meter) grass runway, and bounced into the air. Thirty seconds later, the temperature of the engine coolant went off the scale, possibly because a bump on takeoff had broken a glycol-coolant connection and caused it to spill. Richmond throttled back, made a wide circle around the aerodrome, and lined up to land on a runway too short for such a fast airplane. He dropped down with a thump, breaking off the landing gear and the tail.

The airplane was too badly damaged to be rebuilt, though another airplane was well along toward completion. The next day, however, the German Army occupied Paris. The Germans were now perilously close to the English Channel. Speed records were no longer important, and the second Napier-Heston was never completed. The Napier Sabre engine was rushed into production for the Hawker Typhoon fighter-bomber and, after a long period of problems, developed into a potent engine for both the Typhoon and the subsequent Tempest.

In France, interest in speed records during the 1930s was widespread, with no fewer than six different companies involved in such projects. Of those, three airplanes were completed and only one flew. The variety of original aeronautical ideas was unmatched, however. In 1933, the Avions Bernard firm, which had built the highly successful V.2 in which Florentin Bonnett set the Absolute World Air Speed Record of 278 mph (448 km/h) in 1924, got back in the sport. It built two H.V.120 seaplanes for the 1931 Schneider Trophy Race but could not get them ready for the event. When the Schneider Trophy was retired by the British that year, and the series came to an end, a Bernard seaplane was converted into the V.4 land-plane racer.

The V.4 had a length of 24.6 feet (7.5 meters), a wingspan of 28.4 feet (8.7 meters), a height of 11 feet (3.4 meters), a wing area of 129 square feet (12 square meters), and a flying weight of 4,188 pounds (1,897 kilograms). With a Hispano-Suiza 18SB engine of broad-arrow design and somewhat over 1,000 horsepower (sources disagree on the exact figure), it should have had enough power to break the land-plane record, which then stood at just over 300 mph (480 km/h). One authority claims that the float-equipped version achieved 530 km/h (329 mph).

To motivate French aviators, the government offered a prize of 500,000 francs for breaking the record for land planes in 1933. The Bernard V.4 arrived at the test center of Istres in late 1933. There, the pilot, Jean Doumerc, waited for the hot, dry mistral winds to subside. By the time the weather was suitable for speed flying, and some technical problems had been overcome, it was 1934 and the prize had expired. With that stimulant gone, the project was dropped, and the airplane did not fly.

The other land-plane project for the Absolute World Air Speed Record undertaken by an established organization with racing experience was the Caudron C.714R. After the loss of Caudron's C.712 record aspirant in a crash, Marcel Riffard, the company's chief designer, set out to build an even faster airplane—the C.714R. Construction began in the summer of 1937 but was delayed. To facilitate work on the airplane, it was presented as a close relative of the C.714 fighter plane, of which twenty were ordered for the French Air Force in 1938. It wasn't until the summer of 1939 that the C.714R was completed.

The final result appeared to be worth the wait, however. The C.714R was a small, superbly streamlined craft with a 900-horsepower supercharged Renault V12 engine displacing 1,160 cubic inches (19 liters). Its estimated top speed at sea level was 494 mph (795 km/h). It was 28.5 feet (8.7 meters) long, with a wingspan of 22.1 feet (6.7 meters), a wing area of 75 square feet (7 square meters), and a flying weight of a mere 2,695 pounds (1,221 kilograms).

By the time the C.714R was ready, France was so busy trying to build obsolescent fighter planes for protection against the Luftwaffe that sport flying got lost in the shuffle. It was never sent to the Istres test base, instead remaining at Issy-le-Moulineaux, near Paris, until the start of the war. As German forces approached Paris, the C.714R was moved to the cellars of the Renault building in downtown Paris, where it remained, undetected, throughout the occupation. After the liberation of Paris in 1944, it was brought out and displayed in various places, including the Renault car showroom on the Champs Elysses. Today, the beautiful untested racer is part of the permanent display of the Musée de l'Air.

The only French speed-record airplane of the 1930s to fly was the Dewoitine D.550, which was developed from the standard D.520 fighter plane. Of conventional design, the D.550 was smaller than its military counterpart and was built with the Absolute World Air Speed Record foremost in mind. When design work on it began, the record stood at about 380 mph (611 km/h), well within its projected capabilities; but by the time the airplane flew, in June 1939, the Germans had upped the record near 470 mph (755 km/h). The D.550 was a more conservative concept than either German record-breaker and it should have been much easier to fly. About the same size as the Heinkel He-100V-8, the D550 was considerably lighter, with less wing area. The lighter weight should have balanced out the somewhat less extreme streamlining and — with about the same power as the Heinkel, might have produced almost as much speed.

The D.550 had a wingspan of 26.9 feet (8.2 meters) a length of 26.3 feet (8 meters), a height of 8.9 feet (2.7 meters), a wing area of either 116.4 or 97 square feet (10.8 or 9 square meters), depending on the source. Empty, it weighed 3,274 pounds (1,483 kilograms); its gross weight was 4,012 pounds (1,817 kilograms).

The Dewoitine racer flew on June 3, 1939. In November of that year, it demonstrated an ability to climb to nearly 20,000 feet (6,000 meters) in an impressive 4 minutes 30 seconds. During the same flight, the D.550 is said to have flown 436 mph (702 km/h) at that altitude, which must be a record of sorts for an airplane of such limited power. The test program was flown with a 900-horsepower Hispano-Suiza V12 engine instead of the special 1,800-horsepower, souped-up Hispano-Suiza for which the airplane was designed. There is no evidence that the special engine was ever installed in the D.550, and it must be assumed that further testing was forestalled by the urgent military work. A follow-on design, the D.551, a larger airplane that more closely resembled the D.520 fighter, was captured by the Germans before it could be test flown.

Easily the most spectacular airplane to be built in France — or anywhere, for that matter — with the goal of the Absolute World Air Speed Record was the Bugatti 100P. Ettore Bugatti was an eccentric genius who had made his reputation building racing and touring cars with outstanding performance. His passion was beating the powerful, ponderous German roadracing cars with his small, nimble speedsters. In late 1938, the French government gave Bugatti a contract to develop two prototype fighter planes, the larger of which seems to have had virtually no practical military applications. In terms of originality, though, Bugatti's airplanes were, like his cars, in a class of their own. They were designed for Bugatti by Louis deMonge, a veteran of speed-plane engineering. DeMonge used two engines, placed at the center of the fuselage, to drive counterrotating propellors by means of articulated drive shafts passing on either side of the pilot and meeting in a gearbox in front of his feet.

The cooling system used air intakes in the leading edges of all elements of the Y-shaped tail, as well as outlets at the rear of the wing roots. The pilot was seated in the extreme front of the airplane, where vision was enhanced by placement forward of the wing but slightly restricted by the canopy, which was flush with the fuselage's top. The more carefully one studies the Bugatti 100P and 110P, the clearer it becomes that Bugatti's goal was maximum speed within the power limit of the engine. Any talk of military uses of the aircraft was merely politics to disguise the expenditure of government funds for speed-record airplanes when the nation's most obvious need was for combat airplanes.

The Bugatti 100P was designed with a length of 25.4 feet (7.7 meters), a wingspan of 26.9 feet (8.2 meters), and a wing area of 123 square feet (11.4 square meters). The 110P had the same fuselage but an even smaller wingspan (22 feet [6.7 meters]), which gave it an area of only 88 square feet (8.2 square meters). Both airplanes were to be powered by two Bugatti Grand Prix Type 50B supercharged straight-8 engines whose cylinder blocks would be of lightweight magnesium instead of the usual aluminum; in addition, the superchargers would be of lightweight material. The engine was rated at 450 horsepower at 4,500 rpm, despite a displacement of only 287 cubic inches (4.7 liters). With the 100P's superior streamlining, two such engines could have propelled the aircraft near its design speed of 500 mph (800 km/h).

But it was never to be. As the marching formations of the German Wehrmacht flooded the Champs Elysees on June 1, 1940, and streamed under the Arc de Triomphe, workmen in the small Bugatti factory could watch them from the windows of their nearby shop. The almost finished Type 100P was quietly evacuated to Ermenonville, 30 miles northeast of Paris, where it spent the war hidden from the Germans. There is no evidence that the smaller Type 110P was begun.

After the war, the Bugatti 100P was acquired by an American automobile enthusiast, who removed the priceless engines and eventually sold the airframe to a man who has offered it to the museum of the Experimental Aircraft

Association in Oshkosh, Wisconsin. Restoration of the airplane was undertaken by a small Connecticut firm that specializes in antique car work.

Almost as radical as Bugatti's designs was the Payen "Flechair," which got as far as a full-size mock-up. It was one in a long line of beautiful, tandem-wing airplanes designed by Roland Payen, whose work with delta-wing airplanes dates from the early 1930s and who was still developing radical airplanes in 1977. Payen's specialty in the thirties was airplanes with a delta wing at the rear and a small canard surface in front. His "Flechair" was intended for the 1939 Coupe Deutsch Race, canceled when the war started, and for an attempt on the Absolute World Air Speed Record. The airplane was so sleek as to appear, at first glance, to be a caricature. The long, pointed nose was tipped by a sharp spinner housing two counterrotating, two-blade propellors. The pilot's compartment was set so far back that the windshield blended into the upward slope of the vertical tail. To simplify storage of the landing gear when retracted, there was only one wheel in the center; just how the pilot was supposed to steer the airplane on the ground was never revealed.

Originally, power for the Payen Racer was to be supplied by two six-cylinder Salmson engines of 110 horsepower each (the Coupe Deutsch Race had a top limit on engine displacement). This powerplant was soon dropped in favor of a single engine, variously described as a 397-cubic-inch (6.5-liter), 400-horse-power, vertically opposed 12 Bearn, or a Regnier V12 of the same size and power. After the Coupe Deutsch Race, the engine was to be replaced by a new one of greater power for an attempt on the record. According to a respected aviation newsletter of the day, the Payen was to have a length of 24.3 feet (7.4 meters), a wingspan of 15.8 feet (4.8 meters), and a wing area of 108 square feet (10 square meters). With the 400-horsepower engine, its top speed was expected to be about 315 mph (507 km/h). There is no evidence, however, that the racing Payen was built. Its contemporary, the Pa-22, was flown in 1942, then confiscated by the Germans, in whose hands it disappeared. The Pa-22, though less extreme in its design, was still very much in the tandem-wing style.

Japan almost got into the Absolute World Air Speed Record race. Its impressive Kawasaki Ki.78 "Ken-San," or High Speed Test Aircraft, was designed with the dual purposes of research and record-setting. It might have done much to dispel the prewar image of Japanese aeronautical backwardness had not its existence been kept secret. The Ki.78 was built between September 1941 and November 1942. It flew for the first time on December 26, 1942. Late in 1943, the airplane achieved a maximum speed of 435 mph (700 km/h) at an altitude of 11,500 feet (3,505 meters); no indication of its top speed near sea level has been found.

The Ki.78 was a conventional, low-wing monoplane powered by a Japanese-built version of the Daimler Benz DB 601A—a liquid-cooled, inverted-V12 engine of 2,070 cubic inches (33.9 liters) displacement, with surface evaporation cooling. According to Kawasaki, takeoff power was about 1,500 horsepower. The Ki.78 was 26.6 feet (8.1 meters) long and had a wingspan of 26.2 feet (8 meters), a wing area of 118 square feet (11 square meters), and a gross weight of 5,345 pounds (2,421 kilograms). In view of the fact that design work did not begin until after the start of the Pacific war, it is not clear why the

Japanese thought they could use the airplane to set an official speed record, although it did provide them with useful data on high-speed flight.

Yet another airplane designed with the Absolute World Air Speed Record in mind was the Fiat CS.15. Little is known about the airplane. Work on it was begun in 1939, but was set aside because of the war. The CS.15 was to have used a 2,200-horsepower Fiat AS.8 engine, which, according to a Fiat Company list of projects, would produce a top speed of 528 mph (850 km/h). Just how this remarkable speed was to be accomplished can only be imagined, since convincing data are lacking. The only specifications found show a wing area of 124 square feet (11.5 square meters), an empty weight of 4,223 pounds (1,913 kilograms), and a flying weight of 5,070 pounds (2,296 kilograms).

Subsonic Jets

Sometime during World War II, airplanes became scientific. To be sure, the design and development of flying machines had long been scientific; but it wasn't until the early 1940s that the individual, human element lost its dominance to equations and computation—and to committees. This development was inevitable, of course, for the problems accompanying the achievement of high speeds are too complex, and potentially too catastrophic, to be dealt with on the basis of practical, common-sense engineering. The traditional way of pushing back the limits—shove the throttle to the stops and see what happens—was no longer up to the challenge. Things happen so fast at 400-plus mph (650 km/h) that the pilot has no time to analyze all the factors involved in, say, the sudden fluttering of the ailerons.

The route to flight at 400 mph or greater was a long and difficult one. Few big steps were made between 1903, when the Wright brothers flew for the first time, and 1931, when George Stainforth achieved it in the Supermarine S.6B. Reaching 500 mph was even harder; the law of diminishing returns made each mile per hour costlier in terms of increasing power and reducing wind resistance. This was the nature of the struggle until the introduction of the jet engine. In one fell swoop, the problem of greater power was virtually eliminated. Early jet engines were nearly as powerful immediately as the piston engine had become only after decades of painstaking development. They were also lighter, and were rapidly becoming more powerful, without the greater weight and complexity that had plagued piston engines.

The problem seemed on the way to solution—except that now the need for power increases was growing at an astounding rate. An airplane that can fly

400 mph (650 km/h) using 2,000 horsepower needs almost 7,000 horsepower to fly 600 mph (965 km/h). Moreover, as an airplane's speed approaches the speed of sound (at sea level, about 750 mph [1,200 km/h]), strange things begin to happen. Wind resistance builds at an alarming rate, and the control surfaces on the wings and the tail not only lose their effectiveness, they tend to become counterproductive. The answers to these problems lay not merely in the sky but in the laboratory as well. The new jet engines could push airplanes faster than they had ever flown, but first, the airplanes had to be shaped to take advantage of the new source of power. Although streamlining was already well developed, great effort had to be devoted to designing exotic new airfoils (the extremely critical shape of a wing's generally teardrop-shaped cross section).

Probably the greatest single step in perfecting wing shapes for high-speed flight was the invention of the laminar-flow airfoil — a highly symmetrical shape with its maximum thickness almost halfway back from the leading edge, rather than up front (as had so long been effective). With this development came the swept-back wing, which delays and reduces the sound-barrier problems known as "compressibility effects." Much of the trouble that occurs as an airplane approaches the speed of sound is caused by the refusal of the air to part cleanly as it encounters airplane surfaces moving through it; instead, the air tends to bunch up and compress rather than flow smoothly around the wings, fuselage, and tail.

As World War II drew to an end, it was becoming clear that many airplanes were capable of surpassing the Absolute World Air Speed Record with relative ease. The United States and Great Britain had both propellor-driven and jet airplanes that could do it, and some captured German airplanes were just as fast. For reasons of pride and nationalism, however, the revolutionary, fast Messerschmitt Me-163 rocket plane and the Me-262 jet were not considered. Among the airplanes in the best position to break the record were the British Gloster Meteor and deHavilland Vampire and the American Lockheed P-80 Shooting Star, the McDonnell FH-1 Phantom I, and the Bell XP-83. It was little more than a question of who moved first and fastest. Thanks to their greater recent experience in record flying, the British had a jump on the Americans, and they began preparing a pair of late-model Meteors for record runs almost as soon as the German surrender was signed.

The airplane chosen was closer to a standard military machine than any previously used for speed-record attempts. It was already so fast that extreme modifications such as the Germans had made in 1939 were not needed. Two Meteor Mark IVs were culled from a group just produced and cleaned up somewhat: gun ports and other unnecessary holes were covered, external radio masts were removed, and a special, glossy paint was applied. The engines used were the new Rolls Royce Derwent V, which was not a special powerplant but one about to be installed in production airplanes.

Design of the Meteor began during the Battle of Britain. Serious engine problems were encountered, however, and it wasn't until March 1943 that the first Meteor flew. Numerous difficulties delayed production until 1944, not long before the Germans put their first jet into combat. About that time, the first of the V-1 "buzz bombs" were launched toward London.

The first use of a Meteor (or any Allied jet) in combat occurred in August

1944; one of them flipped a V-1, causing it to crash and explode harmlessly. Because the British were afraid a Meteor would fall into German hands, no Meteors were permitted near enemy-held territory, and none engaged in air-to-air combat with a German jet fighter. The early Meteors were seriously underpowered. They were capable of a top speed even below that of some Allied and German propellor-driven airplanes. Soon, though, more powerful engines were available, and by the time the war ended and the Absolute World Air Speed Record was again of interest, the power was there in abundance.

A course was laid out for the record attempt along the south shore of the Thames estuary, east of London and not far from Eastchurch, site of the Gordon Bennett Trophy Race in 1911. Although the timed portion of the course was less than 2 miles (3.2 kilometers) long, the entire area used for the runs stretched 28 miles (45 kilometers). The fast airplane would need to make wide 180-degree turns at each end of the course without having to slow down unnecessarily. To time the flights with sufficient accuracy, a complex system of cameras was installed. A movie camera was placed at each end of the course; there, it would photograph an airplane as it passed a timing wire, as well as a clock that could be read to an accuracy of 0.002 second. With the course measured to plus or minus 1.5 centimeters (0.6 inch), the overall precision of the system was vastly superior to any system previously used.

Another matter for concern was the safety factor involved in flying at 10 miles per minute (16 kilometers per minute) at an altitude of only 245 feet (75 meters). At the Meteor's anticipated speed, it would take but a split second to crash if something went wrong. In addition, there were still questions concerning longitudinal stability. If the Meteor suddenly acted nose-heavy at Mach 0.8 (Mach 1 is the speed of sound in the prevailing atmospheric conditions), it could plow into the ground before the pilot realized what had happened.

Preparations for the record attempt by the two Meteors began in early August 1945. The Gloster factory had modified the airplanes, and in late September they were ready for practice runs. The pilots chosen were RAF Grp. Capt. Hugh Wilson, commanding officer of the Empire Test Pilots School and one of the RAF's most experienced jet test pilots, and Eric Greenwood, Gloster's chief test pilot. The first serious runs were made October 31, when the weather had improved enough to permit fast flying at low altitude. Greenwood made three passes, clocked at an average speed of 525 mph (845 km/h) — well above the record but so far below what was expected that the effort was considered insignificant. Next, Wilson flew two passes at an average speed of 605 mph (974 km/h), close enough to the target speed to convince everyone they were ready.

After a week of inclement weather, on November 7 the skies improved. The Meteors were given a final check and pronounced ready. Because of unknown factors in the areas of structure and control, the engines were limited to 3,600 pounds (1,631 kilograms) of thrust rather than the 4,000 pounds (1,812 kilograms) they were capable of. Even so, a top speed of 610 mph (982 km/h) was thought possible.

Wilson was the first to take off. Visibility was 7 to 12 miles (11 to 19 kilometers). It was cold and overcast, but the wind was fairly calm as the camouflaged airplane sped along. No rough air was expected. Just a few hard bumps at that speed could cause damaging stress in the airframe. Wilson raced past the timing markers four times, watched by cameras and officials of the Royal Aero Club. His path was marked by a long plume of black smoke from the engines and by the roar that hit the observers after the jet passed. Wilson's speeds for the four runs were 604, 608, 602, and 611 mph (972, 978, 969, and 983 km/h). Greenwood was to have taken off as soon as Wilson landed, but a minor electrical problem kept him on the ground for an hour. When he finally got the go-ahead, he turned in runs of 599, 608, 598, and 607 mph (964, 978, 962, and 977 km/h). Well before the complex calculations were complete, it was apparent that both men had surpassed the Absolute World Air Speed Record by a greater margin than had ever been done before.

The final figures revealed Wilson as the new recordholder, with a speed announced by the FAI of 606.260 mph (975.675 km/h), beating the Messerschmitt record by an amazing 137 mph (220 km/h). The British thus captured the Absolute World Air Speed record for the first time since 1933, and for the first time with a land plane. In marked contrast to the almost unflyable Messerschmitt Me-209 that set the earlier mark, the Meteor was little more than a cleaned-up production aircraft. It had required minimum maintenance, and the only damage done during the runs was a few loose rivets. The record-setting Meteor had a wingspan of 37.2 feet (11.3 meters), a length of 41.3 feet (12.6 meters), a height of 13 feet (4 meters), and a wing area of 350 square feet (32.5 square meters). In military configuration, an empty Mark IV weighed 9,980 pounds (4,521 kilograms), fully loaded, 15,175 pounds (6,874 kilograms).

The next British attempt on the speed record would depend on what the United States did. Rumors were rife of plans to make an attempt, using America's Republic XP-84 Thunderjet or the Lockheed P-80 Shooting Star. The real opponent, however, was a technical one: the "sound barrier." As an airplane approaches the speed of sound, problems multiply. The speed of a particular aircraft was now being expressed not in miles or kilometers per hour but in fractions of the speed of sound. The Meteor's top speed was thus Mach 0.81, or 81 percent of the speed of sound at the altitude and temperature a particular flight was made. The sound barrier was viewed as both an obstacle and a dividing line beyond which flight was supposed to be simpler. Obviously, one way to break the record was to fly under conditions when the speed of sound was at its highest: at a low altitude and high temperature. For the British, altitude was no problem; they had ample coastline at sea level. But high temperature was another matter. In Great Britain, it seldom gets above the 75°F (24°C) level even in midsummer.

In August 1946, it appeared that no other country would make an attempt on the British-held record; so two more Meteors were prepared for the task. Called "Star" Meteors, they were Mark IVs with special Rolls Royce Derwent engines rated at 4,200 pounds (1,903 kilograms) of thrust (a unit roughly equal to 1 horsepower at 375 mph [605 km/h] and 2 horsepower at twice that speed). This time, the site was just offshore at Littlehampton, on Britain's south coast. It was hoped the temperature would be maximum here, and without the turbulent air that often accompanies such heat. If those conditions prevailed, a speed increase of 15 mph (24 km/h) might be expected.

On August 14, at the nearby RAF command base of Tangmere, the first "Star" Meteor received its new engines. Late that day, Grp. Capt. Edward Donaldson, commander of the RAF's High Speed Flight, tested the airplane and recorded a true air speed of 626 mph (1,007 km/h) for three minutes at an altitude of 3,000 feet (914 meters), this despite a temperature of 64°F (17°C), which kept the critical speed down considerably. The next day, although the air was cooler, Donaldson made several runs at nearly 600 mph (965 km/h) in a practice Meteor and was bumped around badly. His accelerometer registered 6 Gs positive and 3 Gs negative; that is, he was pushed down into his seat with a force six times that of gravity, then lifted up with a force three times that of gravity.

Lack of suitable weather conditions forced one postponement after another. It wasn't until September 7 that everything was ready, and even then conditions were far from ideal. In a steady drizzle periodically interrupted by driving rain, Donaldson took off from Tangmere just before 6:00 P.M. He made five smooth runs over the course at an altitude of less than 100 feet (30 meters). Later, he said that things were so well under control, and the airplane handled so well, that he could "watch the countryside going past and glance at my instruments" despite the speed and proximity to the water.

After Donaldson's runs, Sqdrn. Ldr. W. A. Waterton made several passes over the 3-kilometer (1.86-mile) course in the other "Star" Meteor. His speed worked out to 614 mph (988 km/h); but Donaldson's was better, at 615.81 mph (991.04 km/h). Thus, Donaldson became the newest Absolute World Speed Recordholder. At the record speed, each Meteor engine produced the equivalent of about 6,900 horsepower.

Edward Donaldson, born in 1912, joined the RAF in 1931. During World War II he served as a gunnery officer, working closely with the U.S. Army. He commanded an RAF jet base and completed his service as commandant of the RAF Flying College. In 1961, Donaldson became air correspondent for the *Daily Telegraph* newspaper.

One day before Donaldson set the second Meteor record, the first sign of official interest on the part of the United States appeared, in the form of a series of practice runs by the XP-84 Thunderjet. The second prototype of the XP-84 was timed at 611 mph (983 km/h). Because the mark was less than 1 percent over the existing record, however, it was not submitted to the FAI for recognition; nevertheless, it was an American record, adding 259 mph (415 km/h) to the mark of 352 (567 km/h) set by Howard Hughes in 1935.

It was now clear to the British that any major increase in the Absolute World Air Speed Record would require more than a slightly cleaned-up production fighter plane. In view of the need for specially designed aircraft to be used solely for research flying, Britain already had an airplane that might be able to break the record even in cool weather. That airplane was the deHavilland deH. 108 Swallow, an airplane that looked futuristic even in 1946. It was a well-streamlined, tailless creation, with sharply swept-back wings, the fuselage of a Vampire fighter, a single swept vertical tail, no horizontal tail, and a wing based on research in wartime Germany. The deH. 108 was powered by a deHavilland Goblin 2 rated at 3,000 pounds (1,359 kilograms) of thrust—considerable power for such a small, light craft. The deH. 108 had a wingspan of 39 feet (11.9 meters), a length of 24.5 feet (7.47 meters), a wing area of 328 square feet (30.5 square meters), and a gross weight of 8,960 pounds (4,059 kilograms).

The first deH. 108 flew in May 1946, at the hands of 36-year-old Geoffrey deHavilland, Jr., whose father was the founder of the firm and a pioneer of British aviation. The fast airplane provided a wealth of data for more advanced airplanes then being designed.

It is not clear how definite plans were to make an attempt on the Absolute World Air Speed Record with the deH. 108, but on September 27, 1946, deHavilland took the prototype up for trial runs preparatory to timed tests on the speed course at Littlehampton. Presumably, if the speeds attained were high enough, an attempt at the record would follow. Sometime after 5:30 P.M., the whine of a jet engine was heard, followed by a sharp cracking noise. Pieces of the airplane were later recovered, and an investigation pointed to a tendency of the tailless airplane, when flying near Mach 0.9, to experience a sudden pitch-down of the nose, a fluctuating loss of stability, and a decrease in the effectiveness of the combined ailerons and elevators (called elevons).

The tragic loss of one of Britain's foremost test pilots pointed up the vital need to coordinate wind-tunnel research and flight testing, for there had been indications of these problems before deHavilland's fatal flight. The other two deH. 108s later made further contributions to aeronautical science, and one set a 100-kilometer (62-mile) speed record of 605 mph (974 km/h). There were no more tries for the Absolute World Air Speed Record, mainly because by the time initial tests on the second airplane were completed, the record was beyond the aircraft's capability. By May 1950, all three Swallows had been lost in accidents.

When the RAF set its second Meteor record in September 1946, a great clamor arose in the United States for something to be done. If the Air Force's publicity was to be believed, the United States had the fastest airplanes in the world; so there was no excuse for "allowing" the British to hold the Absolute World Air Speed Record. In the fall of 1946, the XP-84 Thunderjet and a special Lockheed P-80R were at the Muroc (California) test base, ready to go. A productive rivalry was expected. The XP-84 reportedly bettered the 616-mph (991-km/h) British record on a flight rendered unofficial when the timing system failed. Following this, the weather turned cold and windy, which put an end to thoughts of record flights that year.

In the spring of 1947, an attempt at the record was delayed again, this time so the Allison Company could provide a more powerful engine. With the installation of the Allison Model 400 — with water/methanol injection for cooling — the P-80R was ready. It was a special record version of America's first true jet fighter, one used to equip numerous Air Force squadrons through the late 1940s up to the Korean War. The P-80 was almost ready in time for use in World War II; four service-test prototypes were sent to Europe for tests while fighting was still in progress. No P-80 saw combat, though a pilot of one of them reportedly went looking for a fight.

The sleek Lockheed was the result of the Army Air Corps' need for someone to produce the first American jet — Bell Aircraft's P-59 Airacomet. This innovative craft never amounted to much from a military standpoint; a subsequent version, however, seemed to hold promise, and it was suggested to Lockheed that the company pick up where Bell left off. Lockheed preferred to build a plane of its own design, though, and thus the first Shooting Star came into being in January 1944. An immediate success, the jet hastened the demise of the Airacomet. Thousands of P-80s were ordered, though most were canceled when the war ended. Although approximately 1,000 P-80 fighters were built, the T-33, a two-seat trainer version, became the world's first standard jet trainer, and more than 5,000 were built.

The special version of the P-80, unofficially called "Racey," retained the super-slick paint job of the early production airplanes, which was subsequently discarded because it was so difficult to maintain. The teardrop bubble canopy was replaced by a lower one with less wind resistance, but which would have dangerously hampered a pilot's vision in a military airplane. To supply the more powerful new engine with sufficient oxygen, the air intakes on the sides of the fuselage were enlarged and reshaped. A new leading edge was built for the wing that gave a sharper edge and greater area while changing the airfoil shape to one more conducive to near-sonic speed flying. The special P-80R had a wingspan reduced to 37 feet (11.3 meters), a length of 34.5 feet (10.5 meters), a height of 11.3 feet (3.4 meters), a wing area increased to 271 square feet (25.2 square meters), and an empty weight of about 7,920 pounds (3,588 kilograms).

At Muroc Air Base, in the Mojave Desert northeast of Los Angeles, the course for this and later record attempts—an elongated runway at the barren desert airfield—was built and measured with great accuracy. By mid-June 1947, everything was in readiness for an attempt on the Absolute World Air Speed Record. No American had held the record since 1924, when the French broke Al Williams' mark of 267 mph (427 km/h). On June 17, the sleek jet was taxied out by Col. Al Boyd, chief of the Army Air Forces Flight Test Division and a veteran P-80 pilot. Boyd flew two runs that day, the faster at about 647 mph (1,041 km/h); four were required, and these were no more than practice.

Two days later, the NAA officials and their precise timing gear were in place and checked out. The two check pilots took off in older training planes and climbed to their assigned altitudes, so observers could determine visually that Boyd did not exceed the maximum permissible altitude at any time during his runs. Then Boyd eased forward the throttle of the P-80R and began his takeoff. Weather conditions were almost ideal, with winds of only a few miles per hour and a temperature of 87°F (31°C)—conditions that lifted the airplane's critical limiting air speed well above 625 mph (1,006 km/h). Boyd made four passes, with the special engine turning out an estimated 4,600 pounds (2,084 kilograms) of thrust, under those conditions, comparable to 7,500 horsepower.

The slowest pass was made at more than 614 mph (989 km/h), and the fastest was over 632 mph (1,017 km/h), resulting in the first official speed over the 1,000-km/h (620-mph) level: 623.608 mph or 1,003.60 km/h. The Absolute World Air Speed Record was back in American hands for the first time in 23 years.

Immediately after his flight, Boyd told the press: "It keeps you busy as hell! There are so many things to do and so many instruments to watch. You have water injection to turn on and off for more power. And you must not exceed the prescribed altitude and must keep on the course. But it's a great feeling. . . ." Much of the credit must go to the people at Lockheed, who created an airplane that could better the speed of the more powerful Gloster Meteor. After a slow start, the American aircraft industry was catching up in the jet race. And this was just the beginning. There were other Army and Navy airplanes that should be able to beat the P-80R. It was a period of considerable interservice rivalry, and how better to demonstrate superiority than by setting world records?

The record-setting airplane went into storage and was eventually transferred to the U.S. Air Force Museum, where it is on permanent display.

Boyd, born in Rankin, Tennessee, in 1906, completed his Army Air Corps flight training in 1929 and worked his way up through a variety of engineering positions, becoming commander of Edwards Air Force Base (formerly Muroc Air Base) in 1949. He retired in 1957, a major general and the deputy commander of the USAF Research and Development Command. He worked for aerospace firms until his death in 1976.

Boyd's record stirred interest in Great Britain, where the record had resided for a year and a half, as well as in the U.S. Navy (Navy Lt. Al Williams was the last American to hold the record). The British had no airplane capable of challenging the P-80R at the time, but the U.S. Navy certainly did: the Douglas D-558-I "Skystreak," the first American jet-propelled airplane designed expressly for research in the problems of flight at speeds approaching that of sound. The novel creation resembled a tube with wings. It consisted of an Allison J-35 turbojet engine and no more airplane than was necessary to carry a pilot, a few hundred pounds of test instruments, and enough fuel to fly for about an hour. It had no guns, no armor plate, no elaborate navigational equipment. It was a vehicle designed to carry humans closer to the mystifying problem of the sound barrier.

The first of three Skystreaks was completed in January 1947 and flown in May of that year. By the middle of August, Gene May, a Douglas test pilot, pronounced the airplane airworthy and ready for a record attempt. At the time, it had been flown only nine and a half hours. On August 20, Navy Cdr. Turner Caldwell prepared himself for the effort at Muroc Air Base. The Army would provide the equipment and the trained technicians for timing Caldwell's flight. Though an experienced military pilot, Caldwell had flown a jet for the first time just two weeks earlier and had logged a mere hour and a half in the Skystreak. For the flight, the airplane carried about 230 gallons (870 liters) of jet fuel and 640 pounds (290 kilograms) of special instruments for recording various information. The engine, a standard powerplant with no special modifications for the record runs, was actually performing slightly below par. A specially tuned engine was available for the D-558-I but was not installed, because the original one was working well and a change would have delayed the flight.

Caldwell took off just before 9 A.M. The ground temperature was 77°F (25°C), considerably cooler than usual in the California desert and thus a handicap, since the airplane's critical Mach number would be reached at a lower speed. The Navy/Douglas team was confident, however, and went ahead. Four passes produced speeds ranging from 628 mph (1,011 km/h) to

653 mph (1,052 km/h), with an official average of 640.743 mph (1,031.178 km/h). The record was back in Navy hands by a margin of 17 mph (27 km/h) over its Army rivals and 25 mph (40 km/h) over the British.

Caldwell, born in Narbeth, Pennsylvania, in 1913, graduated from the U.S. Naval Academy in 1935 and became a pilot in 1939. He served in the Pacific during World War II, then headed training units. Caldwell, the first Navy pilot to fly faster than sound, became a vice admiral in 1967.

The Douglas Skystreak was built mainly of aluminum, with some structural parts of magnesium alloy. Its wing had a 10-percent-thick laminar-flow airfoil, and its Allison J-35-A-23 engine was rated at 4,000 pounds (1,812 kilograms) of thrust. It had a wingspan of 25 feet (7.6 meters), a length of 25 feet (7.6 meters), a wing area of 150 square feet (14 square meters), and a loaded weight of 9,750 pounds (4,417 kilograms). Of three airplanes built, the recordholder (number 37970) is in the Naval Aviation Museum at Pensacola, Florida, and another (Number 37962) is at the Marine Corps Museum, in Quantico, Virginia.

If the Skystreak would do better than 640 mph (1,030 km/h) in cool air and with its engine delivering less than full power, it followed that under better conditions, the airplane would fly even faster. Therefore, on August 25, five days after Caldwell's record-setting flight, Marine Corps Maj. Marion Carl got the nod. Again, the site was Muroc Air Base, but this time the temperature was 94°F (34°C) at 11:30 A.M. when Carl took off. Eighteen minutes later, he was the new holder of the Absolute World Air Speed Record. With barely 2 miles per hour of wind blowing and the engine turning up 101 percent of its rated power, the Skystreak made four runs over the 3-kilometer (1.86 mile) course at an average speed of 650.76 mph (1,047.356 km/h). Another 10 mph (16 km/h) had been added to the record and the U.S. claim to supremacy in high-speed flight made firmer.

Carl, born in 1915 in Hubbard, Oregon, completed pilot training in the Marine Corps in 1939. During World War II he was credited with shooting down eighteen enemy airplanes. As a test pilot, Carl, the first Marine helicopter pilot, made some of the first aircraft carrier landings in a jet. After commanding a photoreconnaissance squadron in Korea in the 1950s, he was assigned to Marine Corps headquarters, becoming a brigadier general in 1964.

Navy morale soared after these consecutive records. After decades of playing second fiddle to the Army in the area of fast airplanes, the Navy was finally on top. Its carrier-based airplanes still had to pay the price of speed-killing extra weight and equipment, and thus could not yet claim to be as fast as the Army's. Still, there was no way to deny the Navy credit for developing what was now officially the fastest airplane in the world.

With this success under its belt, Douglas Aircraft made plans to improve the Skystreak by using the new TG-190 engine rated at 6,000 pounds (2,718 kilograms) of thrust, using water injection for cooling. The increase of about 50 percent should result in an airplane capable of breaking the record. As it turned out, the improved D-558-I became a victim of progress. Douglas built the D-558-II "Skyrocket," which, in 1953, became the first airplane in the world to fly at twice the speed of sound (after being launched from a carrier plane).

Less than two months after the second Navy and the third American Absolute World Air Speed Record, there occurred one of the most historic flights in aviation history. On October 14, 1947, U.S. Air Force Maj. Chuck Yeager sat in the cockpit of the rocket-powered Bell XS-1 (later the X-1) as it was secured in the bomb bay of a modified Boeing B-29 high above Muroc Dry Lake. Yeager was cut loose, and he quickly ignited the rocket motor. Moments later, the bright orange research airplane went through the sound barrier, making Yeager the first human to fly faster than the speed of sound (at that altitude, about 700 mph [1,125 km/h]). Though brief, the flight was long enough to dispel the myth that strange and terrible things would happen when humans tried to fly at that speed.

The speed of the XS-1, while it was recorded accurately, was not eligible for record status. It had been achieved on a single pass at high altitude, and with an airplane that did not take off under its own power. As a scientific accomplishment, however, Yeager's flight is among the great flights of aviation history. While others were squeezing out each little fraction of a Mach number by applying better aerodynamic design, the Bell XS-1, a basic airplane, took a big step with brute force.

The U.S. Navy and Marine Corps held the Absolute World Air Speed Record for a year. Meanwhile, the U.S. Air Force concentrated on developing the North American F-86 Sabre, the first truly significant jet fighterplane. Part of that development was in full view of the public. Over Labor Day weekend, September 3-5, 1948, an F-86A performed at near-maximum speed before 125,000 people gathered at Cleveland Municipal Airport for the annual National Air Races. It was a daring move by the Air Force—attempting an Absolute World Air Speed Record in public, where any mistake would instantly become news and where there was always the chance that the high-performance jet would, in a split second, become wreckage. The F-86A, however, performed superbly. On the opening day of the event, Maj. Richard Johnson smoothly made several calibration runs over the course parallel to the packed grandstands and only a few hundred feet in front of them. People had never seen anything move so fast.

The official test was set for Monday, September 5, the last day of the races. Back and forth Johnson went as the crowd watched in amazement. Johnson's first up-wind run was clocked at almost 659 mph (1,060 km/h), better than the existing record despite the unfavorable wind. His first down-wind run was almost 690 mph (1,110 km/h), and the second up-wind run was at more than 660 mph (1,063 km/h). At that rate, Johnson would finish with a speed near 675 mph (1,085 km/h)—if nothing went wrong.

But something did go wrong. A jammed timing camera missed the fourth run, and the fifth was ruined when the camera accidentally followed another airplane. Finally, the sixth run could not be photographed because Johnson flew too close to the cameras. For a record to be official, times must be used from four consecutive passes on the same flight. The record attempt had misfired, through no fault of the airplane. The Air Force and North American Aviation, however, had shown that their new fighter—flown in virtually standard military configuration—could top the best speed by a research airplane with room to spare.

Ten days later, Major Johnson, the F-86A, and many technicians were at Muroc Air Base to try again, but this time without the pressure of a schedule and pleasing a crowd. On the negative side, the temperature in the Mojave Desert was only 70°F (21°C). Also, there was a light crosswind, which would make flying a precise course more difficult. With the experience in Cleveland to guide them, the crew made the second try work. Johnson's four closely packed passes averaged between 670 and 673 mph (1,078 and 1,083 km/h). His average of 670.981 mph (1,079.841 km/h), more than 20 mph (32 km/h) faster than the Navy record, fully made up for the snafu at the National Air Races.

The F-86A flown by Johnson was only the tenth to come off the production line. It had made its maiden flight in June 1948. The airplane was 37.5 feet (11.4 meters) long, with a wingspan of 37.1 feet (11.3 meters) and a height of 14.6 feet (4.5 meters). With a normal, loaded weight of 13,715 pounds (6,213 kilograms), it could climb at a rate near 7,000 feet per minute (35 meters per second). Its General Electric J47 engine produced 5,200 pounds (2,356 kilograms) of thrust. By the time production ended in 1955, more than 9,000 Sabres, in numerous versions, had been built in the United States, Canada, Australia, Italy, and Japan.

Johnson, a native of North Dakota, learned to fly in 1943 and flew 180 missions during World War II. He later became a test pilot in the Air Force's Flight Test Division at Wright-Patterson AF Base.

After the flurry of activity in 1947-48, the Absolute World Air Speed Record business went into a slump. The U.S. Air Force had the record, but the Navy wasn't equipped to challenge it. The British had tried with the Meteor, their first-generation jet fighter, and were now starting development of more advanced airplanes — though not at the American rate. Then, in June 1950, the Korean War put an end to speed-record attempts for several years to come.

By the time the Absolute World Air Speed Record again aroused interest, the U.S. Air Force had a much improved Sabre — the F-86D. Its General Electric J47 engine was rated at 5,400 pounds (2,446 kilograms) of thrust under normal conditions and 7,350 pounds (3,330 kilograms) of thrust with the afterburner, a device located in the tail pipe where it used the tremendous heat of the exhaust to create additional power by the injection of fuel and ignition of the mixture. The F-86D was more than 4 feet (1.2 meters) longer, thanks to a newly designed nose that had a bullet-shaped radar enclosure above the air intake. The radar made possible a much better all-weather airplane, and the afterburner increased its rate of climb by one-third, to 9,200 feet per minute (47 meters per second) and its top speed from 670 to 710 mph (1,080 to 1,140 km/h).

In November 1952, an F-86D was moved to El Centro Naval Air Station, in California, not far from the Mexican border. From there, it was a short flight to a new speed course on the eastern shore of the Salton Sea, 90 miles northeast of San Diego. The course, more than 200 feet (60 meters) below sea level, could be counted on for the high temperatures needed for achieving the maximum speed from the new Sabre. On November 11, Capt. J. Slade Nash climbed into the cockpit. Nash, on the staff of the Air Force Flight Test Center at Edwards AF Base, was a native of Moville, Iowa. He had won his wings in the Army in 1945 and had been a test pilot for the past six years.

Nash took off at 1:40 P.M. and was in the vicinity of the speed course a few minutes later. The course was marked at either end by a white parachute spread over the ground, by bright red panels; a green flare and a red smoke grenade helped Nash find the points at which to enter the course. The 3-kilometer measured section and its 1-kilometer approach zones were between a state highway and the seashore. At Nash's chosen altitude of 125 feet (38 meters), he was approximately 100 feet (30 meters) below sea level. The temperature during the flight, however, was a cool 76°F (24°C). Nash's four runs were as close in time as any in the history of record attempts: less than 2 mph (3.2 km/h) separated the fastest from the slowest—a tribute to Nash's flying skill and to the lack of wind. His average speed was 698.511 mph (1,124.137 km/h), bettering Major Johnson's mark set in 1949 by 27.5 mph (44.3 km/h). The Americans had flown more than 80 mph (129 km/h) faster than anyone else.

Interest in other countries was quiet, as it had been for several years. There was talk of an attempt by the Canadians, using one of their Canadair F-86 Sabres, built under license, as well as an effort by the speed pilot Jackie Cochran to borrow either an American or a Canadian Sabre for a record run. Cochran was turned down by the U.S. Air Force but, through family connections, managed to persuade Canadair, Ltd. to let her use one of their Sabre Mark 3s. In May 1953, powered by a 6,000-pound (2,718-kilogram) Orenda turbojet engine, the Sabre set a 15-kilometer (9-mile) speed record of 675 mph (1,086 km/h). This, the first serious effort by a woman to set an Absolute World Air Speed Record in the 47 years of such flying, was the kick-off event of one of the busiest record years ever.

In July, activity resumed at the site of the last Absolute World Air Speed Record—the Salton Sea—with an improved F-86D Sabre. The main reason Air Force officials felt there was a chance to surpass their record was the expectation of hotter weather, which should allow the airplane to fly well over 700 mph (1,125 km/h) before reaching its critical Mach number. J. Stanley Holtoner, commander of Edwards AF Base, practiced for several days, then was replaced by Lt. Col. William Barns, the Air Force's representative at North American's Los Angeles factory. Barns made a series of runs shortly before noon, July 16, when the temperature was near 100°F (38°C), which worked out to 713.6 mph (1,148 km/h. By 1:40 P.M., the thermometer had risen to 102°F (39°C), and it was decided that Barns would try again. This time, he was clocked at 715.751 mph (1,151.883 km/h), about as fast as one could hope for under the nearly ideal conditions. The papers and timing films were submitted to the FAI and were quickly approved as the third consecutive Absolute World Air Speed Record by the U.S. Air Force.

The British now reappeared, after an absence of more than six years, with two promising swept-wing jet fighters. They were developed to replace the North American F-86 Sabres, 400 of which had been acquired by the Royal Air Force to fill a gap created by the lack of a suitable replacement for the Meteors and Vampires of the late 1940s. The two leading builders of British fighters had come up with impressive new airplanes: Supermarine, with its Swift, and Hawker, with its Hunter. These airplanes were intended to equip the RAF with first-line fighters until it could move into the supersonic age.

The Hunter was the latest in a series of Hawker pursuits and fighters that began with the Sopwith Camel of World War I and included the venerable Hurricane, which, along with the Spitfire, bore the brunt of the Battle of Britain. The prototype Hunter, WB188, flew for the first time on July 20, 1951, with Neville Duke, Hawker's chief test pilot, at the controls. Intended as a short-range interceptor, the Hunter went into production in May 1953.

In August of that year, the prototype was based near Littlehampton, ready to challenge the American-held Absolute World Air Speed Record. But whereas the most recent American record airplanes had been carefully maintained in service condition, even to the extent of carrying not only their guns but (allegedly) ammunition as well, the Hunter was a special airplane. In place of its original Rolls Royce Avon engine producing 7,500 pounds (3,398 kilograms) of thrust, the Hunter had an Avon equipped with an afterburner which developed a maximum of 9,450 pounds (4,281 kilograms) of thrust — an increase of 25 percent. The airplane's nose had been reshaped to a sharp point, to reduce wind resistance, and the standard, flat windshield was replaced with a curved one so as to better split the wind.

Record trials began on August 31, with Duke flying four runs at an average speed of 722.3 mph (1,162 km/h), 6.5 mph (10.5 km/h) faster than the record but not quite the 1 percent, or 7-plus mph required by the FAI. During other attempts on September 6, Duke could not do even that well; but the next day, he and the red Hawker Hunter streaked along the coast of the English Channel four times, averaging 727.6 mph (1,170.76 km/h).

After spending several years in the shadow of the United States in speed flying, the British at last had an airplane capable of keeping company with the Sabre. Whereas the Hunter fighter that set the record wasn't quite a standard airplane, it had nevertheless achieved the feat under less favorable conditions than the Americans had experienced. The temperature at Littlehampton during the record runs was about 73°F (23°C), compared with 100°F (38°C) in the Mojave. Had the Hunter been flown in such heat, the British estimated that it would have flown near 750 mph (1,200 km/h).

The record-setting Hunter is painted glossy red overall, with standard RAF insignia on the fuselage and tail. It is on display in the RAF Museum's branch collection at St. Athans, in southern Wales. Its length, including the special pointed extension of the nose, is approximately 47 feet (14.3 meters), its wingspan is 33.7 feet (10.3 meters), and its wing area is 340 square feet (31.6 square meters). Modifications for the record attempt turned the prototype Hunter F.1 into the sole Mark III.

Neville Duke was born in 1922 in Kent, England. He became an RAF pilot in 1940, and shot down 28 German airplanes during the war. He later served as a test pilot for Hawker Aircraft from 1948 to 1956.

For several years, there had been growing concern over the safety of airplanes at near-sonic speeds within 330 feet (100 meters) of the ground. No one had yet been killed in an attempt, but everyone agreed that it was only a matter of time. With the improved timing of fast airplanes, using high-speed cameras and radar, there was no longer a technical need for a record airplane to fly so close to the timers. The FAI thus established a new record category — 15-25 kilometers (9.3-15.5 miles) — that can be flown at any altitude.

Although the category made sense, a couple of hurdles had to be overcome before it was accepted. First, the category would have to replace the prestige of the minimum-distance dash that had belonged to the 3-kilometer (1.86-mile) distance for 30 years. Second, pilots would have to wholeheartedly accept that low-level runs were unjustifiably dangerous; only then would they relinquish the glamor and pride associated with tearing along at treetop level.

The first major record set according to the new category was by H. Collins, an Air Force pilot. Collins flew the F-86D Sabre at 708 mph (1,139 km/h) at the National Aircraft Show in Dayton, Ohio, in 1953. Three days later, Lt.Cdr. Mike Lithgow, of the Royal Navy's Fleet Air Arm, flew a Supermarine Swift from England to Libya. The plan was to make a series of record runs in temperatures comparable to those the Americans had taken advantage of, but which do not exist in England. To get the proper weather conditions, the British moved to the desert of western Libya, 50 miles (80 kilometers) southwest of Tripoli. There was nothing but sand, glaring heat, and a straight, narrow road that would make an ideal flight course. Once timing equipment had been brought in, installed, tested, and calibrated, it was up to the mechanics, Mike Lithgow, Supermarine's chief test pilot, and the stock Supermarine Swift Mark IV.

The effort was mounted so hastily that there was not time to clean up the Swift, as the Hunter had been prepared. The Mark IV had no super-slick paint job; there were even rivet heads sticking up, which would interfere with the smooth flow of air over the fuselage. The airplane was well designed, however; its turbojet engine (identical to that of the Hunter) had the necessary power; it also had the not inconsiderable advantage of flying in dry, hot air.

The airplane used for the British attempt was a standard Supermarine Swift Mark IV with a length of 41.5 feet (12.6 meters), a wingspan of 32.3 feet (9.8 meters), and a wing area of 306 square feet (28.5 square meters). The Hawker Hunter proved a better fighter, though, and only about a hundred Swifts, of all versions, were built, most as tactical reconnaissance airplanes. The record airplane can now be found, minus a few parts, in the collection of the North East Aircraft Museum, in Sunderland, southeast of Newcastle, England.

The first serious attempt was set for September 25, 1953. To keep the pilot from being cooked by the combination of outside air and heat generated by air friction, he was provided with a special ventilated suit (the Swift's air-conditioning system wasn't designed for such unusual conditions).

Before takeoff, Lithgow was buckled in place and carefully cooled off by flowing air from a compressor over dry ice. Once the aircraft was airborne, however, the suit malfunctioned, and the cockpit temperature rose to 180°F (82°C). With a flight time of only 15 minutes, the problem was not as serious as it might sound. During the runs, Lithgow's oxygen mask became jammed by perspiration, forcing him to remove it in order to breathe. He then had trouble holding the controls. The four runs were completed without serious incident. (The failure of a fuel gauge forced Lithgow to use his afterburner less than had been planned, as he could not tell how much kerosene remained. As a result, he had to turn on the afterburner later than planned, and he was still accelerating as he entered the course, instead of being at top speed.) The runs averaged 735.54 mph (1,183.74 km/h), enough to oust Neville Duke as the world's fastest human. National pride was preserved, however, since both pilots were British and both were flying British aircraft.

Another attempt was made the next day, September 26, after some technical problems had been solved; but the timing cameras disagreed, and the runs could not be considered official. That same day, a U.S. Navy Douglas F4D "Skyray" was preparing to break whatever record then stood. Only high winds had prevented it from making an attempt earlier.

The British were aware of the American attempt; they also knew the Skyray was capable of higher speed under comparable conditions. On September 28, however, a fierce, hot wind sprang up, keeping the British on the ground until it was too late. While they sat and fidgeted, trying to protect themselves from the stinging sand, the U.S. Navy took over.

On September 27, Lithgow and the Swift were back in the air. The first two runs averaged 743 mph (1,196 km/h), probably fast enough to break the British mark; but on the third run, the afterburner failed to ignite, and the attempt was called off. Meanwhile, at the Salton Sea, in southern California, a faulty fuel gauge caused the canceling of a second day of attempts by the Skyray.

Mike Lithgow served with the Fleet Air Arm during World War II, then joined Vickers Supermarine, becoming its chief test pilot in 1948.

Two consecutive British records within a month was a bitter pill for the U.S. armed services to swallow. After six years of supremacy in speed flying, this was not the sort of news Defense Department public-relations officers wanted. Even with the stakes high in terms of international prestige and domestic morale, however, an element of sportsmanship remained. With the British at a disadvantage in trying to set records, either in England or in the North African desert, the United States offered the facilities at Edwards AF Base. The offer was never taken up, mainly because, after the Libyan adventure, the record was beyond the reach of even the fastest British airplanes available. Then, too, there must have been a feeling on the part of the British that any credit for a record set in the United States would have to be shared, however slightly, with their hosts.

Even as the Supermarine Swift struggled against the wind and sand, and the long supply lines, in North Africa, two prototype American jet fighters were being prepared to return the record to the United States: the Douglas XF4D-1 "Skyray" and the North American YF-100A Super Sabre. Although both airplanes had the power and sleek lines required for the task, near-sonic speed within 100 feet (30 meters) of the ground was sure to pose serious problems. The Skyray, the first of two record aircraft to get into action, introduced a novel shape into speed-record flying. Based on original work by the Germans during World War II, in designing a delta-wing airplane with a triangular wing and no tail, the final product emerged as a cross between a true delta shape and a broad swept-wing design. With an extremely thick wing, it was possible to use an airfoil of minimum thickness in relation to its fore-to-aft dimension, or chord. Such a relatively thin (actually, quite thick) wing provides ample internal space for a sturdy structure and for storing the retractable landing gear and housing fuel (something the increasingly powerful turbojet engines use at a tremendous rate). The Skyray had just such a roomy wing, plus a sharply swept leading edge for delaying the onset of compressibility effects as the aircraft neared the speed of sound.

On the negative side, the Skyray was the first carrier-based airplane to seriously be considered for speed records. Navy airplanes were traditionally of lower performance than land-based airplanes. Much more than old-fashioned interservice rivalry was involved, since a carrier-based airplane must carry the additional load of its arrestor gear, heavy-duty landing gear, and wing-folding mechanism. Moreover, a low landing speed is vital for any airplane that operates from a floating runway sometimes less than 1,000 feet (300 meters) long. Compromises must be made with the requirements of high-speed flight.

Nevertheless, only three days after Mike Lithgow, in a Swift, upped the Absolute World Air Speed Record to 735.54 mph (1,183.74 km/h), the Skyray unofficially broke it. U.S. Navy Lt.Cdr. James Verdin was clocked at 743 mph (1,195 km/h) in four runs over the Salton Sea course. His first three runs were at a rate that would have brought him the record at around 744 mph (1,198 km/h); but the final run was slowed by a sudden precautionary climb caused by concern over fluctuations in the engine gauges. Thus Verdin came up marginally short of the FAI's 1-percent-margin rule.

On October 3, 1953, after replacing the Skyray's pitot tube (which picks up outside air and sends it to vital instruments), Verdin made another try at the record. He took off from El Centro Naval Air Station shortly after 3:00 P.M. By 3:27, when Verdin began his runs, the temperature at ground level (240 feet [73 meters] below sea level) was 97°F (36°C). The Skyray's critical Mach number thus permitted about as high a speed as was possible under those conditions, since temperature any greater would begin to reduce the engine's output.

In a mere seven minutes, Verdin and the second prototype Skyray achieved speeds ranging from 745 to 761 mph (1,199 to 1,224 km/h), with an average of 752.949 mph (1,211.746 km/h)—a new record that replaced Lithgow's 737 mph (1,186 km/h). It was the first Absolute World Air Speed Record to be set by a true naval airplane and the first by an airplane of radical design.

The prototype Skyray had a wingspan of 33.5 feet (10.2 meters), a length of 45.4 feet (13.8 meters), and a wing area of 557 square feet (52 square meters). It was powered by a Pratt & Whitney J57-P-8 turbojet engine rated at about 10,500 pounds (4,756 kilograms) of thrust without afterburning, and 14,500 pounds (6,569 kilograms) with it. The XF4D-1 number 124587 was retired from service in 1960 and broken up for scrap.

The British were said to be considering sending both the Hunter and the Swift to North Africa for more record trials, but Verdin's record put the required speed over 760 mph (1,223 km/h)—beyond the reach of either airplane; so the plan was dropped. The U.S. Air Force, however, had no thoughts of quitting. Two days after Verdin set his record, a North American YF-100A was streaking along the Salton Sea in preparation for official trials. On October 5, it reportedly was timed at a speed less than 1 mph slower than Verdin's Skyray had achieved on the same 1.86-mile (3-kilometer) course.

The YF-100A, albeit a more conventional airplane than the stingray-shaped F4D, proved far more significant, becoming the first supersonic airplane to go into production (as the F-100). Although it began as a redesigned F-86 Sabre, before long, the YF-100A became an entirely new airplane. The prototype Super Sabre flew for the first time on May 25, 1953, and achieved supersonic speed within a few minutes of taking off. Never before had an airplane flown so fast on its first flight, and perhaps never before had an airplane so impressed the test pilot that he pushed it to see how fast it would go.

The development of the F-100 was disappointing after the initial success. Several crashes forced the grounding of all Super Sabres for three months just after the first ones were delivered. On the other hand, problems were to be expected in such an advanced airplane. The problems were solved, and the F-100 became the world standard for the first generation of supersonic fighter planes.

Less than five months after the first flight of the YF-100A, the aircraft was at the Salton Sea to attack the Absolute World Air Speed Record. The pilot was Lt.Col. Frank Everest, chief of flight test operations at Edwards AF Base. On October 5, 1953, Everest made several runs at about 752 mph (1,210 km/h) on the 3-kilometer course, and another series a few days later on the same course, at 758 mph (1,220 km/h). Neither speed, however, was fast enough to top the existing record by the 1 percent demanded by the FAI.

Then North American Aviation and the Air Force found a loophole in the rules. While the FAI insisted that a new record on a course of a given length be at least 1 percent faster than the previous record, it also said the highest speed achieved on a course of *any* length would be recognized as the Absolute World Air Speed Record. In the past, the highest speed had always been accomplished on the shortest possible course, since 1923, a straight 3 kilometers. The necessary margin of speed was now more than 7 mph (11.3 km/h); therefore, it might be easier to fly a fraction of a mile per hour faster on a longer course than to fly 7-plus mph faster on the standard short course.

North American promptly had a 9.3-mile (15-kilometer) course surveyed along the Salton Sea shore, and in mid-October 1953, Everest began practice runs. As an advantage, only one run in either direction was required for the 15/25-kilometer (24/40-mile) record, rather than two in either direction for the 3-kilometer record.

On October 29, just before 3:00 P.M., having averaged 751 mph (1,208 km/h) in tests, Everest took off. The surface temperature was 89°F (32°C). He made a down-wind run on the 15-kilometer course in 43.896 seconds and an up-wind run in 45.216. Extremely accurate high-speed cameras made it possible for the NAA timers, under the direction of Charlie Logsdon, the Records Board secretary, to catch such times while the airplane was traveling more than 12 miles (19 kilometers) per minute.

Everest's average speed was 755.149 mph (1,215.298 km/h), only about 2 mph (3 km/h) faster than Verdin's mark set in the Skyray; but because it was more than 1 percent faster than the existing record for a course of that length, it was perfectly legal and a new Absolute World Air Speed Record. The Navy and the Douglas Aircraft Company protested, accusing the Air Force of sneaking through a loophole. The YF-100A, however, was officially the fastest airplane in the world (not counting air-launched, rocket-powered craft), and there wasn't a thing anyone could do about it except read the rules more carefully in the future.

The F-100 eventually became one of the significant airplanes of the 1950s.

Late versions of it were capable of speeds in excess of 1,000 mph (1,609 km/h) in level flight. The YF-100A had a length of 45.2 feet (13.8 meters), a wingspan of 36.6 feet (11.2 meters), and a wing area of 376 square feet (35 square meters). It was powered by a Pratt & Whitney J57-P-7 turbojet engine rated at more than 12,000 pounds (5,436 kilograms) of thrust using its afterburner.

Everest, born in Fairmont, West Virginia in 1920, graduated from USAAF pilot training in 1942. He flew Curtiss P-40s in Europe and was then sent to the Pacific, where he was shot down and captured by the Japanese after destroying four of their airplanes. From 1946 to 1954, he was an Air Force test pilot, holding the unofficial rocket-plane speed record (1,957 mph [3,150 km/h]) in the Bell X-2. Everest served in a variety of staff positions, becoming a brigadier general in 1965.

Everest's speed in the prototype Super Sabre was equal to 96 percent of the speed of sound. The last few record attempts had seen the approach to the "sound barrier" by the tiniest of steps — 1 percent at a time. It was obvious that for reasons of safety, future attempts should be made at high altitude (the runs by Everest's airplane had resulted in significant damage to private homes near the course). Also, there was growing concern for the safety of the timers and observers who would be exposed to supersonic shock waves at close range if future runs were made near the ground. Finally, the faster an airplane flies, the less time the pilot has to react in emergencies. From then on, the Absolute World Air Speed Record would trade some of its glamor for the safety and efficiency of high-altitude flight.

The Supersonic Era

Between late 1953 and summer 1955, no attempts were made on the Absolute World Air Speed Record. It wasn't that there was no interest in flying faster, simply that FAI rules required that records be set by airplanes flying within 330 feet (100 meters) of the ground, and that was both too dangerous and too inefficient for the supersonic jets being introduced.

When Frank Everest set his near-sonic official record in October 1953, the fastest an airplane had flown under any conditions was 1,238 mph (1,992 km/h), which Bill Bridgeman, a test pilot for Douglas, had accomplished in the D-558-II "Skyrocket." Bridgeman flew at great altitude, where the air is extremely thin and is thus less of an impediment to speed than is the thick air at sea level. Bridgeman's flight was made at almost Mach 1.9, nearly twice the best that had been done under FAI rules.

Among the problems to be solved before records could be set at great altitude, however, was lack of equipment precise enough to track an airplane with sufficient accuracy to satisfy the FAI *and* potential rivals. Timing an airplane that comes within a few hundred feet of timing officials is one thing; timing an airplane 8 miles high is another. Moreover, the need for accuracy increases along with the speed flown by airplanes, whether production or research.

Finally, in the summer of 1955, the FAI agreed to accept records set in its new 15/25-kilometer category, which were flown at any altitude. Equipment had been devised that could track and record an airplane several miles away with the precision required. The standard 3-kilometer (1.86-mile) distance remained limited to airplanes flying at low levels.

While pilots, manufacturers, and military public relations people waited for the FAI to come to grips with a rapidly progressing technology, the speeds achieved at high altitude rose steadily. By summer 1955, a Bell X-1A rocket plane had been flown at Mach 2.5, equal to Yeager's speed of 1,650 mph (2,655 km/h). Although such rocket craft had to be air-launched and thus could not qualify for official records, the newer fighters could also fly considerably faster than the existing mark. The first of these to be tried was the improved North American F-100C, a refinement of the YF-100A that held the record for nearly two years. The F-100C closely resembled the earlier F-100A, but numerous modifications had been made in the latter's structure to permit carrying more equipment. In place of the early-model Pratt & Whitney J57, the prototype F-100C had a J57-P-39 rated at considerably more power than the YF-100A.

Two basic problems were posed by high-altitude record attempts: timers had to see the airplane, and the pilot had to see the speed course, either visually or electronically. Ground-based radar could provide electronic tracking, but it was a far more difficult task to see the airplane from the ground. Eventually, engineers from North American solved the problem. On a concrete pad at each end of the timed portion of the course, they mounted a camera with a 40-inch (10,160-millimeter) lens. On each side of the camera were 50-foot (15.2-meter) steel towers, between which were stretched two thin wires, one above the other. When the wires were aligned precisely, a camera pointed upward would see them merely as a single line. The camera, on a swivel mount that permitted it to move across the airplane's flight path, was aimed with the aid of two telescopes. One, with a magnification of six times and with a broad field of view, was used to find the aircraft; the other, with a magnification of fifteen times, was used to center the airplane in the crosshairs. As the field of view of the second telescope passed the wires strung between the towers, it tripped the shutter on the camera, which, in turn, started the timing mechanism.

The new device, tested at Edwards AF Base for a year before a record attempt, was certified by the FAI on the basis of the device's demonstrated ability to determine the location of an airplane at high altitude within 3 feet (0.9 meter). The total error in the system reportedly was plus or minus 0.02 percent.

Cameras, towers, and miles of telephone lines were installed for the new Mint Canyon Speed Course, an 18.111-kilometer (11.25-mile) stretch from Palmdale Airport southwest toward Los Angeles. The course covered a distance of about 200 miles (322 kilometers), from the southwest corner of Death Valley to San Nicholas Island, 60 miles (96.5 kilometers) out in the Pacific Ocean. At better than 13 miles (21 kilometers) per minute, a Super Sabre would require several miles to turn around at the maximum of about 3 Gs, since a tighter turn would reduce its speed too much.

At about 8:00 A.M., August 20, 1955, Col. Horace Hanes, director of flight tests at Edwards AF Base, took off and climbed quickly to 40,000 feet (12,200 meters). The temperature at Edwards was 82°F (28°C), but that didn't matter; at 8 miles (12.9 kilometers) above the surface, the temperature is about −60°F (−51°C). At that altitude, Hanes would run the new speed course, keeping within 330 feet (100 meters) of his chosen altitude while being checked by orbiting airplanes carrying NAA observers.

Hanes made the required two runs in opposite directions. The down-wind run began at 40,330 feet (12,293 meters) and finished at 41,250 feet (12,573 meters), demonstrating that, unlike the record-breakers of the 1930s, he *climbed* through the course rather than diving to gain speed. The first run was made at 870.8 mph (1,401.1 km/h). The up-wind run, against a 50 mph (80 km/h) wind, started at 40,255 feet (12,270 meters), finished at 40,310 feet (12,286 meters), working out to 773.8 mph (1,245 km/h). Hanes' official speed — the first at high altitude — was 822.266 mph (1,323.026 km/h). The sophisticated timing equipment produced times to the fifth decimal place: 47.21766 seconds for the first run and 52.86590 seconds for the second. Aviation had come a long way since that day in 1906 when Alberto Santos-Dumont was timed with simple stopwatches for a flight of about 90 yards, a few feet above the ground.

Hanes, born in 1916 in Fayette, Illinois, became an Army pilot in 1939. During World War II he flew P-47 and P-38 fighters, then led the Air Force's first jet unit based outside the United States. From 1953 to 1957, he was director of flight tests at Edwards AF Base, retiring as a major general in 1973.

Once the high-altitude timing system had proved effective, the opportunity presented itself for any of a half-dozen new, fast airplanes to have a go at the Absolute World Air Speed Record. Technical obstacles to building more powerful airplanes with better streamlining were being attacked with great energy. Soon the results would be there for all to see.

The military value of high-speed flight led to a new problem, one that must be confronted by those interested in setting records: official disfavor. It had been tacitly agreed that American attempts on the Absolute World Air Speed Record would alternate between the Air Force and the Navy. The Navy planned to make an attempt on the record in late 1955, using its new Chance Vought XF8U-1 Crusader fighter. Practice runs had shown it capable of 1,050 mph (1,690 km/h), about 200 mph (322 km/h) faster than the record. Then, only 48 hours before an official series of runs was to begin, Secretary of Defense Charles Wilson, concerned that a potential enemy of the United States would learn too much about the performance of U.S. warplanes, announced his opposition to such interservice rivalry, even when the rivalry would enhance national security. Perhaps some information of a sensitive nature would be released as a result of excessive exuberance on the part of some manufacturer who wanted to set as fast a record as possible with a new airplane.

For several years, Great Britain had lagged behind the United States in high-speed research. Although America had produced three different airplanes that could exceed Mach 1.5 in level flight, the first British airplane to do that did not make its initial flight until October 6, 1954. That plane, the Fairey Delta 2, was a pure delta wing with a slim, tubular fuselage, air intakes in the leading edges of the wings, and a novel drooping nose section that gave the pilot fairly good visibility for takeoffs and landings while producing unusually low drag in high-speed flight. This unusual concept proved so workable that it was later adopted for the Concorde supersonic transport and by the Soviets for their Tu-144 SST. It was the first British airplane designed expressly for research in the problems of supersonic flight. True, the fast (but doomed) deHavilland Swallow had flown faster than sound at least one time; but that airplane was designed to study the problems of controllability and stability at speeds below supersonic. Nevertheless, the Fairey Delta 2 was, for its day, an advanced airplane.

By the time the British were ready to attempt the Absolute World Air Speed Record in the Fairey Delta 2, the severe drawback of lack of sufficient space for an adequate course had been eliminated. There was no longer any need to build a speed course that could be flown safely at ground level. Now, runs could be made at altitudes so great that few people would be aware of them. There was also no need to send a crew to North Africa for runs over the desert, to take advantage of higher temperatures.

The course chosen for the F.D.2, as it was called, lay along Britain's south coast: a 15-kilometer (9.3-mile) stretch that followed the perfectly straight railroad track between Chichester and Ford, a mile south of the RAF base at Tangmere. After taking off, the pilot, Peter Twiss, climbed at subsonic speed to an altitude of 38,000 feet (11,600 meters), beginning his first run about 25 miles (40 kilometers) from the start of the course. Ten miles (16 kilometers) from the entry point of the timed course, Twiss turned on his afterburner. Trial attempts were made on March 8 and 9, 1956, as well as the morning of March 10. Only then was everyone satisfied that conditions were right. At 11:20 A.M. on the tenth, Twiss took off, climbed to an altitude where the combination of temperature and humidity would produce a white contrail to aid the official spotters on the ground and headed for the course. A few minutes later, having completed the required runs, he headed home. The British achieved everything they could have hoped for: an Absolute World Air Speed Record of 1,132.13 mph (1,821.98 km/h). The first official record over 1,000 mph (1,609 km/h), the mark was also the largest increase over an existing record since the FAI began officiating in 1910. Twiss topped the American F-100C mark by an impressive 310 mph (499 km/h), bringing glee to both the Royal Air Force and the British aircraft industry.

The airplane Twiss flew was one of two designed for research in high-speed flight. WG774, the record machine, had a wingspan of 26.8 feet (8.2 meters), a length of 51.6 feet (15.7 meters), a height of 11 feet (3.3 meters), and a wing area of 360 square feet (33.5 square meters). It was powered by a single Rolls Royce Avon R.A.14 turbojet engine rated at 9,500 pounds (4,304 kilograms) thrust. Midway through a long, productive career, the airplane was modified for further research and was eventually retired to the Fleet Air Arm Museum at Yeovilton. The other F.D.2 is on display at RAF Cosford, where it is part of the reserve collection of the Royal Air Force Museum.

Any American interest in recapturing the Absolute World Air Speed Record had been stifled by a security-conscious Department of Defense. Had Chance Vought's XF8U-1 Crusader been allowed to make an official attempt in late 1955, as planned, the British would still have taken the record with their F.D.2 but the gap in speed would not have been as embarrassingly wide. In the summer of 1956, the Navy and Chance Vought appealed to the Secretary of Defense. This time, Secretary Wilson approved an attempt — as long as the airplane was held well under its maximum speed. The airplane chosen for this limited attempt was the production version of the Crusader, the F8U-1, and the occasion included the awarding of the Thompson Trophy, once the most prized trophy in American speed flying but which was now presented to the military pilot who made the most significant advance in high-speed flight during the preceding year.

The Navy chose China Lake as the site for the test, a 1,000-square-mile (2,600-square-kilometer) tract north of Los Angeles housing the U.S. Naval Ordnance Test Center. Laying out a 9.4-mile (15.1-kilometer) course in such a desolate area was no problem; the few people who lived in the area were long since accustomed to fast airplanes and the noise they make.

Cdr. Robert W. "Duke" Windsor made the required opposite-direction passes shortly after 7 A.M., August 21, 1956. The top speed of his Crusader, the U.S. Navy's first carrier-based airplane with a speed in excess of 1,000 mph (1,600 km/h), was about the same as that of the Fairey Delta 2 — 1,130 mph (1,820 km/h) — but regulations forced him to hold back more than 100 mph (161 km/h) to disguise the airplane's true maximum performance. Windsor's two-run average speed worked out to 1,015.4 mph (1,634 km/h), more than enough to break the three-year-old American record of 822 mph (1,323 km/h). Still, it fell considerably short of the Absolute World Air Speed Record; the British held the record by a margin of 117 mph (188 km/h). Insiders knew the Crusader was as fast as the F.D.2 and that the American craft was a standard military combat airplane; but that didn't help the nation's image.

The F8U-1 that set the U.S. record differed from a production-line airplane only in its paint job. To make it easier for NAA officials on the ground to see it, the outer portions of the wings, and all the vertical tail, were painted a fiery orange. Otherwise, the airplane had the standard F8U-1 dimensions: wingspan, 35.2 feet (10.7 meters), length, 54.5 feet (16.6 meters); wing area, 350 square feet (32.6 square meters). It was powered by a Pratt & Whitney J57-P-4A turbojet engine that delivered 16,200 pounds (7,350 kilograms) of thrust with the afterburner on.

Two and a half months after the American speed mark was set, the Navy decided to show the top brass that it had at least one airplane capable of taking the Absolute World Air Speed Record away from the British. It was all done quite unofficially, and there was no effort to have the flight certified by the NAA. Although there is no thick file in the NAA office in Washington for this speed mission, no one has suggested that the results are anything but accurate. Once the speed of the airplane became common knowledge, it was clear that such an achievement was well within its range.

The airplane used for this unusual flight was the new Grumman F11F-1F Super Tiger. Two were built from the basic F11F Tiger, using an engine of twice the original power in an effort to achieve the level supersonic speed Grumman had promised but not delivered. The first Super Tiger flew May 25, 1956 and approached Mach 1.5 within two weeks. The second one flew August 16, and soon it was being prepared to show just how great was the increase in its performance, once the original Wright J65 (an Armstrong-Siddeley Sapphire engine built under license from Britain) had been replaced with a Pratt & Whitney J79 rated at 15,000 pounds (6,800 kilograms) thrust.

On November 7, 1956, Lt.Cdr. George Watkins, a U.S. Navy test pilot, achieved a speed of approximately 1,220 mph (1,960 km/h, or Mach 1.85), and an altitude of 72,000 feet (21,945 meters) on a single flight. The altitude exceeded the standing Absolute World Air Speed Record of 65,876 feet

(20,078 meters) set by an English Electric Canberra bomber in the summer of 1955. Never before had an airplane set two such significant records, even unofficially, on the same flight.

Specialists insisted there was nothing of a security nature revealed by a flight at maximum speed that was made well below the airplane's optimum cruising altitude. In fact, later flights by Super Tigers produced speeds over Mach 2 (1,300 mph [2,100 km/h]) and altitudes higher than 80,000 feet (24,400 meters), but none of these accomplishments could be considered for record purposes, because proper FAI formalities had not been followed.

Because of excessive weight, the F11F-1F was never accepted for production by the Navy. On April 16, 1958, near Edwards AF Base, the second airplane was used to set its only official World Record. Watkins flew the F11F-1F to an altitude of 76,831 feet (23,417 meters). At the time Grumman Super Tiger was showing it had the speed to break the Absolute World Air Speed Record, several other airplanes in the American military arsenal were in a position to set an official record. Not for 13 months after the unofficial F11F-1F record, however, was the go-ahead received for an official attempt. The U.S. Air Force could confidently look over its McDonnell F-101 Voodoo, Lockheed F-104 Starfighter, and Convair F-106 Delta Dart to see which it preferred for the attempt. The F-101, the most highly developed of the trio, was chosen.

The Absolute World Air Speed Record attempt was planned as part of a series of record trials for the finale of the Air Force's fiftieth anniversary. Chosen for the attempt was one of the first F-101 Voodoos built—a model F-101A single-seat, long-range fighter developed from the McDonnell XF-88. It was a military-standard airplane of considerable size, with sufficient power to propel it at high speed. The course it was to fly was a 16.1-kilometer (10-mile) beeline at Edwards AF Base.

In early December 1957, Maj. Adrian Drew was clocked unofficially at 1,199 mph (1,929 km/h). In an attempt on December 10 that was spoiled by a timing camera that malfunctioned, Drew averaged 1,180 to 1,190 mph (1,900 to 1,915 km/h). These speeds were a solid 50 mph (80 km/h) over the record, whereas only about 11 mph (18 km/h) was needed to satisfy the FAI.

Finally, on December 12, 1957, Drew went back up and made two more runs. Drew's times for the two runs were under 30 seconds for the 10 miles (16.1 kilometers). His speed was calculated at 1,207.6 mph (1,943.5 km/h). The record fell by a margin of 75 mph (121 km/h), and the titles of the world's fastest human and airplane was returned to the United States after a year and a half. The new record-holding airplane was a production military fighter with no modifications intended to increase its speed for record purposes. Clearly, the F-101 could do the job with no special modifications, and none were made.

The F-101A was a hefty airplane. It had a wingspan of 39.7 feet (12.1 meters), a length of 67.3 feet (20.5 meters), a height of 18 feet (5.5 meters), and a wing area of 368 square feet (34.2 square meters). It was powered by two Pratt & Whitney J57-P-55 turbojet engines, each producing 15,000 pounds (6,795 kilograms) thrust. Only 50 of this original version of the F-101 were built before it was replaced by fighter-bomber and reconnaissance versions. The airplane of record eventually was sent to the storage depot at Davis-Monthan AF Base, near Tucson, Arizona.

Major Drew, a native of Carroll County, Georgia, was an instructor in fighter planes during World War II. He flew more than a hundred missions in Korea, after which he became a flight commander in a strategic fighter squadron.

Now that the United States had broken its taboo and set an Absolute World Air Speed record, it was time to take the wraps off an airplane everyone suspected was much faster than the Voodoo—the Lockheed F-104. The Starfighter was a cylindrical fuselage containing a large engine, associated parts, and stubby straight wings, this in an era when everything else intended for high speed had either highly swept-back wings or radical delta wings.

Unknown to more than a few insiders, the F-104 had been flying at a record pace for several years. Even before Horace Hanes set the world's first supersonic record in an F-100 Super Sabre, Lockheed test pilot Ray Goudey pushed a prototype XF-104 to a speed of 1,150 mph (1,850 km/h). And only a few weeks after the British Fairey Delta 2 surprised the world by boosting the Absolute World Air Speed Record to 1,132 mph (1,822 km/h), another Lockheed pilot, Joe Ozier, became the first to fly at twice the speed of sound (about 1,300 mph [2,100 km/h]) in a jet airplane. At the time, these marks, however, were not only unofficial but highly secret.

Thus, when Lockheed received permission from the Air Force to try to make some record attempts, it knew it had the airplane. With so much speed available, it should have been a routine matter to set a record well above the existing one, yet one not fully indicative of the speed the still classified fighter plane was capable of. The Air Force hoped to announce the results on Armed Forces Day.

In 1958, Armed Forces Day fell on Saturday, May 17; time was so short that the NAA's equipment wasn't at Edwards AF Base, ready, until Thursday morning, May 15. Capt. Walter Irwin, an F-104 pilot from the 83rd Fighter Interceptor Squadron, knew how to fly the airplane, but his military training had not prepared him to keep within the limits of the strict FAI rules. Irwin's first start was at 6:00 A.M., Thursday, May 14. He received radar headings from the ground, then position reports, as he tore along at about 2,000 feet (600 meters) per second, trying to stay within the 330 feet (100 meters) of the prescribed altitude. At that speed, a slight twitch of the hand on the control stick would shoot him far above or below the proper altitude. In a mere one-tenth second, Irwin traveled almost the length of a football field.

At 40,000 feet (12,192 meters), Irwin had to concern himself with the "thermal thicket," a combination of speed and air density where the friction heating caused by air compressing as it entered the engine's air intake might be so great that it would melt parts of the engine. To avoid this dread possibility, Irwin used less than full power, and thus on his first run, failed to reach the desired speed.

Irwin landed and changed airplanes. The second pair of runs was better but still not fast enough. The third began well, with an initial run better than 1,500 mph (2,400 km/h). Irwin made a wide, sweeping turnaround at a steady 3-G acceleration and headed back toward the course. Suddenly, a wire broke in the mechanism that controls the afterburner, and he was again forced to abort the effort.

Before the airplane could be repaired, high clouds moved into the area, making it impossible for officials to track and photograph the Starfighter. The last chance to set a record in time for a formal announcement Saturday was the morning of Friday, May 16. As the time remaining dwindled, the pressure increased.

Irwin was back at the task early the next morning in an airplane with the latest-model engine. He took off at 6:47 A.M. and made two fast, smooth passes, holding his altitude along a pencil-thin line in the sky eight miles above the desert. Early figures gave an average of about 1,435 mph (2,310 km/h), far above the existing record. Then came bad news: the timing cameras had failed; thus there was no permanent record of the flight. It would have to be done again.

Added to that disappointment was the news that a small part in the F-104 had failed and would have to be replaced. There was no time to change the part, and so Irwin climbed into yet another F-104, one which, unfortunately, did not have the improved engine. As he headed for the course a few minutes before 8:00 A.M., a Lockheed T-33 jet trainer that had been orbiting over the course, carrying NAA observers, reported that its canopy had been damaged and that it would have to return to Edwards. Fortunately, a spare T-33 was already in the air.

Irwin made his next down-wind run in less than 25 seconds for the 10.1 miles (16.25 kilometers), equal to 1,465 mph (2,358 km/h). He made as tight a turn as possible, keeping in mind that too many Gs would cut into his speed, and headed back against a wind of about 50 mph (80 km/h). The up-wind run took 27 seconds to complete, equal to 1,343 mph (2,161 km/h).

Irwin's official average speed, determined after what seemed like an unusually long delay, were computed as 1,404.09 mph (2,259.65 km/h). The previous record, set six months earlier, was left nearly 200 mph (320 km/h) behind. The F-104 obviously had speed in reserve. On Armed Forces Day, the record was revealed to the public, along with the news that a similar F-104 had recaptured the Absolute World Altitude Record from the French, of 91,249 feet (27,811 meters). It had been quite a day for Lockheed and the U.S. Air Force.

The F-104, known as the "missile with a man in it," was delivered to the Air Force in January 1958 but did not prove satisfactory, being hampered by limited range and foul-weather fighting capability. Many F-104s were turned over to the Air National Guard and to other countries. Lockheed developed a significantly improved version, and more than a thousand of them were built on license in Japan, Canada and Europe. The basic F-104 had a wingspan of 21.9 feet (6.7 meters), a length of 54.8 feet, (16.7 meters), a height of 13.5 feet (4.1 meters), and a wing area of 179 square feet (16.6 square meters). Its gross weight was 23,590 pounds (10,686 kilograms). The F-104's service ceiling, the altitude at which its rate of climb drops off to 100 feet per minute (30 meters per minute), was 58,000 feet (17,675 meters). In the later versions, power was supplied by a Pratt & Whitney J79 engine of 15,800 pounds (7,157 kilograms) thrust.

Until about 1957, Absolute World Air Speed Record attempts were made solely by the United States and Great Britain. The French were developing an impressive aircraft industry, as were the Swedes; but neither France nor Sweden was known to be involved to the extent that it could challenge the

Americans or the British. What the Soviet Union was doing in the area of high-speed flight was, as usual, clouded in mystery. Throughout World War II, the Soviets had been considered backward, though an occasional airplane hinted at progress. The almost total lack of precise information, plus the USSR's eagerness to accept even second-rate airplanes offered through Lend-Lease, indicated that the country was backward technologically.

The first surprise came in 1950, when the swept-wing MiG-15 jet fighter challenged American air superiority over Korea. While the MiG-15s flown by Korean and, later, Chinese pilots suffered considerably at the hands of American F-86 Sabres, the Soviet design was marginally faster and unquestionably well built. Under combat conditions it had some shortcomings that put it at a disadvantage compared with the sophisticated F-86. The MiG-15, however, was a first-rate airplane, which was all the more surprising, in view of the widely held belief that the Soviet aircraft industry was inferior.

In late 1959, the international aviation scene was greeted by another surprise when the FAI announced that a Soviet E-66 had broken the Absolute World Air Speed Record with a speed of 1,483.85 mph (2,388 km/h). Aside from the pilot's name — Georgi Mossolov — however, nothing more was revealed.

The first question Western aeronautical experts asked was: "What the hell is an E-66?" The answer was a long time coming, for it was common practice for the Soviets to treat almost everything as a state secret. In this case, one of the reasons for the secrecy was to delay the world learning about the USSR's latest jet fighter, the MiG-21. The E-66 seems to have been little more than an early model of the MiG-21, perhaps with some modifications intended to increase the airplane's sprint speed in record runs.

It took three years to gather the elementary information that the MiG-21 was a delta-winged airplane rather than a swept-wing machine, as most had concluded. In those days, much of what was known (or surmised) about Soviet airplanes came from the annual flyover of airplanes during the May Day parade in Moscow. Experts would pore over even the graniest photographs, trying to determine which airplane was which and attempting to estimate the performance of each from the size of the air intakes and the angles of the wings. Eventually it became known that the E-66, commonly assumed to be a unique airplane, was simply a MiG-21 (a "Fishbed," in NATO terminology). Details of the E-66's record attempt were never made public; but there is little doubt that the speed claimed was actually achieved. The basic MiG-21 was not a large machine; thus, using the power of its 12,500-pound (5,670-kilogram) Tumansky R37F turbojet engine, it may well have reached Mach 2.25, as represented by the record flight. On the other hand, it is known that a variation, the E-66A, used to set an Absolute World Altitude Record of 113,892 feet (34,714 meters), used an additional 6,615-pound (2,997-kilogram) thrust rocket motor for extra boost; the same could have been done for the speed run.

The MiG-21/E-66 had a wingspan of 25 feet (7.6 meters), a length of 55 feet (16.8 meters), and a takeoff weight, with a full load of fuel (certainly not the condition in which the speed record was set), of 16,700 pounds (7,565 kilograms). Although the airplane was obviously fast because of its power and streamlining, the MiG-21 was considered a second-rate fighter plane, because of a lack of range and a limited weapons capacity. Nevertheless, at least 5,000 MiG-21s were built, and they have served as the main fighter in the air forces of East European countries, as well as some Third World nations.

Before the Soviet Union had a chance to file the extensive paperwork required by the FAI in claiming a major record, the U.S. Air Force challenged the speed of the MiG-21. The hottest airplane in the U.S. Air Force arsenal at the time was the Convair F-106 Delta Dart, the first production versions of which were delivered in the summer of 1959. The airplane was considerably larger than the MiG-21 or the Lockheed F-104 (which had most recently held the Absolute World Air Speed Record). It was also much more powerful, with a single Pratt & Whitney J75 turbojet producing 24,500 pounds (11,100 kilograms) thrust.

A reportedly stock F-106 was pulled off the flight line of one of an Air Defense Squadron flying the type and sent to Edwards AF Base, along with Maj. Joseph Rogers, a test pilot who most recently had held a desk position at Air Defense Command headquarters. During the week preceding the official attempt on the record, Rogers made some half-dozen runs along the course, primarily to familiarize himself with the strict FAI rules. On the morning of December 15, 1959, all appeared ready. The airplane had been performing well, and Rogers was reasonably comfortable on the 11.2-mile (18.1 kilometer) course over the Mojave Desert. He took off at 9:30 A.M. and entered the timing course at 9:56. Fifteen minutes later, it was all over, and he headed back to base to await the computations.

When word finally arrived from the NAA officials, an Absolute World Air Speed Record had been set: 1,525.965 mph (2,455.736 km/h). Both runs were at speeds over 1,500 mph (2,414 km/h), and they were completed in less than 24 seconds. In one week the U.S. Air Force recaptured the Absolute World Altitude Record (Capt. Joe Jordan took a Lockheed F-104C up to 103,395 feet [31,513 meters]) and the Absolute World Air Speed record for a 100-kilometer (62-mile) closed course (Brig.Gen. Joseph Moore flew a Republic F-105B Thunderchief at 1,216.4 mph [1,957.6 km/h]). A French Mirage 3A delta-winged jet fighter held the previous 100-kilometer record, while the altitude record was held by a U.S. Navy McDonnell F4H Phantom II for only a week. The old policy of restricting military airplanes to less-than-maximum performance for security reasons had given way under pressure from international competition.

Major Rogers, a native of Chillicothe, Ohio, became an Army Air Forces pilot in 1944. After flying P-51 Mustangs and P-80 Shooting Stars in Korea, he was sent to Edwards AF Base as a test pilot.

The F-106 made its inaugural flight on December 26, 1956 and was a major interceptor by 1960. It has a wingspan of 38.3 feet (11.7 meters), a length of 70.7 feet (21.5 meters), a height of 20.3 feet (6.2 meters), and a wing area of 631 square feet (58.7 square meters). It is an evolutionary development of Convair's earlier work on delta-winged jets, especially the F-102 Delta Dagger.

In 1958, an airplane appeared on the scene that permanently changed the relationship between the Air Force and the Navy, and one that became the leading Mach 2 fighter for many of the Western world's air forces during the

1960s and 70s. The McDonnell F4 Phantom II dominated an entire generation of combat aviation and may be one of the last military airplanes to be built in such quantity. It began life as a U.S. Navy attack bomber but was converted to an interceptor when its performance became evident. Not long after it became the standard Navy fighter the Air Force ordered the carrier-based airplane as a replacement for its Convair F-106s. The Phantom II, the first major type of airplane to be used by both U.S. air services, was soon in use by Canada, Great Britain, West Germany, and other nations.

Barely 18 months after the first F4 flew (May 1958), its career as a record-breaker began. On December 6, 1959, over Edwards AF Base, a Phantom II reached the record altitude of 98,557 feet (30,039 meters), breaking the Soviet mark. The next year, a Phantom II set a record for a 310-mile (500-kilometer) closed-course flight, at 1,216.76 mph (1,958 km/h), followed by an Absolute World Air Speed Record for the 62-mile (100-kilometer) closed-course flight with a speed of 1,390.24 mph (2,237.36 km/h).

To start 1961 with a supersonic bang, a flight of five F4s took off from Ontario, California, refueled in flight three times, and reached Floyd Bennett Field, in Brooklyn, New York, in about three hours. The fastest plane in flight made the 2,446-mile (3,936-kilometer) coast-to-coast journey in 2 hours 48 minutes, averaging 870 mph (1,398 km/h).

Still not satisfied that the world appreciated the speed of their new fighter, McDonnell Aircraft and the U.S. Navy continued to go after records. This time, they resurrected the low-level 3-kilometer (1.86-mile) category, ignored since 1953, when James Verdin turned in 753 mph (1,212 km/h) at the Salton Sea, setting the last Absolute World Air Speed Record near the ground.

The Salton Sea course was no longer available. Considerable damage had been done to nearby homes by the near-sonic blast of the last series of runs there. A vast, empty tract of land in New Mexico was available, though: White Sands Missile Range. There, noisy, dangerous flying would disturb no one. A 3-kilometer course was laid out near Trinity Site, where the first atomic bomb was tested in 1945, and test runs began in mid-August 1961. The tests soon ran into trouble, however. In order for the F4 to maintain maximum speed at the relatively low altitude of about 4,700 feet (1,433 meters) above sea level, a pilot had to use his afterburner the entire time and control the up-and-down motion of his airplane during the high-G turnarounds with the elevator trim button on his control stick. On one practice flight, the trim mechanism failed and the Navy airplane crashed, killing the pilot. The Navy recruited another pilot and proceeded with the test runs. This time, Lt. Hunt Hardisty was the pilot; Lt. Earl De Esch was his radar operator. The McDonnell Phantom was modified slightly for the record attempt, since it would be flying under conditions quite different from those for which it had been designed: high speed, not at high altitude but at almost no altitude, where the density of the air causes both aerodynamic drag and severe heating. Thus, the engine was augmented with water injection for increased power, and the windshield was reinforced with stainless steel to reduce the chance of it deforming and breaking from the heat generated.

After several practice runs to get the feel of the airplane and the course they had to fly (four times in a few minutes), Hardisty and De Esch got the OK to go for the record. Early on the afternoon of August 28, 1961, they took off to do some hazardous flying: 900 mph (1,450 km/h) at about 125 feet (38.1 meters) altitude. They knew the altitude instruments would be of limited value; they lacked the accuracy and responsiveness needed. It would be up to the pilot to keep on course and absolutely level.

The four runs were made with great precision, the fastest being just one-tenth second faster than the slowest. No run took as long as 7.5 seconds. When the runs had been completed, and Hardisty and De Esch could breathe easily, they were informed that they had set a new world speed record for 3 kilometers (1.86 miles) of 902.719 mph (1,452.777 km/h). At about Mach 1.2, it was the first official supersonic record at low altitude.

The McDonnell F4 Phantom II (then called the F4H-1F) used for the 3-kilometer record was one of the first of thousands built. Its length is 56 feet (17.1 meters), its wingspan 38.5 feet (11.7 meters), and its takeoff weight approximately 40,000 pounds (18,120 kilograms). Power was supplied by two General Electric J79 turbojet engines, each developing 17,000 pounds (7,700 kilograms) of thrust. The airplane flown by Hardisty and De Esch is on display in the National Air & Space Museum's Garber Restoration Facility, in Silver Hill, Maryland, near Washington, D.C.

Once McDonnell and the Navy had the 3-kilometer record in hand, the logical next step was to try for the Absolute World Air Speed Record, and this they did at once. A Phantom II was used, though not the same one used for the 3-kilometer record. The pilot was Marine Corps Lt.Col. R. B. Robinson; the site was Edwards AF Base, since its 10-mile (16.1-kilometer) course was still current and because it had been so useful in the past. The Phantom II would fly in its familiar regime, above 40,000 feet (12,200 meters), and thus would need no major modifications. The airplane, however, would need a lot of fuel, since most of the flight would be made with the twin afterburners on. The Phantom carried not only full internal fuel but three streamlined, disposable tanks, providing the aircraft with an additional 1,340 gallons (5,072 liters) of fuel. The largest tank would be used for the full-power climb to altitude, then dropped. As Robinson began his first top-speed run toward the course's entry gate, he would drop the other two tanks and, in this more streamlined configuration, begin his final acceleration.

Robinson passed through the first gate, still picking up speed. He covered the 10 miles (16.1 kilometers) in 23.5 seconds, for a speed of 1,564 mph (2,517 km/h), then had to turn off his afterburners for the 180-degree turn, which slowed the airplane below Mach 1. The acceleration for the second run was easier, since there was no need to jettison fuel tanks this time. The pass was made in slightly more than 22 seconds, at a speed of 1,649 mph (2,654 km/h). Average speed for the two runs was 1,606.505 mph (2,585.425 km/h) and a new Absolute World Air Speed Record, replacing the Air Force's F-106 mark by 80 mph (130 km/h). The Phantom II's hold on major international flying records had been strengthened; it was already more extensive than that of any airplane in history. Within a few months, more records would be added: the Sustained-Altitude Record, as well as a string of records for the fastest climb from ground level to altitude, ranging from 9,843 feet (3,000 meters) to 98,430 feet (30,000 meters).

If the Phantom II was one of the best-known military airplanes, the E-166, which challenged and took the Absolute World Air Speed Record, was one of the least known. For nearly five years after it won the premier speed record, nothing was known of its appearance – only the bare minimum of specifications required by the FAI. Suddenly, the E-166 was revealed to the public; displayed on the ground during a major air show near Moscow, it was later sent to the museum of the Gagarin Military Air Academy, where it was studied and photographed in detail.

The record set in this strange machine occurred on July 6, 1962. Col. Georgi Mossolov, the pilot of the record-setting E-66 in 1959, was the pilot. His speed, as reported to the FAI, was 1,665.89 mph (2,680.97 km/h). The runs were reported to have included one at 1,865 mph (3,000 km/h).

Everything else reported about the E-166 is vague and frequently contradictory. The FAI was told that the engine of the E-166, thought to be a Tumansky TRD Mark P-166, had a maximum power of 22,046 pounds (9,987 kilograms) thrust; later reports put the power output at 30,000-plus pounds (13,590-plus kilograms). Even the basic dimensions of the airplane are in doubt. Its length is either 55.5 or 65.5 feet (16.9 or 20 meters), and its wingspan is either 22.5 or 29.5 feet (6.9 or 9 meters).

Whereas the Soviets have said nothing about the purpose of the E-166, Western experts assume that it is research – a type of aircraft the USSR must have explored. There is no evidence of armament on the E-166, but there are some devices on the vertical tail that appear to be military electronics. In addition, a clear panel is evident in front of the pilot, which could be for the display of test data (then again, it could be a sophisticated gunsight). The presence of military equipment on essentially nonmilitary airplanes has long been noted, such as the bomberlike glass noses on Soviet airliners.

A few months before the record set by the E-166, the initial test flight of a new American airplane occurred behind a curtain of secrecy. So sensitive is this airplane and its use that, more than 20 years later, the whole story still hasn't been told. The airplane is the Lockheed A-11 (or is it the A-12?), which became the YF-12A and led to the similar SR-71 (which was supposed to have been called the RS-71). Its original, and still most important, function is long-range strategic reconnaissance – in other words, aerial spying. With a design top speed of something over 2,600 mph (4,200 km/h) and a design cruising altitude that may be as high as 120,000 feet (36,500 meters), the SR-71 has, for two decades, been the highest-performance jet airplane in the world.

It is also, without doubt, the most complicated and difficult to build of all successful airplanes in aviation history. To create it, an elite team of engineers working in Lockheed's super-secret "Skunk Works" under Clarence Johnson solved more basic problems than had ever confronted the designers of an aircraft. Called the "Blackbird," it had to be able to fly for hours at speeds that raise the temperature of its skin above 450°F (230°C), something not encountered in designing earlier airplanes, even though such research rocket planes as the X-15 flew faster for a few minutes at a time.

"Kelly" Johnson and his Skunk Works built the U-2 spy plane that cruised with impunity over the USSR and elsewhere for four years until one was shot down in May 1960. From then on, mere altitude, even in the 80,000-foot (25,000-meter) range was no protection. An airplane that combined altitude with great speed and range was needed, and that is what Lockheed explored.

On April 26, 1962, in the Nevada desert, the first A-11 (the factory designation) flew in complete secrecy. It is as peculiar a flying machine as anyone has been prevented from seeing. It consists of a fuselage more than 100 feet (30.5 meters) long, a delta wing at the extreme rear, and a pair of massive engines whose diameter is greater than that of the fuselage. The twin vertical tails are canted inward, whereas the wings' leading edges extend forward past the cockpit, giving the front of the airplane a flat-fish look. Inside, the SR-71 is just as radical. Every part must withstand tremendous heat for hours without losing its shape or strength, a requirement that led to innovative techniques for machining new alloys of titanium. The engines, built specially for the airplane by Pratt & Whitney, can operate at extremely high altitudes where there is little oxygen. The entire airplane uses what has come to be known as "stealth technology," aimed at reducing an aircraft's susceptibility to tracking by radar and by other detection techniques.

So great is the speed of the "Blackbird" that it was approved for a record attempt at considerably reduced power. The first YF-12 fighter flew in August 1963, and record attempts began in the spring of 1965. If the lid was to be lifted from this hush-hush project even partially, it might as well be done with a flair; therefore, the program called for challenging six records.

Using two YF-12As, three Air Force crews laid siege to the FAI record book on May 1, 1965, at Edwards AF Base. Maj. Walter Daniel (pilot) and Maj. Noel Warner (defense systems officer) set three records in a single 1,000-kilometer (621-mile) flight: 1,688 mph (2,716 km/h) for a run with no payload, with 1,000 kilograms (2,200 pounds), and with 2,000 kilograms (4,415 pounds). Daniel then teamed with Capt. James Cooney to set a 500-kilometer (310-mile) closed-course record of 1,642 mph (2,642 km/h).

The most important records were set by Col. Robert Stephens (the pilot) and Lt.Col. Daniel Andre. They ripped up the 16.1-kilometer (10-mile) straightaway course (for the 15/25-kilometer category) with two runs under 17.5 seconds. Their average speed of 2,070.115 mph (3,331.507 km/h) was almost 400 mph (635 km/h) faster than Mossolov had flown three years earlier. On the same flight, Stephens and Andre took the record for a flight at the greatest sustained altitude: 80,334 feet (24,485 meters).

America's super spy plane, whose actual mission was kept secret for many years, had shown that it could outperform any manned airplane flying. At a speed of Mach 3.14 and an altitude of 80,000 feet (24,400 meters), the airplane was well short of its maximum performance; thus, no vital secrets were revealed.

The YF-12A flown by Stephens and Andre is 101 feet (30.8 meters) long, with a wingspan of 55.6 feet (16.9 meters) and a height of 18.5 feet (5.6 meters). Its empty weight is about 60,000 pounds (27,180 kilograms), its gross weight more than 140,000 pounds (63,420 kilograms), most of the difference being accounted for by fuel. Power is from a pair of specially developed Pratt

& Whitney J58 turboramjets rated at 32,500 pounds (14,723 kilograms) thrust each, using special JP-7 jet fuel.

A decade later, the Defense Department felt the performance of the "Blackbird" needed to be demonstrated again, and on July 27, 1976, an SR-71A reconnaissance plane was flown over the course at Edwards AF Base on the required two passes in opposite directions. The up-wind run was completed in 16.7 seconds and the down-wind in 16.21 seconds, for an average speed of 2,193.64 mph (3,529.56 km/h)—an increase of nearly 125 mph (200 km/h) over the previous Absolute World Air Speed Record. At this rate, the SR-71A flew almost 1 kilometer per second—85 times as fast as Santos-Dumont flew while setting the first speed record with an airplane. And it can be assumed that the airplane's speed of Mach 3.3 was well below the speed the airplane is actually capable of.

The pilot was Capt. (later Colonel) Eldon Joersz, assisted by Maj. George Morgan, the reconnaissance systems officer. Other SR-71As set records in two other categories: 2,092 mph (3,367 km/h) for 1,000 kilometers (621 miles) in a closed circuit, and a sustained altitude of 85,069 feet (25,928 meters).

Colonel Joersz later told the author:

I'm not really sure when the planning started for these missions, [but] I've got a feeling the date is pretty close to . . . October 1967. That's when the "Foxbat" (the Soviet MiG-25) set the 1,000-kilometer closed course record. Ever since, every SR-71 crew member and almost everyone associated with the airplane has been itching to let us put in the books, officially, what we do nearly every day we fly the bird. However, for all those years, due to security reasons, we'd had to wait.

The countdown began with about a week to go before the big day. We spent hours studying the missions that had been prepared by the men back in the Plans Shop. Because of the impact on the normal weekly training schedule and the sonic-boom problem along the route, we were not allowed to practice the mission in the aircraft beforehand. The simulator is an excellent training aid, with three-dimensional motion and performance characteristics identical to the aircraft. After two practice runs, we satisfied ourselves with every aspect of the overall plan and felt ready for the real thing.

As I climbed into the cockpit and sat there while the . . . staff finished strapping me in . . . I realized that I was just a bit excited and maybe even a bit nervous (I would never have admitted it then). From that point on, things started to get busy, and I forgot about the butterflies. . . .

The engines were slowly advanced and the brakes were released at the scheduled takeoff time—to the second. A slight pause and we were at maximum power, roaring down the runway like a three-wheeled dragster. Our acceleration was a little slower than usual today, because we were taking off a little heavier than normal, but we still reached 220-plus mph [350-plus km/h] [at] a little over 4,000 feet [1,200 meters], where we lifted into the air, accelerating and climbing on our way toward the entry gate over Edwards Air Force Base.

I started a slow left turn, heading east into Nevada, climbing at slightly less than the speed of sound until we were above 30,000 feet [9,150 meters]. Then, with a slight forward pressure on the stick, the rate of climb was slowed to allow the Mach indicator on the instrument panel to jump through Mach 1. It wasn't long until we were passing through Mach 2 and accelerating south through Nevada. This was a busy time in the cockpit due to the constant checking and cross-checking of engine and inlet instruments to be sure everything was working properly.

Passing 60,000 feet [18,300 meters] and Mach 2.6, everything was right on schedule. Just about then, "Sport Control" gave us a call advising of "radar contact." So far, not a single deviation from the plan. Taking a second to look out the canopy window, I could see Fresno, California off to my left, and the San Joaquin Valley . . . all around [it]. Looking skyward, I could see black sky and a bit of the earth's curvature.

We were now heading almost straight south, aiming at Los Angeles. Our altitude was right at 80,000 feet [24,400 meters]; our Mach indicator was stable at over three times the speed of sound. Fifteen seconds more (about eight miles) and we began a 90-degree left turn. Immediately after rollout, we entered the first timing gate. The aircraft was still running very smoothly and we expected no problems — after all, we've flown these same speeds under similar situations, routinely, for years.

OK, this was it! The wings were level . . . our Mach was just a little less than planned, so a little increase in throttle position . . . there was the Mach we were looking for. The ground speed was just under 2,200 mph [3,540 km/h], but we knew we had a headwind, and it would be a tailwind coming out, so we were all set. A call from "Sport Control" reconfirmed that they had radar contact and that we were over the entry gate. I made every effort to hold the altitude and speed; we didn't want to have to do it over again.

Wouldn't you know it! The right inlet encountered some roughness, then cleared quickly. Our speed and altitude were still right on. Twenty seconds later, we had "Sport Control" confirm our position. Now all we had to do is turn around and fly the course in the opposite direction, average out the two speeds, and we're down. To turn around, we had to turn 90 degrees left and 270 degrees right. That took 750 miles and more than 20 minutes! We flew north out of California into Nevada and right down the "strip" of Las Vegas, then began the big right turn that took us into Utah, Arizona, and finally back into California, heading west.

We flew the exact same course we flew the first time. The ground track was the same, the altitude had to be nearly identical, and we looked for, basically, the same Mach number as [we did] during the first pass. We used some fuel in our turn, and the aircraft was lighter; but because the rules restricted us to our first altitude of approximately 80,000 feet [24,384 meters], it was . . . hard to keep the machine from going faster than we are programmed to go. Therefore, as we approached the entry gate for the second time, the throttles were pulled back and, I assure you, there was no time for sightseeing.

"Good run . . . looks A-OK," says "Sport Control" as we exited [from] the course and started a slow right turn and began our 250-mile [400-kilometer] descent and deceleration for the landing at Beale Air Force Base. The pressure was off. The landing was a piece of cake. The double-delta wing design allows you to float a little and, actually, makes a bad landing difficult. When we landed, the record was still unofficial, but all the data looked like we had a real world speed record.

Indeed, Colonel Joersz had an Absolute World Air Speed Record — one that stands a good chance of being in the FAI record book for a long time. Together with the record set by the fighter version of the "Blackbird," the Lockheed airplane has held the classic speed record since 1965, longer than any other airplane.

Propellors Prevail

The era of privately financed attempts on the Absolute World Air Speed Record ended in 1931 with Lady Houston's donation of a half-million dollars which made possible the Supermarine S.6B. The seaplane's 1931 Schneider Race victory and subsequent speed record of 407 mph (655 km/h) was the only nongovernmental effort in a decade; after that, no private group made a serious attempt. For reasons of economics, and because of the technology available, only governments captured major speed records, beginning with Francesco Agello's 1933 record of 424 mph (682 km/h), set in a Macchi-Castoldi MC.72.

As detailed in Chapter 4, there remained considerable interest in the land-plane record when seaplanes dominated the Absolute World Air Speed Record. When the technological explosion of World War II brought jet-propelled airplanes to the fore, private interest focused on the record for piston engines, since jets were the exclusive preserve of the military.

Even if the Absolute World Air Speed Record was beyond reach, there remained the challenge of making a propellor-driven airplane go faster than it had ever gone. What made that such an appealing goal was the existing record: 469 mph (755 km/h), still held at the end of World War II by Fritz Wendel flying the Messerschmitt Me-209V-1 in 1939. Whatever else the Messerschmitt stood for during the war, its speed record was intact.

Many better designed and more powerful propellor-driven airplanes were built during World War II. And then there were the jets. Although the latter were meant for high speeds at high altitudes, most had proponents who insisted they could surpass the record held by the Me-209V-1. In the aftermath of the war, most fighter planes were destroyed. No one had any use for them. The military was delighted with the new jets, whereas civilians had little use for single-seat airplanes that could fly more than 400 mph (644 km/h). Flyers returning from the war who wanted to remain in aviation thought more in terms of small, inexpensive Piper Cubs for joyriding, or surplus transport planes with which to start a new airline.

The weekend that World War II began, the National Air Races were held at Cleveland, Ohio. When the races were resumed on Labor Day weekend 1946, the availability of cheap surplus warplanes injected new life into the classic aerial extravaganza.

Brightly painted P-38 Lightnings, P-39 Airacobras, P-51 Mustangs, P-63 Kingcobras, and F4U Corsairs filled the hangars and ramps near packed grandstands at Cleveland's Hopkins Airport. Although some had been specially modified for the Thompson, Bendix, Sohio, and other trophy races, many were still in military makeup. Yet even the slowest of these "racers" was much faster than the finest of custom-built prewar racers; thus the weekend was dominated by machines that had cost their owners as little as $1,000.

The first postwar Thompson Trophy Race was won by Alvin Johnston in his well-modified Airacobra, "Cobra II," at 374 mph (602 km/h) around a closed course and in heavy traffic. He flew his qualifying lap at 409 mph (658 km/h), which suggests a straight-and-level speed about 435 mph (700 km/h). With a few changes for record flying, "Tex" Johnston's airplane probably could have challenged the propellor-driven record. There was no money in setting speed records, however, whereas plenty of cash could be won in pylon racing at Cleveland. The first prize in the Thompson Trophy Race was over $15,000 — too much to be ignored by a speed flyer not satisfied with ordinary flying.

An airplane that had been prepared for pylon racing was, of course, also in good shape for setting records. A pylon racer had been lightened by removing such items as guns, armor plate, and radios. With less weight to be lifted, the airplane needed less wing area; thus its wing could be shortened, which cut the weight even more. With no guns, its gun ports could be filled in and smoothed over. With less concern for the pilot's reduced visibility, the canopy could be lowered and thus streamlined. The engine no longer had to be highly dependable; so it could be souped up.

The first ex-military airplane to make an attempt on a speed record was a Goodyear-built FG-1D Corsair. In the 1946 Thompson Trophy Race, Cook Cleland, a retired Navy pilot, flew it at a speed of 357 mph (575 km/h). Cook saw immediately that his racer wasn't fast enough to threaten the German-held piston record (which was more than 100 mph [160 km/h] faster), but other records were waiting to be broken.

One of those records was the American Air Speed Record, held since 1935 by Howard Hughes, at 352 mph (566 km/h). Even more vulnerable was the Women's World Speed Record, held since 1938 by Jackie Cochran, at 292 mph (470 km/h), in a prototype Seversky P-35 Army pursuit. Obviously, Cook was not eligible for the women's record; but one of his associates was. Marge Hurlburt had been a schoolteacher, flight instructor, mechanic, and WASP ferry pilot.

Cleland, who didn't need the Corsair for racing, replaced it with two F2G-1

Corsairs. The F2G-1 was an experimental version of the FG-1D, but with nearly twice its horsepower. So, in March 1947, with the small airport at Cleland's hometown of Willoughby, Ohio covered with frozen slush, Marge, the ground crew, and the Corsair FG-1D "Lucky Gallon" were in Tampa, Florida.

A three-kilometer (1.86-mile) course was laid out from Peter O. Knight Airport, east-northeast across an arm of Tampa Bay to a spit of land. On the afternoon of March 16, a pair of Aeronca light planes were positioned above the course at each end to ensure that Hurlburt did not exceed the altitude limits or dive onto the course. At the airport, a large crowd waited. They had been drawn by the All-Women Air Show, which included stunt flying, a small aerobatics contest, and novelty acts.

Hurlburt took off a few minutes before 4:00 P.M. and headed to the course for the first speed record attempt in the United States in more than a decade. After four official passes, she turned back to the airport. She was in the air only 20 minutes, but it was long enough to bring her the Women's World Air Speed Record, at 337.63 mph (543.61 km/h). Although Hughes' U.S. mark held firm, the handwriting was on the wall: before long, a faster pylon racer would take the title away from him.

Hurlburt hoped to fly a new Goodyear "midget" racer* she had helped build in September 1947, but at the time the rules forbade women and men entering the same pylon race. After some successful racing of a modified North American AT-6 Texan trainer in events exclusively for women, Hurlburt died in the crash of a plane at an air show. Her Corsair FG-1D was soon dismantled and substantial parts of it went to Walter Soplata, a private collector who has a museum near Newbury, Ohio.

If Marge Hurlburt was a lucky young woman who got a chance at a record because of a friend, the next person to challenge a major record was quite different. In 1938, Jackie Cochran raced in several prewar Bendix Transcontinental Derbies, beating nine men. The wife of a wealthy industrialist, she was the most famous woman flyer since Amelia Earhart. When Cochran decided to try for a record, she had the talent, reputation, and connections to get the finest in equipment and crew available. Choosing a highly modified P-51C Mustang, she placed second in a field of 22 in the 1946 Bendix Race, from Los Angeles to Cleveland. Although it resembled an early Mustang, Cochran's green number 13 was lightweight, clean, and powerful.

The first record on her agenda was not the classic three-kilometer dash, but the 100-kilometer closed-course run. A course was laid out between the ranch at Indio, California, which she and her husband owned, and the small town of Hemet, 31 miles (50 kilometers) away. She would fly the course in one direction, make a fast 180-degree turn, and head back to the starting point, with her total time counting. Because of the elevation — nearly a mile above sea level — she would gain some advantage from the thinner air, yet the runs could be timed with stopwatches, since she would come close to the timers.

Just after 11:00 A.M., December 10, 1947, Cochran took off from Thermal

---

*A racing airplane with an engine not more than 190-cubic-inch (3.1-cubic-centimeter) displacement.

Airport. She made the single flight around the 100-kilometer course and landed with two important records: 469.549 mph (755.668 km/h). Cochran took the women's piston-engined speed record from Marge Hurlburt by a wide margin and set an Absolute World Air Speed Record for propellor-driven airplanes on a closed circuit of any distance. Actually, by topping the Messerschmitt record of 1939 by a fraction of a mile per hour, she set the Absolute World Air Speed Record for piston-engine airplanes, though no such record is formally recognized by the FAI.

A week later, Cochran was at it again, this time going for the three-kilometer record — the most important speed mark anyone can hold. A course was laid out in the Coachilla Valley, 3 miles (5 kilometers) west of the Salton Sea. Again, she used the P-51C, which had performed flawlessly on the 100-kilometer run. She took off from Thermal at 9:40 A.M. and headed south. Her first two runs were for practice, to get acquainted with the course and the markings she would have to follow at better than 7 miles per minute (11 kilometers per minute) at an altitude of only a few feet. The third run was a good one, but on the fourth Cochran flew behind the timing cameras, then suddenly climbed to avoid a wandering private plane. This put her above the maximum altitude allowed by the FAI rules.

Because she needed four consecutive satisfactory passes to qualify, she made five, just to be sure. The last four were the best, averaging 412.002 mph (663.054 km/h). Cochran's speed was well below the record (469 mph [755 km/h]), but she took the American three-kilometer speed record for propellor-driven airplanes.

Cochran flew her Mustang to third place in the 1948 Bendix Trophy Race, at 446 mph (718 km/h). As it was being ferried home to California by another pilot, however, it crashed and was destroyed. Cochran carried on with a second Mustang, a converted F-6C photoplane. In 1949, Joe DeBona flew the airplane in winning the last civilian Bendix Race, at a record 470 mph (756 km/h). Before she got another crack at a record, however, a promising newcomer emerged: Betty Skelton. Skelton flew a tiny Pitts Special biplane in the air show at Cleveland in 1947. The bright-red aerobatic plane was a startling contrast to the large, powerful racing planes surrounding it.

Aerobatic and air-show flying was Skelton's first love; but speed in the air, on the ground, and on the water was starting to take over. For an attempt on the Women's World Air Speed Record, she arranged to fly the racing P-51D Mustang that belonged to Woody Edmondson, the 1948 All-American Aerobatic Champion. Though not as highly modified as Cochran's long-distance racer, the P-51D still had enough power to put a dent in Cochran's mark of 412 mph (663 km/h).

Betty made her first try on July 11, 1948, over the same three-kilometer (1.86-mile) course at Tampa, Florida that Marge Hurlburt used a year earlier. Taking off from Peter O. Knight Airport, she turned official runs of 389 and 405 mph (626 and 652 km/h). As she started the third run, the water-injection system failed, and she had to make an emergency landing. The damage, however, could be repaired. The next day, July 12, she went at it again. This time, her first two runs reportedly averaged 421.6 mph (678.5 km/h). Suddenly, the well-worn Rolls Royce Merlin V12 blew up! Cochran, deciding not to bail out over Tampa Bay (she didn't know how to swim), managed a dead-stick landing.

Skelton had been so near to the Women's World Record, yet there was nothing to show for it. She tried to make arrangements for a new record attempt, to be made the day after the September 1948 Cleveland Air Races; but the management turned her down, claiming there would be too much cleaning up to do, and that most of the officials needed would have gone home.

Undaunted, Skelton changed her plans. This time, she wanted to make the attempt during the January 1949 Miami All-American Air Maneuvers, second only in prestige to the Cleveland National Air Races. To give herself a better chance of breaking several important records, she talked Cook Cleland into letting her fly one of his F2G-1 Corsairs. Cook and his partner Dick Becker had swept the 1947 Thompson Trophy Race in the Corsairs. They might have repeated the feat in 1948 had not both blown cowling air scoops loose during the race. The Corsairs appeared capable of much more than 400 mph (645 km/h) around a pylon race course, and even more in straight flight. In case something happened to interfere with Cochran's plans to fly a Corsair, she arranged to borrow a friend's deHavilland Mosquito bomber for the attempt.

Skelton made no more tries for an air-speed record. Her attention turned increasingly toward aerobatics and air-show flying. In her Pitts Special, she won the Women's International Aerobatics Championship in 1949 and 1950, then moved away from flying into land- and water-speed records, where she set numerous marks.

In the spring of 1949, another woman began making plans to go after the women's record and, hopefully, the overall propellor-driven record. Dot Lemon, like Betty Skelton and Marge Hurlburt, a pilot in women's air races, convinced J. D. Reed, a wealthy Texas industrialist, to let her fly his newest racing plane, a highly modified P-51D. The airplane was not only the finest modified Mustang of the Cleveland Air Races era, its performance wasn't surpassed until the 1970s, when the Reno Air Races stimulated innovation in racers of the Unlimited Class. The P-51D, christened "Beguine," had the usual improvements for reducing weight and wind resistance—with one big difference: the bulky air intake and radiator under the airplane's belly were removed and replaced by slim, cylindrical radiators on the wingtips that resembled small jet engines.

Lemon hoped to make her attempt—which, in view of the later performance of the airplane, stood a good chance of success—on the weekend of July 4, 1949, on a three-kilometer course near La Porte, Texas, not far from Houston. For some reason, the flight never took place. It could have been that the airplane wasn't ready for all-out speed flying, and was being held in reserve for the more newsworthy Thompson Trophy Race two months later.

As it turned out, fame never came to the "Beguine" despite the $100,000 rumored to have been spent on it. Bill Odom, a successful round-the-world flyer, was chosen to race the airplane at Cleveland. Odom qualified at 406 mph (653 km/h) and then won the preliminary Sohio Trophy Race easily at 388 mph (624 km/h). On the second lap of the final civilian Thompson Trophy Race, on September 5, 1949, Odom failed to negotiate a pylon turn and crashed into a house, killing himself and two occupants. The dark-green "Beguine" was gone, and so was the traditional Cleveland Air Races, though the two were not related. Their fate was sealed when the military, preoccupied with the Korean War, withdrew support from the races, and they faded from the aviation calendar.

The final major propellor-driven speed record set by Jackie Cochran was also the first recognized by the FAI for its new 15/25-kilometer distance category. Using a 16-kilometer (9.9-mile) straight course running from the Cochran-Odlum Ranch eastward, she operated out of nearby Thermal Airport. On April 9, 1951, Cochran made six runs over the course, though only two were required. The first run was called a practice run, the next two were missed by some of the officials, the fourth and fifth were acceptable, and the sixth was not recorded by the cameras. Her speeds were 466 mph and 463 mph (750 and 745 km/h), for an official average of 464.38 mph (747.19 km/h). The airplane used was the modified P-51B Mustang purchased from DeBona.

One of the world's best-known flyers, Jackie Cochran was the most prolific record-setter in FAI history. She was raised in a foster home in Georgia and began flying while in her early twenties, placing well in numerous air races before World War II. She was a leader of the WASPS, women pilots who ferried military airplanes during the war; later, she headed a cosmetics firm that bore her name. Cochran was the first woman to fly an airplane faster than the speed of sound, and she carried on a considerable rivalry with Jacqueline Auriole of France. Cochran retired from active flying in 1970 after suffering a heart attack, and died in 1980.

Until now, all the postwar speed record attempts had been made by women pilots — probably more a coincidence than anything else. Scores of men were flying fast, piston-engined airplanes, but none had yet shown an interest in an assault on speed records. That is, not until Anson Johnson arrived on the scene. In 1948, "Johnnie" Johnson entered an innocuous P-51D Mustang in the Thompson Trophy Race, emerging the surprise winner when all but three of the ten starters dropped out with mechanical trouble. A pilot for National Airlines, Johnson had suddenly achieved a measure of fame and some cash. He therefore set out to turn his racer into a truly competitive machine.

Foremost among the changes Johnson made was relocation of the under-fuselage radiator in the wings — though not at the tips, as was done in the "Beguine." He used Bell P-39 radiators mounted inside the wings, with air scoops cut in the leading edges and outlets on the upper surfaces of the wings, near the trailing edge. With power from a souped-up Rolls Royce Merlin Mark 225 engine, Johnson was in a good position to compete with experienced flyers and, possibly, win a race on his own rather than by default. In 1949, however, Johnson had his own troubles. He had difficulty retracting his landing gear. When he was finally able to do so, and give the airplane full throttle, he turned in an estimated 450 mph (725 km/h) on the straight stretches of the Cleveland race course, meanwhile trying to catch the 4,000-horsepower Corsairs of Cook Cleland and Ron Puckett. On the ninth lap, he heard strange noises, then saw smoke in the cockpit. The airplane was on fire, and he had to land at once.

That was the last of the classic Thompson Trophy Races; thereafter, the award was restricted to achievements in military flying. With the end of the

Cleveland Air Races, there were no more pylon competitions for the large Thompson-class airplanes. Interest in authentically restored former military airplanes had not yet emerged; about the only event available to a fast, expensive airplane was the 10-year-old speed record still held by Fritz Wendel.

Johnson, with limited financial backing, had his Mustang ready for its big test on June 6, 1952. He would be using Shell tri-methyl triptane fuel rumored to be 200 octane. A 3-kilometer (1.86-mile) course was laid out near Key Biscayne, Florida. The trials were set for early morning, but by the time NAA officials had their timing apparatus ready, it was midmorning and the air had warmed up considerably. Still, because Johnson had turned in an unofficial 500-plus mph (800-plus km/h) in practice the day before, he thought a little loss of power due to the heat wouldn't hurt.

Taking off about 9:00, Johnson made his first pass at what the local newspapers said was 510 mph (821 km/h). The second run was at 503 mph (810 km/h). Because his engine was beginning to overheat, he canceled the remainder of the runs. Just how fast he flew was not preserved in NAA files; in view of the far superior power and streamlining of the airplane that eventually flew that fast officially, it seems unlikely that it was as fast as reported. Not realizing this, Johnson was satisfied with the P-51's performance. He determined to make more runs on June 8, beginning at 6:35 A.M., when the air would be cool and calm — ideal for the purpose. That day, he tore through the course eight times in 30 minutes. His fastest single run was at 444.5 mph (715 km/h), with the best four consecutive runs averaging 428.9 mph (690 km/h), well under the speed announced at the time.

Johnson probably would have laid claim to a new American propellor-driven air-speed record — if not the World Record he coveted — had not an NAA official loaded the film incorrectly in a timing camera, rendering the data unsuitable for verifying the record. The Mustang performed well, and all eight passes were uneventful; yet Johnson had nothing to show for his effort. Since the fault was its own, the NAA offered to forego its usual fee of several thousand dollars for another attempt at a later date. Johnson planned another attempt with the same airplane for February 1953, then canceled it, deciding instead on early 1954. He first talked about a course at Wayne Major Airport, near Detroit, Michigan, then one at Boca Raton, Florida, during the Carnival of Speed Week, January 31 to February 7, 1954. Along the way, however, he lost a sponsor; then the Mark 225 engine required a major overhaul during which it vanished. That may have been the last straw, for it forced him to switch to an engine of less power and greater weight.

The P-51D Mustang passed through several owners' hands, then sat out in the salty air of southern Florida. When the sport was resurrected at Reno in the 1960s, two racing pilots considered rebuilding the airplane, but it was so corroded that nothing could be done. At last report, the P-51D was in the collection of the Connecticut Aeronautical Historical Association at Hartford, awaiting restoration to display status.

As the Cleveland National Air Races became only a memory, a few enthusiasts kept up interest in sport racing. Around 1962, Cook Cleland, winner of the 1947 and 1949 Thompson Trophy Races, held out some hope of rebuilding an F2G-1 Corsair for a speed-record attempt. The project got as far as shipping the pieces of the late Ben McKillen's number 57 to Philadelphia, where Martin Decker, an NAA executive and a manufacturer, would arrange for the costly reconstruction. The airplane was in such poor condition, however, that it had to be scrapped.

In September 1964, in the barren desert northeast of Reno, big-time air racing came back to life after 15 years. Although it wasn't Cleveland, it was racing by Thompson- and Bendix-class airplanes and by small, fast "midgets." Not a single man flying the "Unlimited Class" airplanes had raced them before, nor had any of their airplanes been on a pylon race course. Once they learned how, though, the sport picked up where it left off in 1949, with the introduction of clever, effective ideas in powerplants and streamlining.

The most interesting of these new airplanes was the Grumman F8F Bearcat, the last propellor-driven fighter manufactured in the United States, and an airplane not available to private owners in the heyday of the Cleveland Air Races. The Bearcat was fast and highly maneuverable — two important traits in closed-course racing. Of several Bearcats entered at Reno in 1964, the most significant was owned and flown by Darryl Greenamyer, a test pilot for Lockheed. That first year, most Unlimited racers sported bright paint schemes but evidenced little in the way of meaningful modifications. By contrast, Greenamyer's was natural aluminum in color but had a small plexiglass canopy and a complete clean-up.

Greenamyer's racing performance at Reno in 1964 was only so-so; but he won the Unlimited race in 1965, at 396 mph (637 km/h), equal to the best turned in at Cleveland in the "old days." With continued improvements, Greenamyer added sufficient speed during the winter of 1965-66 to justify an attempt on the German-held piston-engine record. The Bearcat had power similar to that of the Messerschmitt Me-209V-1; in addition, it was a more flyable, modern airplane.

The first test was set for the Los Angeles Air Races, May 29-31, 1966, at Fox Field, near Lancaster, California. Originally, Greenamyer was to be one of three pilots going for the 27-year-old record; the others were Tommy Taylor, in a Hawker Sea Fury, and Chuck Lyford, in a P-51 Mustang. When the time arrived for the test, however, only Darryl was on the line, his Bearcat gleaming in its white paint with light metallic blue arrows running the length of the fuselage and wings. The change most evident in the airplane was a shortened vertical tail (to reduce drag). During the air show, Greenamyer made only two runs on the 3-kilometer (1.86-mile) course. Retiring from the event, he said the airplane lacked lateral stability because of the smaller tail and jokingly suggested that it might be trying to follow the arrows on the wings instead of those on the fuselage as it snaked from side to side at high speed. Greenamyer said he had also been plagued by the high winds and blowing sand prevalent during the show.

Greenamyer was determined, though, more determined than anyone had been in a long time. He wanted the 3-kilometer record badly. While he made plans, Greenamyer also worked on his airplane, flying it in every Unlimited Class race he could get to. In late 1966, he won at Reno for the second time and repeated the win the next two years, bringing his record in the Unlimited Class to four straight and dominating the field.

Greenamyer's second record attempt was set for late August 1968, not long before he was to be at Reno trying to win enough prize money to pay for the attempts at the record. On August 24, the Bearcat was filled with a special blend of gasoline and nitro-methane tailored to the temperature and humidity. It was towed out to the end of the runway and started (the racer had no starter of its own, and had to use a portable unit).

Using less than full power, Greenamyer streaked through the course at what looked to the few spectators present like at least 500 mph (800 km/h). The NAA timers said otherwise, that the speed was 447.5 mph (720 km/h). A real disappointment; but there was still time — and power — in reserve. A second try was somewhat faster; but the timers missed the first run, and the flight counted for naught.

Late in the day, with time running out, a third try was scheduled; but the engine refused to start because of the failure of the fuel pump. Sunday, August 25, remained. A flight at 11:00 A.M. was aborted when the engine began to run rough due to excessive nitro-methane fuel additive. After a quick pit stop to change the fuel mixture, Greenamyer went back up. The first run was a beauty, with a speed of 498 mph (801 km/h); the engine ran rougher than ever, however, and this time the problem was more serious — a burned piston.

Back home, Greenamyer and his crew of friends and co-workers changed two pistons and cylinders, then scheduled another record attempt for September 8. This time, the entire engine seized up after a short test run. They now had to face the obvious need to replace the engine. Back in Los Angeles a standard Pratt & Whitney R-2800 engine was installed, which, though it did not develop the power of the special engine, had enough to give Greenamyer another win at Reno.

In August 1969, one month before the sixth annual Reno Air Races, Greenamyer and his now famous number 1 "Conquest I" were at Edwards AF Base, familiar to Greenamyer, who at the time was flying the super-secret SR-71 "Blackbird" for Lockheed. He was in the Mojave Desert for another try at Wendel's durable propellor-driven record of 469.224 mph (754.981 km/h).

Greenamyer's first set of four passes over the 3-kilometer (1.86-mile) course, made shortly before noon on August 16, produced an oil-pressure problem. The four-pass average was an unofficial 475 mph (764 km/h). Whereas that was fast enough to break the record (474 mph would have done it), Greenamyer was so sure he could do better that he scheduled another run that afternoon. He took off from Edwards at 3:38 P.M. and made four runs in 25 minutes. The fastest (with the wind) was 510 mph (821 km/h), the slowest (against the wind) 454 mph (730.5 km/h). His average speed was a satisfying 482.462 mph (776.449 km/h), breaking a record that had stood for more than 30 years. A determined individual with a clear view of his goal had finally outsped the Third Reich's heavily financed propaganda Messerschmitt. Five years' work on a surplus U.S. Navy fighter plane had produced the world's fastest piston-engined airplane and the first to be clocked officially in excess of 500 mph (805 km/h).

The Bearcat continued racing long after Greenamyer's goal had been achieved. A variety of mechanical problems held down his speed at Reno in 1970, but Greenamyer was back in the winner's circle in 1971 with a winning speed of 414 mph (666 km/h). In 1972, the Bearcat was raced at Reno by Richard Laidley, whose excellent flying was negated by a disqualification for low flying. Greenamyer's final race in the number 1 (now painted yellow) occurred at Reno in 1975, when he set a one-lap qualifying record of 436 mph (702 km/h) but was prevented from further racing by mechanical problems.

In January 1977, the Bearcat was used for a purpose far from normal: Greenamyer made a transcontinental flight to deliver it to the National Air & Space Museum. Despite the airplane's limited fuel capacity and the lack of a radio, as well as other necessities for a winter flight, he made it in a week of difficult flying.

The special Grumman F8F-2 has undergone a long series of modifications, most of them highly successful. Its length is about 30 feet (9.1 meters), including the propellor spinner from a P-51H Mustang and the specially designed tail cone; its wingspan is 29.7 feet (9 meters), clipped down from the standard 35.5 feet (10.8 meters), including computer-designed Hoerner wingtips. The empty weight, while not known, is considerably less than a standard Bearcat's 7,700 pounds (3,488 kilograms).

The oil coolers, which had been in the leading edges of the wings, were relocated inside the water-alcohol tank in the fuselage. The normal bubble canopy was replaced by a tiny one made from the same mold as those for "Cosmic Wind" Formula One racers. Because the electrical and hydraulic systems were removed, the landing gear had to be raised with compressed nitrogen and lowered by gravity. The propellor was from a Douglas A-1 Skyraider attack bomber. The Pratt & Whitney R-2800 engine was modified with parts from numerous different versions, to produce an estimated maximum power of about 3,000 horsepower.

As for Darryl Greenamyer, his love for flying low and fast brought him fame and notoriety in the sporting aviation community. At Reno, he was invariably the lowest man on the race course; his Bearcat had so little downward visibility that he had to fly lower than the others in order to keep them safely in sight. Greenamyer, the undisputed king of Unlimited Class pylon racing, was now the holder of the World Speed Record for propellor-driven airplanes. He was also a very experienced test pilot, with considerable time in such high-performance jets as Lockheed's F-104 Starfighter and the Mach 3-plus YF-12A and SR-71 Blackbird. What challenges were left for a speed-oriented flyer?

About 1966, when Greenamyer began to take charge of Unlimited Class air racing, he quietly got himself wrapped up in an unusual project: building an F-104. Of course, Lockheed, Greenamyer's employer, had been doing this for years; but Greenamyer had something special in mind for an airplane which, at the time, was solely for military purposes. Slowly gathering parts as he found them, he methodically accumulated the parts for his own Starfighter. Why was he doing that? The answer was, to go after the "absolute" 3-kilometer (1.86-mile) speed record at low altitude, long considered the permanent possession of Navy Lt. Hunt Hardisty and the McDonnell F4H Phantom II he flew 902.115 mph (1,451.503 km/h) in 1961. The danger of further attempts at such speed and so near the ground had prevented any air force from seriously contemplating an assault on that particular record.

Either the danger was of little concern to Greenamyer, or it was part of the challenge. He spent 10 years creating his private F-104. Now that he had a magnificent airplane painted in surrealistic swirls of red, white, yellow, and orange, Greenamyer wasn't about to let it gather dust. On October 2, 1976, the airplane was finally ready for its debut. It would make the traditional four runs over a 3-kilometer course near Mud Lake, southeast of Tonopah, Nevada, on the perimeter of an Air Force gunnery range. Although the airplane was as ready as it could be, given the limited finances of its owner/builder/pilot, other matters had to be contended with. Probably the most crucial matter was fuel. The special F-104 carried more than 1,000 gallons (3,758 liters), enough to fly at least 1,000 miles (1,600 kilometers) at its cruising altitude of 40,000 feet (12,200 meters). The speed runs, however, must be made within 100 meters (328 feet) of the ground, where a modern jet engine is outrageously inefficient. The runs should take no more than a few minutes, yet there was concern that the tanks would not hold enough fuel to do the job with safety reserve.

Test runs over the course were made on Saturday, October 2, in preparation for the official trials the next day. On Sunday morning, four dashes were flown right on schedule; but trouble with a fuel pump so reduced the afterburner's thrust that the speed was below the existing record. Changes were soon made, and another flight was made that afternoon. This time, the airplane and pilot performed flawlessly. The timing cameras, however, produced only fuzzy images unusable for official verification of a set of passes that reportedly averaged nearly 1,010 mph (1,625 km/h).

It took Greenamyer a year to prepare for more speed runs, even with the financial support of Ed Browning, an Idaho sportsman, whose "Red Baron" air racing team included a highly modified Mustang. Preparing a supersonic jet is considerably more complex than getting a Bearcat ready to race at Reno. But at last, in October 1977, the world's hottest private airplane was ready to go. The crew gathered for the test at Mud Lake, at an elevation of almost 1 mile (1.6 kilometers), where high-speed cameras manned by NAA officials would zero in on the F-104 as it flew at Mach 1.3 no more than 100 feet (30.5 meters) above the ground.

The airplane left the ground at 6:15 P.M., October 24, and was back down at 6:35. In that 20 minutes, Greenamyer flew the 3 kilometers (1.86 miles) four times at speeds ranging from 977 mph to 1,000 mph (1,572 to 1,609 km/h), with the result that he set a record; 988.260 mph (1,590.45 km/h). He missed the 1,000-mph mark by a fraction of a second for his average speed, and by an eyelash on his third run, when he was clocked at 999.971 mph (1,608.953 km/h). Greenamyer, however, held a pair of records that no one before him held — or probably even considered: the fastest human in the world in a piston-engined airplane, and the fastest in a jet at low altitude.

Sadly, another pilot with a dream of a special speed record died that weekend. Bob Reichart, an antique-airplane enthusiast, of Ojai, California, spent several years re-creating one of the great pre-World War II racers, Ben Howard's "Mr. Mulligan," starting with pieces of the original recovered from a plateau in New Mexico where it crashed in 1936. Because Reichart built a new "Mr. Mulligan" from many of the old parts, it was considered a restoration of the original. His goal was to set some speed records and then retire the airplane to a museum. On October 24, he made four runs along the same 3-kilometer course in FAI Class C.l.c., breaking the old record of 239.5 mph (385.5 km/h) with a speed of 284.4 mph (457.7 km/h). The next day, to boost the airplane's weight into Class C.1.d. for another record, he added his wife Shelly. Reichart bore down on the course, skimming the gently rolling terrain at a speed said to have been at least 330 mph (531 km/h), when everything seemed to happen at once. One wheel hit a hillock of dried mud, and the airplane cartwheeled across the desert, destroying itself and killing both occupants. Reichart's first mark went into the book as an official record, but his second could not, even though he made four successful passes over the course. FAI rules have long required that the airplane land intact at the end of a record attempt.

The successful F-104 "Red Baron" probably should have been retired to a museum, but Greenamyer had other plans for it. He wanted to capture the World Altitude Record for Airplanes held by Alexander Fedotov in a special E-266M (a modified MiG-25 "Foxbat" fighter). With as much power as the F-104, and a cleaner, lighter airframe that once held the record, at 91,200 feet (27,810 meters), he felt he could top the current record of 123,534 feet (37,650 meters).

In February 1978, as he completed a flight test of a water-injection system designed to add thrust to the engine, something went wrong with the Starfighter's landing gear. The nose wheel and one of the two main wheels extended and locked, but the other main wheel did not. Greenamyer tried everything he could think of, then flew low past observers, who reported that the left landing gear was not secure. He then flew to Edwards AF Base, where he let down slowly and gingerly felt for the runway. The left gear felt spongy; the control tower said the gear looked like it was not solidly in place. It was considered extremely dangerous to try to belly-land the fast fighter, and Greenamyer chose the only alternative he had: fly to the approved area in the vast test center, climb to 10,000 feet (3,000 meters), and eject. He landed by parachute with no ill effects. The crippled Starfighter hit the ground among the scrub and was destroyed. Greenamyer's plan was finished. The dream of holding two major jet records was gone, with one record untouched.

While Greenamyer's achievements were there for all to see, one of his associates saw this as a challenge. Ed Browning had long supported the most highly modified P-51 Mustang, the Red Baron RB-51. The airplane had been raced with considerable success by several pilots, including Greenamyer, who flew it to a record-setting win at Reno in 1977, averaging 431 mph (693.5 km/h) around a pylon race course. In repeating the win in 1978, Steve Hinton established the potent Mustang as the airplane to beat.

What was so special about number 5? Starting with the front end, it had the first set of counterrotating propellors seen on a speed airplane since the Macchi-Castoldi MC.72 flew 441 mph (708 km/h) in 1934. The propellors were a modified unit from a British Avro Shackleton patrol bomber and were connected to a Rolls Royce Griffon engine with 40 percent greater displacement than the Merlin (with which the Mustang had become a legend). The extra power necessitated extensive changes in the rear; therefore, a much larger (and less graceful) tail was installed to counteract all that horsepower. This gave the airplane, already fitted with a tiny canopy and shortened wings, a disproportionate look. It was meant to be fast, not pretty.

Any airplane that could regularly top 435 mph (700 km/h) around Reno's lop-sided race course should be able to do at least 50 mph (80 km/h) better on a straight run. Browning and Hinton prepared to find out. They knew it would take more than 487 mph (784 km/h) to break the Bearcat's 10-year-old record.

The Red Baron RB-51 and its crew went to the speed course at Tonopah, Nevada, the course Greenamyer had used in setting his jet speed record. On August 9, 1979, test runs of the Mustang produced 477 mph (768 km/h), well under the record but indicative of the airplane's potential once the power of its Rolls Royce Griffon was unleashed. The next day, a full-power attempt was about to begin when, at 3,000 rpm and 100 inches of manifold pressure (both figures were far above the design limits of the engine), some important parts broke. Hinton managed to glide the airplane back to the runway, where he landed. Mechanics set to work replacing the engine.

On August 11, the new engine was flight tested and carefully broken in in preparation for speed runs the next day. After three hours of running, the engine was pronounced ready, and shortly after noon on August 12, Hinton hit the course wide open — at 3,050 rpm and 100 inches. His four runs averaged 489.25 mph (787 km/h), 2 mph (3.2 kilometers) more than was needed for a record. Browning, however, was determined to reach 500 mph (805 km/h); so they prepared to try harder. On August 13, as Hinton prepared to attack the course, a spark plug blew out of the engine while it was turning 3,100 rpm and pulling 103 inches (262 centimeters) of manifold pressure. By the time repairs were made, the air was too warm and turbulent for safe flying.

At last, on Thursday morning, August 14, 1979, everything seemed in order. Hinton was given permission to use maximum power regardless of the risk to the engine. At 9:15 A.M., he took off, pushing the throttle to the limit. The Griffon engine was turning 3,150 rpm and pulling 108 inches of manifold pressure, about 3,800 horsepower. The first pass was completed in just over 13 seconds, for a speed of 502 mph (808 km/h). The next pass took 0.1 second longer, working out to 498 mph (801 km/h). At that rate, not only would Greenamyer's record be broken, but the 500-mph (805-km/h) barrier might be topped. The second down-wind run was somewhat slower, at 500 mph, and the final up-wind run was made at 497 mph (799 km/h). Hinton's average speed was 499.059 mph (803.152 km/h), which beat the record by almost 17 mph (26 km/h). It just missed the 500-mph goal, but that was secondary. An estimated $300,000 had been invested in the RB-51.

Next stop for Hinton and the bright-red racer was Reno, a month later and a few hundred miles northwest. He turned in the fastest lap yet by a propellor-driven airplane on a race course: 442 mph (711 km/h). When another modified Mustang boosted the record to 447 mph (719 km/h), the stage was set for a fast race. It was a nose-to-tail battle all the way, with Hinton trailing John Crocker by a smaller and smaller margin. As the finish line of the last lap came into view, though, the engine in Hinton's RB-51 began to give out. He had enough momentum to make it across the finish line and place second, at 415 mph (668 km/h); but in his eagerness to finish the race, he wasted precious speed that could have been converted into altitude, since it was clear that a forced landing was coming up. When the engine failed completely, the propellors went into flat pitch, causing tremendous wind resistance, and Hinton found himself unable to reach a runway. He disappeared from view behind a hill near the south end of the course, and all that could be seen from the grandstands was a plume of black smoke.

The airplane was demolished by the impact; somehow, Hinton, though seriously injured, was found intact and conscious by the rescue crew. He was rushed to a hospital while his friends at the airport, assuming that no one could have survived the crash, mourned his passing. Eventually he regained his health and flying status, but nothing salvageable remained from the RB-51, much to the chagrin of museum officials.

The dream of 500 mph (805 km/h) in a piston-engined airplane lives on. While once each step to greater speed opened another door to improved transportation and more effective combat, today the practical has stepped aside in favor of pure sport.

The Future of Speed Records

What future is there for efforts directed at new Absolute World Air Speed Records? Will new developments in materials, powerplants, and aerodynamics lead to higher speed records, as they often did in the first two-thirds of this century? Or have the times changed so much that the record has become an anachronism?

There is good reason to expect the Absolute World Air Speed Record, held since 1965 by Lockheed's exotic YF-12A and its near-twin SR-71A, to remain supreme for a long time—for several reasons.

First, the SR-71A, currently an active spy plane, probably has at least 400 mph (650 km/h) in reserve. For reasons of national security, there was no reason to push the airplane to its limit in 1976 when it set the present record of 2,194 mph (3,530 km/h), and numerous reasons not to do so.

Second, there is no indication the Soviet Union has much interest in challenging Lockheed and the United States for the record, even assuming the USSR has an airplane that can do it. The last Soviet Absolute World Air Speed Record was set more than 20 years ago, and no move has been made since. The E-266M did set a 500-kilometer (310-mph) closed-circuit record in 1967, of 1,853 mph (2,982 km/h), which suggests it can fly around a tighter course than the SR-71A. In the area of straight-line speed, however, the U.S. Air Force seems to be in charge.

Third, no country other than the United States and the USSR has shown interest in the absolute record since 1956, when the British turned their Fairey Delta 2 loose to set the first record over 1,000 mph (1,609 km/h). Clearly, however, the British possess no airplane that can approach the current record, and there is no sign that such a craft is being considered.

Fourth, the need for airplanes capable of speeds greater than the SR-71A's 2,600 mph (4,200 km/h) is minimal. Aerial reconnaissance has largely been replaced by satellite reconnaissance. For one thing, satellites are less vulnerable to interception.

Military airplanes such as the latest American and Soviet fighters are gradually approaching the speed of the SR-71A, but a more important need is for airplanes that can maneuver at high speed. The current Soviet-held mark for a 100-kilometer closed-circuit run is 1,619 mph (2,605 km/h), which involved flying for more than two minutes at a steady 4 Gs. Boosting the record to 2,000 mph (3,200 km/h) requires that the pilot experience more than 6 Gs, a force that potentially is destructive.

Thus, combat airplanes find themselves restricted by speed, while reconnaissance airplanes can use their level speed to great advantage. The SR-71A is said to require a radius of 90 miles (145 kilometers) to turn at high speed. Such a turn (of 180 degrees) would cover almost 300 miles (450 kilometers), seriously limiting the airplane's combat value.

Military leaders from all countries have long had to weigh the prestige and psychological advantages of setting speed records against the potential disadvantages, including the risk to pilots' lives, charges of wasting money, and the loss of vital secrets. Today, there seems to be less than ever for a country to gain from speed tests; thus, there remains little chance of there ever again being a glorious spree of record setting such as was seen in France in 1910-13, in the United States in the early 1920s, or between the United States and Great Britain after World War II.

If the Absolute World Air Speed Record looks safe, though, the piston-engine record race continues. Once Darryl Greenamyer broke the 30-year-old German record in 1969, many people assumed he would hold it indefinitely. His reign lasted only 10 years, and now several categories of airplanes are in the running for even faster records:

1. New Unlimited Class "warbird" pylon racers. The one-lap record at the Reno Air Races hit 450 mph (724 km/h) in 1981 and shows no sign of having reached a plateau. More power is being squeezed from modified Mustangs and other former military airplanes whose airframes are steadily being improved in streamlining. As it has long been, the main obstacle is money.

2. Custom-built Unlimited Class racers. These are still on the drawing boards and in the workshops, but they will soon emerge to challenge the 35-year supremacy of the large, powerful airplanes that attract crowds in the Nevada desert each September. The United States has many experienced, talented airplane designers and builders, thanks to the highly successful program of the Experimental Aircraft Association of encouraging individuals to build sport airplanes on their own.

With much less power than the souped-up (and thus temperamental) Rolls Royce and Pratt & Whitney engines that have long ruled the class, small custom-built racers should eventually take over. An unlimited racer with as little as 600 horsepower should be able to fly as fast as a modified fighter plane with 3,000, and with twice the power — 1,200 — it should be able to top 550 mph (885 km/h).

3. Custom-built speed-record airplanes. Since they have so little to justify

their existence economically, these are the most exotic of all. After all, one can fly faster than Mach 2 for the price of a ticket on a Concorde supersonic transport.

The challenge of flying faster than anyone has ever done with a given form of propulsion remains strong. And practicality has never played that important a role in racing or record setting.

The famous Italian industrial designer Luigi Colani has designed a shape for an airplane which he thinks can reach 560 mph (900 km/h) with a piston engine. Like all Colani's designs, be they airplanes or pencil sharpeners, this design resembles nothing previously seen, except perhaps on the scratch pad of a daydreaming schoolboy.

The fuselage is a tube squeezed narrow in the center and pointed at both ends. The small, thin wing has a sharply swept back leading edge, straight trailing edge, and thin winglets sticking up from the wingtips. The tail has four small, swept-back surfaces which form a cross, while there is a small canard surface at the front. At both ends are small, nonretractable wheels supported by streamlined struts, as well as small wheels at the wingtips. It is the propellors, however, that evoke the greatest surprise. The one at the rear has five scimitarlike blades swept forward so that they almost are parallel to the fuselage. The front propellor, of four blades, sweeps forward so sharply that it looks like it might be mounted on the nose of a James Bond car to slice up a foe's spare tire. Colani has said nothing about the powerplant for this novel craft, nor about the cost or who might pay it.

Another radical idea, one proposed to the National Aeronautic Association, suggests how far people are willing to go to break the propellor-driven record. One man, who insists on anonymity, asked for relief from the FAI rule that requires all four passes to be made without landing. He claims this would be impossible for the airplane he proposes, as its engine would be so highly souped up that it would likely fail and have to be changed after each run. Presumably, the man contemplates adapting the technology found in drag-racing engines to airplanes, so that a relatively light V8 engine which normally produces 300 horsepower can generate well over 1,000 for a very short time.

Thus, despite the lack of practical applications and the certainty of little publicity for even a successful record attempt, the lure remains. It may be partly for nostalgia, partly because of the conviction that the piston-engine airplane has not reached its limit, and partly because this is an area in which the individual can still try to climb to the top of a mountain without having to call for help from huge corporations or from governments.

For those whose finances preclude anything more than a modest investment, numerous record categories are available that may be within their means. The FAI record book has dozens of pages of speed, distance, and altitude categories that fit the needs of those with sport aircraft of many sizes and horsepower:

Class C.1.a/o—fixed-wing airplanes weighing no more than 300 kilograms (661 pounds), ready for takeoff.
Class C.1.a—300 to 500 kilograms (661 to 1,102 pounds).
Class C.1.b—500 to 1,000 kilograms (1,102 to 2,204 pounds).

Class C.1.c — 1,000 to 1,750 kilograms (2,204 to 3,858 pounds).
Class C.1.d — 1,750 to 3,000 kilograms (3,858 to 6,614 pounds).

Business and executive airplanes may set records in higher weight categories:

Class C.1.e — 3,000 to 6,000 kilograms (6,614 to 13,227 pounds).
Class C.1.f — 6,000 to 8,000 kilograms (13,227 to 17,636 pounds).
Class C.1.g — 8,000 to 12,000 kilograms (17,636 to 26,455 pounds).
Class C.1.h — 12,000 to 16,000 kilograms (26,455 to 35,274 pounds).
Class C.1.i — 16,000 to 20,000 kilograms (35,274 to 44,092 pounds).
Class C.1.j — 20,000 to 25,000 kilograms (44,092 to 57,320 pounds).
Class C.1.k — 25,000 to 35,000 kilograms (57,320 to 77,140 pounds).
Class C.1.l — 35,000 to 45,000 kilograms (77,140 to 99,180 pounds).
Class C.1.m — 45,000 to 55,000 kilograms (99,180 to 121,220 pounds).
Class C.1.n — 55,000 to 65,000 kilograms (121,220 to 143,260 pounds).
Class C.1.o — 65,000 to 70,000 kilograms (143,260 to 154,280 pounds).

These classes are subdivided by type of engine: Group I (piston); Group II (turboprop); Group III (turbojet); Group IV (rocket). Airplanes of different weights may compete at distances up to 10,000 kilometers (6,214 miles), as well as around the world.

Speed records may also be set by amphibians, seaplanes, and flying boats; by helicopters and autogyros; sailplanes and hang gliders; human-powered airplanes; vertical takeoff aircraft; balloons and dirigibles; and by model aircraft and spacecraft.

In addition, there are scores of altitude, distance, and time-to-climb records available to aircraft of many varieties. Including city-to-city speed records, more than 2,000 record categories are listed in the FAI record book.

At the top of the prestige scale, however, is the Absolute World Air Speed Record where it has been since Alberto Santos-Dumont flew his Type 14-bis 25.66 mph (41.3 km/h) at Bagatelle, France, in November 1906.

Appendix 1:
Official Speed Records

Following is a selection of official FAI Speed Records, as of January 1, 1983

Absolute Records (all types of engines, all weights)

Straight Course—2,193.16 mph (3,529.56 km/h); USAF Capt. Eldon Joersz; Lockheed SR-71; USA; July 28, 1976

Closed Course—2,092.294 mph (3,367.221 km/h); USAF Maj. Adolphus H. Bledsoe; Lockheed SR-71; USA; July 27, 1976

Class C.1, Group I (piston engine, all weights)

Three kilometers—499.04 mph (803.138 km/h); Steve Hinton; North American RB-51; USA; August 14, 1979

15/25 kilometers—464.374 mph (747.339 km/h); Jacqueline Cochran; North American P-51C; USA; April 9, 1951

100 kilometers—469.549 mph (755.668 km/h); Jacqueline Cochran; North American P-51C; USA; December 10, 1947

500 kilometers—437.05 mph (703.376 km/h); Jacqueline Cochran; North American P-51C; USA; December 29, 1949

Class C.1.a/o, Group I (piston engine, not over 300 kilograms)

Three kilometers—55.9 mph (89.94 km/h); Zane Myers; Wizard Ultralight; USA; January 3, 1982

15/25 kilometers—51.7 mph (83.18 km/h); Zane Myers; Wizard Ultralight; USA; January 3, 1982

100 kilometers—184.99 mph (297.72 km/h); Charles Andrews; Monnett "Monex"; USA; August 3, 1982

500 kilometers—182.3 mph (293.4 km/h); Charles Andrews; Monnett "Monex"; USA; August 3, 1982

Class C.1.a, Group I (piston engine, 300 to 500 kilograms)

Three kilometers—235.77 mph (379.68 km/h); Charles Andrews; Musso "Real Sporty"; USA; October 26, 1980

15/25 kilometers—234.46 mph (377.32 km/h); Paul Musso; Musso "Real Sporty"; USA; October 17, 1982

100 kilometers—221.81 mph (356.96 km/h); Charles Andrews; Musso "Real Sporty"; USA; August 5, 1980

500 kilometers—203.14 mph (326.92 km/h); Charles Andrews; Musso "Real Sporty"; USA; August 5, 1980

Class C.1.b, Group I (piston engine, 500 to 1,000 kilograms)

Three kilometers—234.64 mph (377.608 km/h); Dan Mortensen; Amsoil-Rutan Racer; USA; May 2, 1982   15/25 kilometers—235.93 mph (379.7 km/h); Vladislav Loitchikov; Qwant; USSR; September 4, 1979

100 kilometers—233.32 mph (375.49 km/h); Dan Mortensen; Amsoil-Rutan Racer; USA; October 10, 1982

500 kilometers—253.23 mph (407.53 km/h); A.J. Smith; Smith AJ-2; USA; August 6, 1982

Class C.1.c, Group I (piston engine, 1,000 to 1,750 kilograms)

Three kilometers — 284.376 mph (457.65 km/h); Robert Reichart; Howard DGA-6 "Mr. Mulligan"; USA; October 23, 1977

15/25 kilometers — 236.68 mph (380.9 km/h); Vladislav Loitchikov; Qwant; USSR; September 18, 1979

100 kilometers — 282.87 mph (455.23 km/h); John Harris; Bellanca Skyrocket II; USA; July 28, 1975

500 kilometers — 296.49 mph (477.15 km/h); John Harris; Bellanca Skyrocket II; July 22, 1975

Class C.1.d, Group I (piston engine, 1,750 to 3,000 kilograms)

Three kilometers — no record established

15/25 kilometers — no record established

100 kilometers — 322.780 mph (519.480 km/h); R.M. Sharpe; Supermarine Spitfire VB; Great Britain; June 17, 1950

500 kilometers — 326.50 mph (525.45 km/h); John Harris; Bellanca Skyrocket II; August 1, 1975

Class C.1, Group II (turboprop-powered, all weights)

Three kilometers — no record established

15/25 kilometers — 501.44 mph (806.10 km/h); USN Cdr. D. H. Lilienthal; Lockheed P3C Orion; USA; January 27, 1971

100 kilometers — 438.68 mph (706 km/h); B. Konstantinov; Ilyushin Il-18; USSR; May 16, 1968

500 kilometers — 453.9 mph (730.61 km/h); Alexander Metronie; Antonov An-10; USSR; April 29, 1961

Class C.1, Group III (turbojet-powered, all weights)

Three kilometers — 988.26 mph (1,590.45 km/h); Darryl Greenamyer; Lockheed F-104; USA; October 24, 1977

15/25 kilometers — 2,193.16 mph (3,529.56 km/h); USAF Capt. Eldon Joersz; Lockheed SR-71; USA; July 28, 1976

100 kilometers — 1,618.7 mph (2,605.1 km/h); Alexander Fedotov; E-266; USSR; April 8, 1973

500 kilometers — 1,852.61 mph (2,981.5 km/h); Mikhail Komarov; E-266; USSR; October 5, 1967

Class C.1.a, Group III (turbojet-engine, below 500 kilograms)

Three kilometers — no record established

15/25 kilometers — no record established

100 kilometers — 279.689 mph (450.115 km/h); Jerry Mercer; Bede BD-5J; USA; March 8, 1979

500 kilometers — 211.85 mph (342 km/h); Jerry Mercer; Bede BD-5J; USA; March 16, 1979

Class C.1.b, Group III (turbojet-engine, 500 to 1,000 kilograms)
no records established

Class C.1.c, Group III (turbojet-powered, 1,000 to 1,750 kilograms)

Three kilometers—no record established

15/25 kilometers—469.13 mph (755 km/h); Rozalia Chikhina; Yakovlev Yak-32; USSR; February 19, 1965

100 kilometers—441.17 mph (724.43 km/h); G. Korchuganova; Yakovlev Yak-30; USSR; January 14, 1965

Class C.1.d, Group III (turbojet-powered, 1,750 to 3,000 kilograms)

Three kilometers—541.6 mph (871.798 km/h); Massino Ralli; Aermacchi MB.326; Italy; August 2, 1967

15/25 kilometers—546.8 mph (880 km/h); Massino Ralli; Aermacchi MB.326; Italy; December 1, 1967

100 kilometers—516.3 mph (831.007 km/h); Massino Ralli; Aermacchi MB.326; December 3, 1967

500 kilometers—483.2 mph (777.67 km/h); Massino Ralli; Aermacchi MB.326; Italy; December 6, 1967

Class C.2, Group I (seaplanes, piston engine, all weights)

Three kilometers—440.681 mph (709.209 km/h); Francesco Agello; Macchi-Castoldi MC.72; Italy; October 23, 1924

100 kilometers—391.072 mph (629.37 km/h); Guglielmo Cassinelli; Macchi-Castoldi MC.72; Italy; October 8, 1933

1,000 kilometers—250.676 mph (403.424 km/h); M. Stoppani and G. Gornin; Cant Z 509; Italy; March 30, 1938

Class E.1 (helicopters, all types of engines, all weights)

Three kilometers—216.839 mph (348.971 km/h); Byron Graham; Sikorsky S-67; USA; December 14, 1970

15/25 kilometers—228.91 mph (368.4 km/h); Gourguen Karapetyan; Mil A-10; USSR; September 21, 1978

100 kilometers—211.35 mph (340.15 km/h); Boris Galitsky; Mil Mi-6; USSR; August 26, 1964

500 kilometers—214.84 mph (345.74 km/h); Thomas Doyle; Sikorsky S-76; USA; February 8, 1982

Appendix 2:
Chronology of Speed Records

25.66 mph, 41.292 km/h; November 12, 1906; Alberto Santos-Dumont; Santos-Dumont Type 14-bis; Bagatelle, France

32.74 mph, 52.69 km/h; October 26, 1907; Henri Farman; Farman Biplane; Issy-les-Moulineaux, France

34.057 mph, 54.810 km/h; May 20, 1909; Paul Tissandier; Wright Biplane; Pau, France

43.385 mph, 69.82 km/h; August 23, 1909; Glenn Curtiss; Curtiss Reims Racer; Reims, France

46.179 mph, 74.318 km/h; August 24, 1909; Louis Bleriot; Bleriot Type XII; Reims, France

47.842 mph, 76.995 km/h; August 28, 1909; Louis Bleriot; Bleriot Type XII; Reims, France

48.205 mph, 77.57 km/h; April 23, 1910; Hubert Latham; Antoinette Monoplane; Nice, France

66.181 mph, 106.508 km/h; July 10, 1910; Leon Morane; Bleriot Monoplane; Reims, France

68.199 mph, 109.756 km/h; October 29, 1910; Alfred Leblanc; Bleriot Monoplane; Belmont Park, New York

69.47 mph, 111.801 km/h; April 12, 1911; Alfred Leblanc; Bleriot Monoplane; Pau, France

74.415 mph, 119.760 km/h; May 12, 1911; Edward Nieuport; Nieuport Monoplane; Chalons, France.

77.671 mph, 125.00 km/h; June 12, 1911; Alfred Leblanc; Bleriot Monoplane; Etampes, France

80.814 mph, 130.057 km/h; June 16, 1911; Edward Nieuport; Nieuport Monoplane; Chalons, France

82.727 mph, 133.136 km/h; June 21, 1911; Edward Nieuport; Nieuport Monoplane; Chalons, France

90.199 mph, 145.161 km/h; January 13, 1912; Jules Vedrines; Deperdussin; Pau, France

100.22 mph, 161.290 km/h; February 22, 1912; Jules Vedrines; Deperdussin; Pau, France

100.944 mph, 162.454 km/h; February 29, 1912; Jules Vedrines; Deperdussin; Pau, France

103.658 mph, 166.821 km/h; March 1, 1912; Jules Vedrines; Deperdussin; Pau, France

104.334 mph, 167.910 km/h; March 2, 1912; Jules Vedrines; Deperdussin; Pau, France

106.116 mph, 170.777 km/h; July 13, 1912; Jules Vedrines; Deperdussin; Reims, France

108.181 mph, 174.100 km/h; September 9, 1912; Jules Vedrines, Deperdussin; Clearing, Illinois, USA

111.735 mph, 179.820 km/h; June 17, 1913; Maurice Prevost; Deperdussin; Reims, France

119.239 mph, 191.897 km/h; September 27, 1913; Marcel Prevost; Deperdussin; Reims, France

126.667 mph, 203.850 km/h; September 29, 1913; Marcel Prevost; Deperdussin; Reims, France

171.041 mph, 275.264 km/h; February 7, 1920; Sadi Lecointe; Nieuport 29V; Villacoublay, France

176.136 mph, 283.464 km/h; February 28, 1920; Jean Casale; SPAD-Herbemont 20bis; Villacoublay, France

181.864 mph, 292.682 km/h; October 9, 1920; Bernard de Romanet; SPAD-Herbemont 20bis; Buc, France

184.357 mph, 296.694 km/h; October 10, 1920; Sadi Lecointe; Nieuport 29V; Buc, France

187.983 mph, 302.529 km/h; October 20, 1920; Sadi Lecointe; Nieuport 29V; Villacoublay, France

192.011 mph, 309.012 km/h; November 4, 1920; Bernard de Romanet; SPAD-Herbemont 20bis; Villacoublay, France

194.516 mph, 313.043 km/h; December 12, 1920; Sadi Lecointe; Nieuport 29Vbis; Villacoublay, France

205.223 mph, 330.275 km/h; September 26, 1921; Sadi Lecointe; Nieuport-Delage Sesquiplane; Ville-sauvage, France

211.902 mph, 341.023 km/h; September 21, 1922; Sadi Lecointe; Nieuport-Delage Sesquiplane; Ville-sauvage, France

222.97 mph, 358.836 km/h; October 18, 1922; Gen. Billy Mitchell; Curtiss R-6; Selfridge Field, Michigan, USA

233.014 mph, 375.00 km/h; February 15, 1923; Sadi Lecointe; Nieuport-Delage Sesquiplane; Istres, France

236.588 mph, 380.751 km/h; March 29, 1923; Lt. Russell Maughan; Curtiss R-6; Wright Field, Ohio, USA

259.148 mph, 417.059 km/h; November 2, 1923; Lt. Harold Brow; Curtiss R2C-1; Mitchell Field, New York, USA

266.584 mph, 429.025 km/h; November 4, 1923; Lt. Al Williams; Curtiss R2C-1; Mitchell Field, New York, USA

278.481 mph, 448.171 km/h; December 11, 1924; Adj. Florentin Bonnet; Bernard V.2; Istres, France

297.817 mph, 479.290 km/h; November 5, 1927; Maj. Mario de Bernardi; Macchi M.52; Venice, Italy

318.624 mph, 512.776 km/h; March 30, 1928; Maj. Mario de Bernardi; Macchi M.52R; Venice, Italy

357.723 mph, 575.700 km/h; September 12, 1929; Sqd.Ldr. A. H. Orlebar; Supermarine S.6; Calshot, England

407.001 mph, 655 km/h; September 29, 1931; Flt.Lt. George Stainforth; Supermarine S.6b; Lee-on-Solent, England

423.824 mph, 682.078 km/h; April 10, 1933; Francesco Agello; Macchi-Castoldi MC.72; Lake Garda, Italy

440.678 mph, 709.202 km/h; October 23, 1934; Francesco Agello; Macchi-Castoldi MC.72; Lake Garda, Italy

463.921 mph, 746.604 km/h; March 30, 1939; Flt.Capt. Hans Dietrle; Heinkel He-100V-8; Oranienburg, Germany

469.224 mph, 755.138 kmh; April 26, 1939; Flt.Capt. Fritz Wendel; Messerschmitt Me-209V-1; Augsburg, Germany

606.26 mph, 975.675 km/h; November 7, 1945; Gp.Capt. Hugh Wilson; Gloster Meteor IV; Herne Bay, England

615.81 mph, 991.04 km/h; September 7, 1946; Gp.Capt. Edward Donaldson; Gloster Meteor F.4; Littlehampton, England

623.608 mph, 1,003.60 km/h; June 19, 1947; Col. Albert Boyd; Lockheed P-80R; Muroc Air Base, California, USA

640.743 mph, 1,031.178 km/h; August 20, 1947; Cdr. Turner Caldwell; Douglas D-558-I; Muroc Air Base, California, USA

650.796 mph, 1,047.356 km/h; August 25, 1947; Maj. Marion Carl; Douglas D-558-1; Muroc Air Base, California, USA

670.981 mph, 1,079.841 km/h; September 15, 1947; Maj. Richard Johnson; North American F-86A; Muroc Air Base, California, USA

698.511 mph, 1,124.137 km/h; November 19, 1952; Capt. J. Slade Nash; North American F-86D-5; Salton Sea, California, USA

715.751 mph, 1,151.883 km/h; July 16, 1953; Lt.Col. William Barns; North American F-86D-35; Salton Sea, California, USA

727.6 mph, 1,170.76 km/h; September 7, 1953; Sqd.Ldr. Neville Duke; Hawker Hunter III; Littlehampton, England

735.54 mph, 1,183.74 km/h; September 25, 1953; Lt.Cdr. Mike Lithgow; Supermarine Swift 4; Azizia, Libya

752.949 mph, 1,211.746 km/h; October 3, 1953; Ltd.Cdr. James Verdin; Douglas XF4D-1; Salton Sea, California, USA

755.149 mph, 1,215.298 km/h; October 29, 1953; Lt.Col. Frank Everest; North American YF-100A; Salton Sea, California, USA

822.266 mph, 1,323.026 km/h; August 20, 1955; Col. Horace Hanes; North American F-100C; Palmdale, California, USA

1,132.13 mph, 1,821.98 km/h; March 10, 1956; Peter Twiss; Fairey F.D.2; Chichester, England

1,207.60 mph, 1,943.5 km/h; December 12, 1957; Maj. Adrian Drew; McDonnell F-101A; Edwards AF Base, California, USA

1,404.09 mph, 2,259.65 km/h; May 16, 1958; Capt. Walter Irwin; Lockheed F-104A; Edwards AF Base, California, USA

1,483.85 mph, 2,388 km/h; October 31, 1959; Col. Georgi Mossolov; E-66; Podmoskovnoe, USSR

1,525.965 mph, 2,455.736 km/h; December 15, 1959; Maj. Joseph Rogers; Convair F-106A; Edwards AF Base, California, USA

1,606.505 mph, 2,585.425 km/h; November 22, 1961; Lt.Col. R. B. Robinson; McDonnell F4H-1; Edwards AF Base, California, USA

1,665.89 mph, 2,680.97 km/h; July 6, 1962; Col. Georgi Mossolov; E-166; Podmoskovnoe, USSR

2,070.115 mph, 3,331.507 km/h; May 1, 1965; Col. Robert Stephens; Lockheed YF-12A; Edwards AF Base, California, USA

2,193.64 mph, 3,529.56 km/h; July 27, 1976; Capt. Eldon Joersz; Lockheed SR-71A; Edwards AF Base, California, USA

Landplane records set when the Absolute World Air Speed Record was held by a seaplane:

294.418 mph, 473.820 km/h; September 5, 1932; Jimmy Doolittle; GeeBee R-1; Cleveland, Ohio, USA

304.522 mph, 490.080 km/h; September 4, 1933; James Wedell; Wedell-Williams number 44; Glenview, Illinois, USA

314.321 mph, 505.848 km/h; December 25, 1934; Raymond Delmotte; Caudron C.460; Istres, France

352.391 mph, 567.115 km/h; September 13, 1935; Howard Hughes; Hughes H-1; Santa Ana, California, USA

379.629 mph, 610.950 km/h; November 11, 1937; Hermann Wurster; Messerschmitt Bf-109V-13; Augsburg, Germany

Piston-engine records set when the Absolute World Air Speed Record was held by a jet-propelled airplane:

482.462 mph, 776.449 km/h; August 16, 1969; Darryl Greenamyer; Grumman F8F-2; Edwards AF Base, California, USA

499.059 mph, 803.152 km/h; August 14, 1979; Steve Hinton; Red Baron RB-51; Tonopah, Nevada, USA

Low-altitude, 3-kilometer (1.86-mile) records set when the Absolute World Air Speed Record was held at high altitude:

902.719 mph, 1,452.777 km/h; August 28, 1961; Lt. Hunt Hardisty; McDonnell F4H-1; White Sands, New Mexico, USA

988.260 mph, 1,590.45 km/h; October 24, 1977; Darryl Greenamyer; Lockheed F-104; Tonopah, Nevada, USA

Index